AF798293

An Approach to Substance Writing
&
Critical Appreciation

An Approach to Substance Writing
&
Critical Appreciation

U. K. BHATIA
SHANKAR NATH SEN

Ababil Books
Kolkata

Published by
Ababil Books
Publishers & Distributors
Indian Leather Housing Complex , Ahmed Villa
15A/1, Gulam Jilani Khan Road
Kolkata-700 039
West Bengal, India
Phone: 9477508834
E-mail: contact@ababilbooks.com
Visit us: www.ababilbooks.com

ISBN: 978-93-91449-90-2

First Published: 2007
Second Revised Edition: 2011
Third Reprint: 2015
Fourth Reprint: 2025

Price: Rupees **Three Hundred** Only

Disclaimer

- The author and the publisher have taken every effort to the maximum of their skill, expertise and knowledge to provide correct material in the book. Even then if some mistakes persist in the content of the book, the publisher does not take responsibility for the same. The publisher shall have no liability to any person or entity with respect to any loss or damage caused, or alleged to have been caused directly or indirectly, by the information contained in this book.
- The author has fully tried to follow the copyright law. However, if any work is found to be similar, it is unintentional and the same should not be used as defamatory or to file legal suit against the author.
- If the readers find any mistakes, we shall be greatful to them for pointing out those to us so that these can be corrected in the next edition.
- All disputes are subject to the jurisdiction of Kolkata Courts only.

Printed by: D. G. Offset, 96/N, Maharani Indira Devi Road, Kolkata-700 060

Contents

The Author's Note

This book is a humble attempt to cater to the needs of the students of English literature in the area of writing substance and critical appreciation. No doubt, it is purely an academic exercise done for an academic purpose.

It is a fact that the art of writing substance and critical appreciation cannot really be taught. All depends upon the literary perception and word power one possesses. However, a few tips and suggestions would not be out of place for the beginners and it is with this object that this attempt is made.

I do not claim hundred percent originality of what views and ideas I have expressed in the following pages. I have borrowed many of the ideas from various books and websites and have tried to assimilate the same to make them a single and comprehensive whole.

Should the book be found helpful to the students for whom it is written, I shall consider my efforts successful.

I welcome suggestions for the improvement of the book in future.

Kolkata
12.07. 07

U. K. BHATIA

Preface to the Second Edition

The critical forum is a place of vigorous conflict and disagreement, but there is nothing in this to cause dismay. What is attested is the complexity of human experience and richness of literature, not any chaos or relativity of taste. A critic is better seen, no doubt, as an explorer than as an 'authority', but explorers ought to be, and usually are, well equipped. The effect of good criticism is to convince us of what C. S. Lewis called 'the enormous extension of our being which we owe to authors.' The present edition will be justified if it helps to promote the same end.

A single volume can represent no more than a selection of critical opinions. The book not only prepares the students for their graduation, but it also paves the way for further advanced study of substance writing and critical appreciation of literary pieces in future. Most of the passages chosen for critical appreciation in this book are drawn from the syllabi of the various universities. At the end of the book a glossary of technical and literary terms has been added to enable students to undertake critical appreciation on their own with confidence.

All these realities have been taken into account while revising the edition of this widely read book. I hope the revised version will live up to your expectations.

Kolkata
10 May 2011

SHANKAR NATH SEN

CHAPTER I

Substance Writing: The Main Ideas

Summary, like paraphrase, allows you to reproduce another writer's thoughts—but in a shortened form. In writing a summary, you focus on the most important statements of the original passage and eliminate the less important material. Three techniques—*selection and deletion, note taking, and miniaturizing*—can help you shorten the material. As you become more adept at summarizing, you will devise your own combination of these techniques for each occasion. But in all cases the summary must be written in readable prose that reflects the essential meaning of the original text. Like paraphrase, summary can be used for many purposes: to help you understand the main points and structure of an author's argument, to convey that understanding to others, to present background information quickly, or to refer to another writer's ideas in the course of making your own original statement.

Writing a Substance

Whereas paraphrase writing leads you to examine all the details and nuances of a text, substance writing gives you an overview of the text's whole meaning. If you look over the whole text too rapidly, however, you may overlook important parts. Good substance writing, therefore, requires careful attention to the meaning and shape of the entire text. As you become more skilled at substance writing, you will become aware of just how much meaning can be distorted or lost by too rushed a substance. You will also become aware how much meaning you can convey in just a few words if you write summarily.

Unlike the paraphrase writer, who must discover new ways to restate the meaning, the summarizer looks for the most compact restatement. To highlight the essentials of another writer's idea—rather than to provide complete and detailed restatement–is the purpose of substance writing. A substance will help you understand the major direction, the main points, and the overall shape of the more detailed original. It restates the essence of the original in as few words as possible, but in different words. In cases, when you use an author's original words, you need to put them in quotation marks. But when you use a substance in the course of your own writing, you must use your own words as far as possible or mark the use of the author's words with quotation marks.

To rewrite a longer piece in short form, you must first understand the piece you are working with. Begin by reading the piece carefully, making sure you absorb the full meaning. If there are words you do not know, since looking them up may not be always possible, particularly in the examination hall, guess their meanings in the context of the entire passage. If some sentences are confusing, paraphrase them mentally. Identify the main ideas and determine how the less important material relates to those main ideas. In short, read.

Once you understand the piece you are summarizing, you must decide which parts you are going to include in the substance and which you are going to leave out. Of course, how much material you select depends on how long you want the substance to be and for what purpose you are going to use the substance. However, unless you have a more specific ratio in mind, you should generally try to create a substance about half to one-third the length of the original.

Our discussion presents three methods for choosing the material to include in a substance–(i) selection and deletion, (ii) note taking, and (iii) miniaturizing. The methods overlap somewhat. By deleting, for example, you in effect select the material that remains. Miniaturizing is only a structurally focused version of note taking. A good substance takes into account all three methods, and in practice people switch back and forth among them. Because each of these methods emphasizes slightly different skills, however, we shall discuss them separately. Through the somewhat artificial separation and isolated practice of these skills, you will master the art of making concise and exact substances. After you gain control of all the methods, you will be able to combine them as you see fit. Before we discuss these methods, however, let us briefly examine the steps in writing a substance.

Analytical and Descriptive Substances

Having selected the material to include in your substance, you must then decide whether your substance will be analytical or descriptive. Analytical summaries adopt the cone of the original full text, simply presenting the information it contains in shorter form. *Descriptive substances* adopt a more distant perspective, describing the original text rather than directly presenting the information it contains. For example, an analytical substance of the Declaration of Independence might begin as follows:

> When people declare themselves independent of their political ties, they should give reasons. Governments are formed to protect equality and rights, including life, liberty, and the pursuit of happiness. If government does not do this, people can change the government.

A descriptive substance of the same passage might begin as follows:

> Nehru opens the Declaration of Independence by stating that a country declaring independence needs to give its reasons. He goes on to discuss the purposes of government in protecting individual rights and the legitimacy of change if government does not live up to its obligations.

Note that the analytical substance does not mention the author or title of the piece but rather gets right down to the content. Thus it can present more information more compactly and more summarily. *To convey the content of a source, analytical substances are preferable to descriptive substances.*

On the other hand, descriptive substances give a more nearly complete picture of the structure of the original. They also establish a certain distance between the writer of the substance and the writer of the original piece. This sense of objectivity is useful whenever the summarized material is to be analyzed, evaluated, or otherwise discussed. *For critical or evaluative purposes, descriptive substances are preferable.* Hence descriptive substances should be used in book reviews, in essays of analysis, and in other essays discussing a text.

Substance Writing

The key to writing an effective substance is combining the material you choose to include into concise, coherent sentences and paragraphs. If your sentences are carelessly formed, not only will the substance be unreadable, you will also lose the connection among the pieces of information in the substance. You could simply wind up with tossed word jumbles. On the other hand, carefully written sentences can help show how the separate facts and ideas fit together to build the meaning of the whole. Thoughtful word choice and sentence structure can help you reduce a substance by half with no loss of information, ideas, or clarity. Incidentally, because the substance form places such a premium on conciseness and clarity, writing substances provides excellent practice for the improvement of your general writing style.

Because you are taking information from many pans of the original text, you could easily lose sight of the logical structure of the whole piece. You need to pay close attention to the new transitions and paragraph structure of the substance. Rather than running all the information together in a series of seemingly unrelated sentences, you can use transitions to show the connection between sentences, and you can create new paragraphs to reflect large divisions in the original material.

Finally, in your finished draft of the substance, be sure you identify the source of the original material in a heading (in case of substance), an introductory phrase, or a footnote. When substances are worked into the course of longer arguments, you can cite the source of your material in an introductory phrase or a footnote without interrupting the flow of your argument.

Steps in Writing a Substance

- Read the original carefully.
- Choose material for the substance.
- Decide whether your substance will be analytical or descriptive.
- Rewrite the material in concise, coherent sentences and paragraphs.
- Identify the source of the original text.

Methods of Choosing Material for the Substance

Method 1: Selection and Deletion

Because a substance moves quickly through the main points of the original, you need to focus on the most important ideas and details and leave out less important material. In preparing to write your substance, you can identify important material by underlining, circling or highlighting it and can eliminate less important material by deleting it or crossing it out.

Look for key words to identify those that express substantial information or make major statements. Ask yourself, "What is central here? What is the author's specific point? What statements draw the whole piece together?" Cross out digressions, repetitions, non-essential background information, extended examples, interest-provoking anecdotes, and other minor supporting details. Thus by selection and deletion, you make the most important material emerge, while you push the less important to the background. This method of choosing material works best where there are direct statements of main ideas, accompanied by much detailed elaboration, wordy examples, expressions, or other clearly less important material.

Method 2: Note Taking

Taking notes on the key ideas for each of the paragraphs of the passage reveals the logic of ideas in the whole piece and the connections among them. As you write down the key idea for each paragraph or so of the original, you will be concerned more with large chunks of meaning than with specific details. As you look over your notes, you may notice that each paragraph owns its own meaning, which is related to the meaning of the paragraph before or after it. You will become aware of the whole piece as a series of ideas, one following another.

Method 3: Miniaturizing

As you read through the original, pay attention to the various parts of the structure: the order of ideas, their relative lengths, and their relationships. Think of a large photograph reduced to wallet size. In a relative sense all the parts remain the same; only the scale has changed. Notice the shape, flow, and overall impression of the original passage so you can create a miniature version of it in your substance. As in the note-taking method, you should jot down the main ideas and key statements of the original, but you should also try to keep the size of your notes in rough proportion to the size of the original. Follow the logic of one idea flowing from another, and re-create the transitions and structure of the original.

When the arrangement, logical development, and balance of parts of the original are important, miniaturizing will help you retain the overall meaning and impression. Generally this method is most appropriate for more complex and subtly argued originals, whose parts fit together in unusual ways or in ways that are difficult to follow.

Methods of Choosing Material for the Substance

- *Select more important information and delete less important material:* This method may be useful when clearly stated main ideas in the piece are immediately followed by many details or examples.
- *Take notes on the main ideas*: This method may be useful when the development of a complex idea in the piece is treated in many subsections. The notes serve as an outline of the flow of the author's thought.
- *Miniaturize the original:* This method may be useful when the logical development is subtly argued and pans of the piece fit together in unusual ways.

The following rules will guide you in writing effective summaries. The substance:

1. Is usually about half the length of the original, though it will vary depending on the content of the original.
2. Begins with the main idea (as in developmental paragraphs) and proceeds to cover the major supporting points in the same sequence as the source, always in complete sentences.
3. Changes the wording without changing the idea.
4. Does not evaluate the content or give an opinion in any way (even if you see an error in logic or fact).
5. Does not add ideas (even if you have an abundance of related information).
6. Does not include any personal comments by the author of the substance (therefore, do not use 'I') and
7. Seldom uses quotations (but if so, always with quotation marks).

Such vocational considerations, though important, are not in our view the most telling, however. The fundamental value of substance is that **it tests and exercises every aspect of linguistic competence.** To write an accomplished substance you need to have mastered eight major skills.

1. Good comprehension

To reduce a long document to its essentials requires a sound understanding of its every point and sentence. This is often more demanding [and therefore more reliable as a gauge] than any standard comprehension exercise.

2. Good prose composition

A substance should be crisp and easy to read. To achieve such at-a-glance clarity you need a muscular style, where everything is pertinent and works efficiently.

3. Discerning judgment

The prime task of substance writing is to distinguish what is really important from what is merely interesting or decorative.

4. An Authoritative vocabulary

Although you must never invent **material** when fashioning a substance, it is entirely in order to recast ideas in your own words. In fact this is often essential, enabling you to cut down a structure of say 15 words to 5 or 6. To do that you need a vocabulary, broad, supple and vigorous.

5. Literary feel

Contrary to certain prejudices, there is nothing 'airy-fairy' about good literature. Indeed, the best literature is always formidably exact; no matter how large or complex their goals, great writers are masters of nuance and substanceion. All good substance writers have something of such qualities; the chances are they acquired them through literary study.

6. A fierce eye for flab

Substance writing is a ruthless business! In most academic substance writing tasks, you may be given an exact and mandatory word limit; even otherwise, in a very real sense, every word counts. And even if you are not constrained by such numerical targets, you still need to be vulture-like in your ability to tear at sentences and reduce them to their bare bones. This is closely analogous to the 'keyword' noting system enabling you to 'gut' a chapter or an entire book, and is a most valuable skill whatever your walk of life.

7. Sound logic

No matter how ruthlessly abridged, a substance has to make sense in its own right. This calls upon clarity of thinking and alertness to the distinct stages of an argument.

Finally, and obviously:

8. Accurate mechanical and grammatical English

This hardly requires a comment! Every task involving the use of English needs to be mechanically correct. None more so than substance, nevertheless: you can sabotage all the above strengths if you misspell, punctuate badly and perpetrate poor or clumsy grammar. Besides, if those things do disfigure your work, it is overwhelmingly probable that you will possess few if any of the seven skills just outlined, because each one depends on a sound knowledge of how language works and how it should be used.

Given that substance writing is a centrally important skill, how do you go about it successfully?

Well, substance writing is as much an art as a science, in that success depends more upon practice than upon the learning of fixed principles and guidelines, valuable though the latter can be. So let us start with an example.

"Gardeners are very frequently asked by persons interested in the cultivation of ornamental trees and shrubs to indicate to them some of the distinctive characters which mark off the common cypress from its near relative, the American arbor-vitae. These are two of the most widely grown ornamental conifers in the British Isles, and there is hardly a garden or park of any size in which one or other is not present.

It is not an easy matter under ordinary circumstances to indicate to the layman the differences that exist between these two species."

This passage is pleasantly written: few would accuse it of flabbiness or tedium. But while it is already tolerably concise, it can be further reduced. Let us look at it phrase by phrase.

1. **Gardeners are very frequently asked**... 'Very' does no real work and can safely be omitted. Perhaps, too, the simpler 'often' might replace 'frequently'.
2. **By persons interested in the cultivation of ornamental trees and shrubs**...the gardeners are unlikely to be asked anything by persons not thus interested! So if economy is the main criterion, the whole phrase can be jettisoned.
3. **To indicate to them some of the distinctive characters which mark off the common cypress from its near relative, the American** *arbor-vitae*...' To them' has to go anyway, because we've omitted Phrase 2. Everything else that precedes 'the common cypress' can be rendered by the infinitive 'to distinguish between'; in addition the term 'its near relative' can go, as it's a mere supplementary descriptor. The amended phrase thus reads: **To distinguish between the common cypress and the American** *arbor-vitae*.
4. **These are two of the most widely grown ornamental conifers in the British Isles**... The first two words can be omitted, provided a comma is placed after the preceding 'arbor-vitae' instead of a full stop. In addition 'widely grown' can be replaced by the single word 'popular'.
5. **There is hardly a garden or park of any size in which one or other is not present**... 'Of any size' is weak; 'or other' is similarly inessential. And if you are feeling really ruthless-and I propose to be!-you could argue that this whole sentence is more or less implied by the word 'popular' that I've just suggested. So we can get rid of all of it.
6. **It is not an easy matter under ordinary circumstances to indicate to the layman the differences may exist between the two species**. Because Phrase 5 has disappeared completely, you can render this simply by 'This is not easy.'

The full substance thus reads:

Gardeners are often asked to distinguish between the common cypress and the American *arbor-vitae*, **two of the most popular ornamental shrubs in the British Isles. This is not easy.**

An original total of 93 words has become 30. To be sure, some elegance, subtlety and sheer information have been sacrificed; but the new version is a clear expression of the salient 'bones' of the passage, and that is what any substance seeks to achieve.

That passage was quite well-written in the first place, which paradoxically made it relatively easy to summarize. The sentences flowed clearly and built into an 'argument' that was comfortable to follow; to dismantle them in the interests of ruthless economy was therefore a straightforward business.

But sometimes you will have to substance material that is difficult to disentangle, where you'll have to work really hard just to understand what the main argument might be. Study this next passage carefully. Just work out what you think it means. Try to identify the key phrases that form the cornerstones of the argument:

"In the affluent society, capitalism comes into its own. The two mainsprings of its dynamic—the escalation of commodity production and productive exploitation—join and permeate all dimensions of private and public existence. The available material and intellectual resources (the potential of liberation) have so much outgrown the established institutions that only the systematic increase in waste, destruction and management keeps the system going. The opposition which escapes suppression by the police, the courts, the representatives of the people, and the people themselves, finds expression in the diffused rebellion among the youth and the intelligentsia, and in the daily struggle of the persecuted minorities. The armed class struggle is waged outside: by the wretched of the earth who fight the affluent monster. "

As I pointed out before, the writing here is jargonesque and top-heavily abstract, making it very difficult to identify those 'key phrases', because one is rarely sure what they actually mean! However, after (at least) two careful readings, you might come up with a list something like this:

1. **affluent society** An old term, now stale, that refers to any industrialized nation, the writer's prime focus.
2. **capitalism; commodity production and productive exploitation** Capitalism is his main target; the other two phrases mean, roughly, 'the manufacture of goods' and 'the ruthless consumption of labour and resources'.
3. **all dimensions of public** and **private existence** Stresses that capitalism dominates our lives in every way.

4. **available resources/have outgrown institutions** To be candid, I still don't really know what this means: the entire sentence is an opaque mess. The suggestion seems to be that capitalism makes very poor use of the potential at its disposal, mainly because (as is implied later) its governments wish to retain power.
5. **increase in waste/destruction/management keeps system going** See my comments for Phrase 4. The idea (I think) is that the status quo preserves itself by purely negative methods, leading to...
6. **opposition/suppression/diffused rebellion**... direct or indirect suppression. Opposition is either tyrannically put down by state machinery or ignored because it is ineffectual.
7. **struggle: wretched of the earth versus affluent monster** The one vibrant moment in the whole piece, graphically reducing the conflict to its ultimate alternatives.

It may take you a long time, both to think out and to write, which is annoying. Nobody minds fruitful hard work: what is irritating here was that the original seems **designed** to confuse or intimidate. However, any substance writer will eventually encounter similarly poor originals, and at least that laborious 'gutting' gives us a clearer sense of what the passage is centrally about.

The next task is to 'translate' those key phrases into fluent and comprehensible English.

Phrases 1-3 present no real problem. I suggest:

Capitalism, the systematic consumer of all resources, dominates affluent society at every level.

One could omit 'all' and 'at every level'; you may include them in an attempt to retain the categorical tone of the original.

Phrases 4, 5 and 6 are murderously difficult, as already noted! The core of their argument seems to be that capitalism is by turns inefficient, deliberately destructive and tyrannical, and that its primary concern is to keep the system going for the benefit of 'the haves'. So we may suggest:

Fundamentally wasteful and tyrannical, it enlarges the range and intensity of its influence, destroying or emasculating most potential rebels.

This takes considerable liberties, may be; but we do not think it distorts the original's thrust or tone, and it covers all the main ideas.

Phrase 7 is blissfully easy in comparison. It makes sense to retain the powerful 'the wretched of the earth'; 'the affluent monster' is perhaps also worth preserving. However,We suggest replacing the full stop after 'rebels' with a comma, and continuing:... 'leaving only the wretched of the earth to fight it.'

We have sacrificed 'affluent monster' in the interests of a simple and punchy structure, but it can be reinstated if that is your taste.

The complete substance thus reads:

Capitalism, the systematic consumer of all resources, dominates affluent society at every level. Fundamentally wasteful and tyrannical, it enlarges the range and intensity of its influence, destroying or emasculating most potential rebels, leaving only the wretched of the earth to fight it.

That is 42 words; the original had 120.

Take the following poem:

Riches I hold in light esteem,
And Love I laugh to scorn;
And lust of fame was but a dream
That vanished with the morn.
And if I pray, the only prayer
That moves my lips for me
Is, 'Leave the heart that I now bear,
And give me liberty!'
Yea, as my swift days near their goal
'Tis all that I implore:
In life and death a chainless soul,
With courage to endure.

Now, this is a poem by Emily Bronte, and it is entitled 'The Old Stoic'. In the poem the poet expresses the philosophy of life of an old stoic philosopher. But as students, you are not expected to know all this, if the title and the name of the poet are not mentioned in the question paper. Hence to avoid all troubles, it would not be wrong to begin the answer with *The poet here expresses his philosophy of life.* In the next place, the close study of the poem at once makes it clear what the speaker does not want and what he really does want in life. Among the former are riches, love and fame. The objects of his desire are freedom of mind and courage to endure the sufferings of life. Hence the substance thus may be attempted:

The poem is put in the mouth of an old stoic philosopher and expresses his philosophy of life. Wealth and amour are not among the objects of his desire. Love of fame was a folly of his youth, which has passed away with it. Now that he is old and near the grave, the only things he prays for are freedom of soul and courage to endure the sufferings of life.

Now that we've thoroughly explored three very different examples, we can begin to identify some of the principles and guidelines that inform substance writing.

1. *Read the original very carefully:*

If it needs two readings, give it two. You should not even start to think in terms of reducing it until you are confident that you have grasped the main points and the thrust of the argument.

All that's obvious enough, perhaps, but it needs to be rigidly adhered to. Sloppy substance writing work invariably hinges on imperfect understanding, and that in turn derives from excessive initial haste.

2. *Once you're ready to begin, isolate the key phrases:*

It is up to you how you do this: you can use highlighter pens, a separate sheet of rough paper, and any method you like. However, it is not recommended the savage crossing out of everything you think you can omit, for two reasons. First, it makes your 'text' look a right mess, which will not assist clear thinking. Second, you may delete a phrase that you subsequently recognize as essential, and reinstating it in your text will both waste time and be tricky anyway.

3. *Start your first draft of continuous prose:*

It is assumed that your 'skeleton' is sound - that you've identified and assembled the requisite 'bones'. But even a substance needs some flesh - ideally, enough to make it attractive in its own right. What else from the original should you keep or efficiently paraphrase?

Well, knowing what to omit is more than half the answer:

3a. *Omit all examples, illustrations and quotations:*

This is often less easy than it might sound, because such material may well be very interesting and thus memorable. However, it must be done: such things illuminate the argument rather than define it. They are secondary, and if you're reducing a piece to a third of its length [or even less], you can only afford to include primary material. That's one of the reasons why it's essential to have grasped the governing thrust of the argument before you pick up your pen.

3b. *Be prepared to strike out all adjectives and adverbs:*

We say 'Be prepared to strike out' rather than simply 'Strike out' because some 'qualifiers' will be necessary. If you look back at the two examples analysed above, you'll see that the adjectives and adverbs that remain really pull their weight: they are definitive, not decorative. However, if you rigorously 'interrogate' all such words as to their true value, you should find that most of them do not have a good enough case.

3c. *Never repeat material, even if the original does:*

Be totally ruthless about this. The only concession you might make to an obsession with a particular point is to isolate it in a paragraph of its own.

4. *In general, write in shortish, crisp sentences:*

Such a style may at times strike you as rigid and bare, and if you can construct longer sentences that are muscular and substancee, go ahead. But remember that you **are** producing a skeleton of the original, and skeletons are rigid and bare! Keeping your sentences short will also promote clarity, allowing you to keep a regular check on where your argument is going and whether each word is doing some real work.

5. *Try to use your own words wherever possible:*

In truth, this is **not** always going to be possible: most passages will include some terminology or phrasing that must remain or simply cannot be improved upon. But look to paraphrase where you can: sometimes neat wording on your part will render an idea in six words that it took the original a dozen to achieve. Besides, if you stick slavishly to what you've 'gutted' from the original, it is likely that such a residue will be stilted, tending to creak rather than flow.

Now for three important **'don'ts':**

6. *Never invent material:*

Whatever you put down, especially when it's in your own words, make absolutely sure that your material exists in the original, or is at the very least strongly implied in it.

7. *Never pass an opinion or judgment on the original:*

Your job is that of a disinterested scribe **and nothing else**. Your opinion is irrelevant: furthermore, expressing it will waste words that should be devoted to central points. Even if the argument you're dealing with enrages you, keep out of it!

8. *Never bring the author's name into your text:*

Substance takes authorship for granted. If you really believe that who wrote the piece is of fundamental importance, then find a way to mention it; do not allow it to clutter up your reduced version.

There are two views about what to do if the original is in the first person. Some authorities say that a substance should always be written in the third person, and that the original must be recast accordingly. Others argue that clarity is the chief criterion, not formalism, and that if the substance will read better in the first person, then use it. We incline to the former view, but either is tenable. Practice, experience and 'feel' will guide you best: do what seems most comfortable, provided the resultant version is clear and apt.

Finally, three guidelines concerning shape and length.

9. *hould a substance be paragraphed?:*

It depends on the length of the finished substance.

Anything under 100 words should be presented as a single paragraph, unless there is a major switch of topic or focus therein.

For reductions of 100-200 words, a single paragraph will often still be appropriate; but be prepared to divide into two or even three, according to the material's range and your sense of the reader's comfort.

Any final version that goes noticeably over 200 words should have at least two and probably three paragraphs; four to six it if climbs to 450 and above. If the substance is any good, it will make for fiercely concentrated reading: a single chunk of prose of 200+ words is distinctly 'user-unfriendly'.

10. *If you're instructed to cite the number of words you've used, do so and don't guess or lie about it!:*

People who set academic substance tasks do so very carefully. When they stipulate a word target or word limit, they are not sadistically adding a further difficulty: on the contrary, they're trying to help you, for they will already have worked out that the job can best be done in the figure they cite. So keep a regular check as you go on the number of words you've used—it will sharpen your performance.

If you're too lazy to do that, don't compound the folly by making a vague guess or, even worse, inventing a number that 'looks good'. The chances are it will look **terrible**: your assessor will not need to count the words to know that you're lying. One rapidly develops a 'feel' for a version that is too short or too long, and you are most unlikely to get away with any such chicanery!

10a. *If given no such target or limit, what should you aim for?:*

The fraction most often mentioned in substance work is **one-third or one-half.** In the two examples explored above, we ended up reducing both originals to that length.

—o—

CHAPTER II

Critical Appreciation

First we need to know the distinction between literary appreciation, interpretation and literary criticism.

- Literary appreciation: The dictionary definition of "appreciate" is "to evaluate the quality or value of a certain thing." Literary appreciation, as we may define it, involves not only evaluation but also personal, impressionistic, or emotional apprehension of the work we read. This emotional/personal aspect of reading is very important for us; it usually decides whether we want to go on studying a work and how we are going to do it. However, personal appreciation can lead to subjective and vague judgment, which is the kind of literary appreciation we want to avoid.
- Interpretation—In a broad sense, interpretation can mean all the action involved in our reading from apprehension, appreciation to analysis. Here we will define it more in terms of "text analysis": that is, to interpret is to "explain and clarify the meaning of" a text so that its rich meanings can be understood.
- literary criticism—Far from being "negative evaluation" as the word "criticism" sometimes suggests, literary criticism develops from the first two steps of reading into a more systematic analysis of a work. "Systematic" mean two things here:
  1. literary criticism has to be developed and presented with sufficient evidence from the text and they have to be logically presented;
  2. literary criticism involves a theoretic framework, which usually the critic is aware of.

Having gained some ideas about the subject relating to criticism and its various nuances let us now turn to area of 'prose' and study its various aspects. This will help us to develop some basic ideas as to how to assess a piece of prose.

Broadly, prose writing may be classified into various categories:

1. Straightforward, utilitarian writing

In such writings some practical advice is given in a practical manner, without stylistic flourishes. Prose is here used, not for artistic effect, not for expression of personality, but for communicating information. In short, prose here does its ordinary and everyday job. Such straight-forward writing we judge by the ease and speed with which we can read and understand it. If it is clumsy and obscure, either the writer does not know his job or else he is writing hastily. The difficulty of writing such prose depends partly but not wholly on the complexity of the subject-matter. It is not always easy to explain a simple matter clearly. On the whole, the success with which a writer composes everyday prose depends on the skill, patience and experience with which he handles the language. In utilitarian prose we do not look to it for style or personality. Its style, if any, consists in absence of literary devices; the personality of the writer is best expressed when it does not obtrude itself.

2. Rhetorical Prose

Here the language is strong and vigorous. Here the author is not one to compress his thought into a short sentence; on the contrary, his style is ample and repetitive. Here the logical argument is not always the strong point of the writer. The author normally attempts to convert by the vigour of his indignation in whatever cause he is advocating, and by the force of his own conviction.

3. Plain Narrative

Here the writer writes, not for artistic effect, but to tell a plain tale of some remarkable incident or adventure. Clarity and exactness are the two things the author aims at while observing literary propriety. Here the style is direct and what is sometimes called 'masculine' free from affectation and obscurity. Here the narrative proceeds naturally and easily, without digression and without excessive bareness; he is mostly not pompous and never dull. It is the style of an educated gentleman using prose purely as a medium for communicating a narrative of fact and discovery to an educated audience.

4. Realism, dramatic reporting

Here the prose is the expression of much more complex thought and more literary writing. Such writing may deceive us into thinking that it is simpler than it is. Here the literary effect is sought to be heightened by use of various figures of speech. This kind of writing may be summed up as a narrative of action, with an undercurrent of psychological comment; this is effected by a combination of vivid, carefully selected physical detail with occasional abstract suggestion.

5. Expressionism, subjective description

Here the writer does not attempt to be detached and objective, but stamps upon every sentence his own feeling, emotion and personality. The objects of his description and the words used to project them on to the reader's eye are deliberately selected to heighten this impression.

6. Impressionism

Here very little feeling is expressed and conveyed directly by the choice of words. The writing is objective. Yet there may be subtle emotional undercurrent. The writing is generally vivid, but not photographically precise. It is impressionistic.

7. Psychological narrative

In such type of prose, the narrative is interwoven with psychological analysis and speculation to a high degree. Here, psychological speculation and the minute analysis of the characters' mind are more important than the narrative. At times the style tends to be rambling series of phrases and expressions loosely strung together, with a minimum of finite verbs. It is especially adapted for rendering the loosely connected, unhurrying impressions and sensations which flow through the mind. This rambling, reflective style in which the exploration of the characters' state of mind is more important than the relation of facts, is one of the most notable characteristics of early twentieth-century fiction and has left its mark on most fiction since.

8. Irony

Irony, which consists in saying the opposite of what you mean or of implying disapproval while you appear to approve, is the weapon of the intelligent obliged to associate with the foolish or barbarous. It enables him to maintain his own private standards while appearing to conform to those of society. It enables him to criticize without this being apparent to those he does not wish to offend. The ironist has an air of superiority. But it may be his only method of retaining reason and sanity.

9. Experimentalism

At first sight the writing may appear incomprehensible farrago, part sense, part nonsense; but careful study shows that the writing is deliberate, highly organized, and perfectly lucid, though difficult. Everyday language is broken up and reassembled to exploit its maximum allusive and suggestive possibilities. Puns and ellipses abound. Most readers find that the passage or the book requires too much concentration and ingenuity to be read in long stretches, but read in short passages it is brilliant and amusing. The style is too original to be imitated, and it is difficult to see how the experimental distortion of ordinary prose could be carried further.

A CHECK LIST FOR CRITICAL APPRECIATION

PROSE

1. Find out whether the style is clear or obscure. If you find the writer obscure, it may be because his style is slipshod or hasty, or may be he has something difficult to say. In that case the fault may be ours; perhaps we should be reading with closer attention.
2. Find out whether the writing is objective or subjective. This appears to be one of the main distinctions to be made in criticizing prose. An objective writer is one whose personality is kept in the background; we may get an impression of the quality of his intellect, his power of mind, but we shall not get a clear impression of his private personality. This is something we derive from reading of subjective prose—prose marked throughout by touches which give away the writer's tastes and temperament. An objective writer appears to write authoritatively, as if what he has to say is true, independently of his personal impressions. A subjective writer makes no attempt to keep his personal impressions to himself; he shows clearly that he is writing of things as seen through his eyes; and how they appear will differ according to his moods. On the whole scientific or factual writing is usually of an objective kind; memoirs, personal narratives and imaginative writings are often subjective. We read the former kind of writing for what it has to say; we read the second kind more for an impression of the writer's personality.
3. Objective writing is factual, objective description we call realistic; subjective description we call impressionistic. The former appears more solid; the latter is more vague, but often more lifelike. Both sorts of writing have their place in literature.
4. We may sometimes say of objective writing that it is detached and unemotional; subjective writing is often emotional. The ironist writes in a detached way; he stands apart from his subject. His emotions are kept below the surface. On the other hand, the subdued emotion may break through to the surface and express itself in the form of ridicule or indignation. One of the points to notice about prose writing is the writer's emotional attitude to his subject–whether the emotion is present or absent, and if present, whether it is below the surface,

betraying itself only by an occasional adjective, or whether it is near the surface, ready to communicate itself at any moment directly to the reader.

5. Find out whether the style is 'masculine' or 'feminine'. A masculine style is direct, sometimes crude, sometimes pompous or dogmatic, full of strong light and shade, concrete and emotionally not subtle. A feminine style is more subtle in emotion and observation, full of suggestions and half-lights, less forceful.
6. Another distinction we shall make in examining prose style is that between the experimental and the traditional. The majority of the prose writers are conservative in style, conforming to the accepted patterns of sentence structure and choice of words. When we read experimental prose, we must decide whether the writer has anything new to say or whether he is only striving for effect.
7. In coming closer to the prose passage and examining in greater detail, the first thing we shall probably be aware of is the vocabulary, the choice of words and phrases. When we come to consider these words in combination, we shall notice first the general rhythm or flow of the passage. If it is jerky, this may be from deliberate intention. Before condemning a style for jerkiness, we must see whether this has any deliberate purpose.
8. Clarity is the great objective in prose writing—the quality of saying exactly what is intended as unmistakably and simply as possible, without false emphasis or straining after-effect. Indeed, we might say—and it is another of the paradoxes of literary criticism—that the great aim of style is to divert attention from itself towards the subject.

POETRY

Critical appreciation of a poem can be made by reading the same several times and by reflecting on what you read. There is no surer way. Every poem has a life of his own. That is why every poem must be criticized individually. We read a poem with a purpose of trying to discover the essential life within it - in other words, the poet's intention, conscious or unconscious. One more thing is to be pointed out. Criticism remains a highly subjective process. Every reader is an individual human being. All his attitudes, especially in aesthetic matters, will be conditioned by his prejudices and preconditions. As such there are no accepted canons of the taste in poetry.

All said and done, from the practical and academic point of view, the following important aspects may be examined while assessing a poem:

- The poet's sincerity and depth of feeling
- The expression of the poet's individuality
- A continuous feeling for aptness and beauty of language
- A vivid sense of concrete objects as metaphors, similes, and symbols for the expression of experience.

But the course of the real essence of a good poem is indefinable.

To sum up: (Some practical advice)

What should be the length of a Critical Note from the examination point of view? The answer to the question is simple. The critical comment on a passage or a poem should be brief and to the point. There is a wrong, although a popular, notion that a critical comment on a passage has to be of a certain minimum length, and that it must be made as elaborate as possible. That, of course, is an absurd idea, as you can easily guess. The length of the critical comment should vary naturally from passage to passage or from poem to poem. But it should be always as brief and precise as possible. It is not possible to lay down specific rules for writing critical comments on passages. There are, however, certain points which should be dealt with whenever you write a critical comment on anything—a piece of prose or a poem. For example, you should point out in your critical comment how far the writer has succeeded in driving home the main idea of the passage. You must also say something about the methods he employs to reach that goal. You should add a few brief remarks on the style and language. Some may think that one must always praise the writer or the poet and eulogize his language and method of presentation. This is a wrong idea. You are free to point out any particular weakness of style or language that you may find in the piece in question. But one thing should be remembered. Most of the passages set in your examination papers are generally taken from the writings of renowned poets and authors. And, the paper-setters generally take care to select for your passages of fine literary excellence. While dealing with such passages or poems, you naturally have little room for adverse criticism. But that certainly does not mean that you are not allowed to make any adverse comment even when there are ample grounds for it. In the case of poems, you should keep in mind a few additional points. While commenting on a poem or an extract from a poem, you should do well to mention the metre. You may sometimes quote a line from the given passage to show how it scans.You may mention the literary type which the passage in question belongs to, and you may also comment briefly on the rhyme pattern.

Now let us briefly recapitulate what a student should do while writing out a critical comment:

- Make your critical comment brief and to the point;
- Clearly state how far the writer has succeeded in making the main idea clear to the readers;
- How does he manage to do this? What are the methods he employs? (He may have achieved through comparisons, contrasts, arguments or sometimes through sheer eloquence.)
- Does the style of presentation do justice to the subject-matter? Is the language simple or is it difficult? Does it facilitate comprehension? You should make all these points clear in your critical comment.
- In the case of poetry passage, you should mention the metre and you may say something about the rhyme pattern

—o—

CHAPTER III

Substance and Critical Note (Prose) Examples Worked Out

Example 1

Perseverance is the very hinge (1) of all virtues. On looking over the world, the cause of the nine-tenths of the lamentable (2) failures which occur in men's undertakings, and darken and degrade (3) so much of our history, lies not in the want of talents, but in the manner of using them, in flying from object to object in starting away at each little disgust, and thus applying the force which might conquer any one difficulty to a series of difficulties so large that no human force can conquer them. The smallest brook on earth by continuing to run has hollowed for itself considerable valley to flow in. Commend (4) me, therefore, to the virtue of perseverance. Without it, all the rest are little better than fairy gold (5) which glitters (6) in your purse, but when taken to market, proves to be stale or cinders (7). (140 words)

Central Idea: Perseverance is essential to success in life. Without it, all other virtues are of no use.

Word-notes: 1. Mechanism by which a door is hung; 2. Regrettable; 3. Lower; 4. Recommend; 5. Gold made by the fairies of which we hear in popular stories; 6. Shines; 7. Ashes.

Substance: Perseverance is key to success in life. Most of the failures in the lives of men are due not so much to the want of powers as to the lack of tenacity of purpose. Without perseverance all other qualities, however brilliant, are of no avail. We should, therefore, cultivate the virtue of perseverance, which is the crown of all virtues. (60 words)

Critical Note: Thematically the passage is about perseverance which the author considers to be the basis of all other virtues and logically concludes that without it all other virtues lose their ground. The author has no pretension about what he wants to say and he speaks out his mind with absolute frankness. He knows that he is didactic in his approach and therefore, tackles the subject accordingly. He seems to address his students from the platform of a teacher.

The treatment of the subject, when considered from the standpoint of style, borders the archaic pattern. The main sentence through which the author drives his point home is unnecessarily lengthy consisting of as many as 80 words. Comparison of perseverance with a brook is rather conventional and therefore, devoid of any novelty. Similar is the comparison of other virtues (without perseverance) with fairy gold. Such literary devices may be educative for school boys but their literary merit is insignificant.

The above piece belongs to the genre of reflective essay whose only purpose is to ignite a sense of awareness among others. Assuming, however, that the author's viewpoint is stretched further in the essay, it is doubtful how many will have the patience of going through the writing in a single-reading. As an open-minded reader, we may consider the passage no better than an academic exercise on a didactic subject.

Example 2

Would you know whether the tendency of a book is good or evil, examine in what state of mind you lay it down? Has it tended to make you dissatisfied and impatient under the control of others? Has it disposed you to relax (1) in that self-government, without which both the laws of God and man tell us there can be no virtue, and consequently no happiness? Has it attempted to abate (2) your admiration and reverence for what is great and good, and to diminish in you the love of your fellow creatures? Has it addressed itself to your pride, your vanity, your selfishness, or any other of your evil propensities? (3)Has it defiled (4) the imagination with what is monstrous (5)? Has it disturbed the sense of right or wrong which the Creator has implanted in the human soul? If so–if you are conscious of all or any of those effects - or if having escaped from all, you have felt that such were the effects it was intended to produce, throw the book into the fire whatever name it may have on the title page! Throw it into the fire though it should have been a gift of a friend. (198 words)

Central Idea: Bad books corrupt the mind and should always be avoided.

Word-notes: (1) Slacken; (2) Decrease; (3) Tendencies; (4) Corrupted; (5) Hateful.

Substance: The value of a book is to be judged by the effect it produces on the reader. If the book tends to make the reader intolerant of control, or rebellious against the laws of God and man, or lessens his admiration for what is good and noble or inflames his pride and selfishness, or corrupts his imagination and disturbs his sense of moral values, then it is a bad book indeed. We should never have anything to do with such books. (81 words)

Critical Note: The role of books in human civilization is an accepted phenomenon. Not that their effects on human mind have always been wholesome. Rather it may be said that books have played their roles in doing and undoing of civilization in their own ways. So their effects have been both negative and positive.

It is in this context that the author sends his cautionary advices to the readers regarding choice of books. But unconventionally he states his arguments the other way round i.e. he cautions the readers about the books not to be chosen and hence to be discarded. He raises certain 'negative' questions the answers to which, if positive, should alert the reader and he should reject the book forthwith without hesitation. This final suggestion, which is not unexpected to the readers, comes at the end of the passage.

It may be imagined that the author has adopted the unconventional method by starting his subject with several questions involving various values, rather the lack of them with a definite purpose in mind, that is to create an interest in the minds of the readers. Further, it is easier to list the negative values in books rather than elaborating the positive values and qualities. This method affords the readers an easier way to select books.

The passage belongs to the genre of literary essay. Its primary virtue lies in the fact that the author does not assume the serious role of a preacher or teacher; rather he establishes a sort of personal contact with the reader as evident from the frequent use words 'you' and 'your' in the passage. The passage is characterized by clarity of thought and expression. The logic is forceful and authoritative.

Example 3

When the time comes for Veneering to deliver a neat and appropriate stammer to the men of Pocket-Breaches, only Podsnap and Twemlow accompany him by railway to that sequestered spot. The legal gentleman is at the Pocket-Breaches Branch Station, with an open carriage with a printed bill, 'Veneering for ever!' stuck upon it, as if it were a wall; and they gloriously proceed, amidst the grins of the populace, to a feeble little town hall on crutches, with some onions and bootlaces under it, which the legal gentleman says are a Market; and from the front window of that edifice Veneering speaks to the listening earth. In the moment of his taking his hat off, Podsnap, as per agreement made with Mrs. Veneering, telegraphs to that wife and mother, 'He's up.'

Veneering loses his way in the usual No Thoroughfares of speech, and Podsnap and Twemlow say 'Hear hear!' and sometimes, when he can't by any means back himself out of some very unlucky No Thoroughfare, 'He-a-a-r He-a-a-r!' with an air of facetious conviction, as if the ingenuity of the thing gave them a sensation of exquisite pleasure. But Veneering makes two remarkably good points; so good, that they are supposed to have been suggested to him by the legal gentleman in Britannia's confidence, while briefly conferring on the stairs.

Point the first is this. Veneering institutes an original comparison between the country and a ship; pointedly calling the ship, the Vessel of the State, and the Minister the Man at the Helm. Veneering's object is to let Pocket-Breaches know that his friend on his right (Podsnap) is a man of wealth. Consequently says he, 'And, gentleman, when the timbers of the Vessel of the State are unsound and the Man at the Helm is unskilful, would those great Marine Insurers, who rank among our world-famed merchant-princes—would they insure her, gentlemen? Would they underwrite her? Would they incur a risk in her? Would they have confidence in her? Why, gentleman, if I appealed to my honourable friend upon my right, himself among the greatest and most respected of that great and much respected class, he would answer "No!"'

Point the second is this. The telling fact that Twemlow is related to Lord Snigsworth, must be let off. Veneering supposes a state of public affairs that probably never could by any possibility exist (though this is not quite certain, in consequence of his picture being unintelligible to himself, and everybody else), and thus proceeds. 'Why, gentlemen, if I were to indicate such a programme to any class of society, I say it would be received with derision, would be pointed at by the finger of scorn. If I indicated such a programme to any worthy and intelligent tradesman of your town—nay, I will here be personal, and say Our town—what would he reply? He would reply, "Away with it!" That's what *he* would reply, gentlemen. In his honest indignation he would reply, "Away with it!" But suppose I mounted higher in the social scale. Suppose I drew my arm through the arm of my respected friend upon my left, and, walking with him through the ancestral woods of his family, and under the spreading beeches of Snigsworthy Park, approached the noble hall, crossed the courtyard, entered by the door, went up the staircase, and, passing from room to room, found myself at last in the august presence of my friend's near kinsman, Lord Snigsworth. And suppose I said to that venerable earl, "My Lord, I am here before your lordship, presented by your lordship's near kinsman, my friend upon my left, to indicate that programme;" what would his lordship answer? Why, he would answer, "Away with it!" That's what he would answer, gentlemen. "Away with it!" Unconsciously using, in his exalted sphere, the exact language of the worthy and intelligent tradesmen of our town, the near and dear kinsman of my friend upon my left would answer in his wrath, "Away with it!'"

Veneering finishes with this last success, and Mr. Podsnap telegraphs to Mrs. Veneering, 'He's down.'

Then dinner is had at the Hotel with the legal gentleman, and then there are in due succession, nomination and declaration. Finally Mr. Podsnap telegraphs to Mrs. Veneering, 'We have brought him in.'

Charles Dickens: from *Our Mutual Friend*

Substance: The passage describes an election meeting for parliamentary candidate in a humorous manner. There is use of a kind of ironic manoeuvre the author appears to write as a political and social reformer; his genially destructive political satire is directed against the tradition of 'Veneering for ever', or the pretence of democracy without the reality. (After all, a 'veneer' is a thin sheet of superior material which is used to hide inferior material.) The author involves his character in an ironic situation, and gives an ironic impersonation of him, and makes ironic comments about him and about other topics. The irony of Mr Veneering's situation is not directed against him personally, but against a political abuse of the period prior to 1832. Pocket-Breeches is a 'pocket borough', in which there is no candidate to oppose him. The result of the election is a foregone conclusion. Mr Veneering's speech is a formality and a sham. The mechanical nature of the process by which he becomes an MP is emphasized by Mr Podsnap's ludicrously unnecessary series of snappy telegrams: 'He's up'...'He's down.'...'We have brought him in.'

Comment: The author's use of the present tense throughout the passage has the effect of conveying the speed and inevitability of the process, rather in the manner of a present-day racing commentator. Moreover, the author's ironic impersonation of Mr Veneering's speech is also not intended to satirize him personally, but spurious political rhetoric generally. This is suggested by the unusually large number of obvious clichés with which his character is driven: *the finger of scorn*, *august presence*, *honest indignation*, and so on. The author also arranges for each part of Veneering's grotesque speech to culminate, not in a splendidly oratorial conclusion, but in an utterly deflating bathos: the extremely banal 'No!' at the end of the third paragraph.

Further on, the author makes a large number of ironic comments, often of a deflationary kind. The author's comments are not only deflating, but also considerably subtle, relying either on obvious bathos or on the implying of meanings which are quite simply the opposites of the ones stated. Bathos is being employed when we are told that Mr Veneering is to *deliver*, not a speech, but a *stammer*, and when we are told that the four men 'gloriously proceed...to a feeble little town hall on crutches'. The following comments mean the opposite of what they appear to state: Mr Veneering 'makes two remarkably good points' (that is, remarkably *bad* points); he 'institutes an original comparison' (that is, an utterly *hackneyed* one); he finishes 'with this last success' (that is, the last dismal *failure*). The author also makes ironic use of clichés, not only in his ironic impersonation of Mr Veneering, but in his own comments as narrator: Pocket-Breaches is 'that sequestered spot'; Mrs Podsnap is 'that wife and mother'; the electorate of Pocket-Breaches are the entire 'listening earth'. The effect here is to draw attention to the hypocrisy which underlies the use of such clichés.

The author makes three comments directly to us: he tells us that 'Veneering's object is to let Pocket-Breaches know that his friend...is a man of wealth', that 'the telling fact that Twemlow is related to Lord Snigsworth, must be let off', and that Veneering's 'picture' is unintelligible to himself and everybody else. These are explanatory comments, designed to guide the reader through the confusions of Veneering's speech, and to make quite sure that he appreciates each bathos when it eventually arrives.

There is not the slightest hint of sympathy for Veneering, Podsnap, and Twemlow: the author's distance from his character is absolute. They are farcical buffoons, presented entirely from the outside, with nothing to suggest that they have the inner fears, doubts and hesitations common to all men. Their names are labels which invite us to regard them as comic *types* to be thought of only in terms of their outward behaviours and appearance. A man with a name like 'Veneering' can only be an oily rascal. 'Podsnap' bespeaks a pompous dogmatist, while 'Twemlow' is both timid and effect is 'tremolo', spoken with a lisp. 'The legal gentleman' is just that, three times, and is endowed with no human characteristics whatsoever. The author writes in the comic tradition of Fielding and Ben Jonson, with their 'humour' characters (that is, highly simplified character types) such as Lady Booby and Sir Epicure Mammon.

To sum up, then: the writer writes in the grand tradition of farcical exaggeration. He employs fairly obvious and repetitious ironies, a restricted narrative technique, highly simplified and exaggerated characters, together with a ludicrous situation, to produce a comically simple political satire. One thing which the writer aims at is, as Sir Philip Sidney put it, 'to teach and delight'.

Example 4

We know little of our greatest men; and the truth is, we want to know all about them. When you come to that time of life when you grow tired of fiction (1), you naturally turn to fact. And the facts you seek and which have greatest attraction for you are the facts in the lives of your fellow-men especially those whom you have come to love or to admire. It has been said with truth that there is an interesting picture to be made out of every human life, the lowest as well as the biggest, but the interesting thing about life is its human side, its passions, hopes, virtues, aspirations, habits, thoughts, and feelings. We all dearly like to see the inside of the mansion (2) where dwells the human soul. We want the blinds (3) taken down, and the windows raised, and the roof taken off that we may see all the particulars of the interior. The same instinct that drives people to an auction drives them to a biography. (170 words)

Central Idea: Man naturally desires to know about the great men of the world. Biographies give such knowledge.

Word-notes: 1. Imagined thing; 2.Large dwelling house; 3. Screens for windows.

Substance: Our knowledge of the greatest men of the world is very meagre indeed, though in reality we are very much eager to know much about them. Nothing can be more attractive than the facts of the lives of those whom we admire or love. But the most interesting facts in them are their hopes and fears, habits and thoughts and feelings. We all like to have an insight into the depths of the soul of a great man. All these we can have from biography. (85 words)

Critical Note: The theme of the passage relates to the study of biography. The study of biography, according to the author, affords a man with an opportunity to know the details of the lives of the celebrities.

The passage begins with a presumption that after a certain age a person gets tired of fiction and therefore, turns to facts in the forms of biographies. This point is debatable and may not apply in all cases. However, this does not dilute the point the author tries to establish. And his point is to establish the need of reading biographies. The author draws the comparison of a mansion and an auction which indicates the fact that the article has been written for the common readers.

The style adopted by the writer is straight-forward and lucid. Clarity of thought and expression is one of the merits of the passage. The reader is able to get to the point of the writer by a single-reading.

Example 5

What is war ? Behold! vast regions desolated, forests rent, villages in ruins, fields left barren and waste! Thousands in their vigour of life, blown up and scattered like chaff before the wind! Thousands again groaning in the agony of broken limbs! Beyond the scene of desolation, roads strewn with the wounded and the dying, harvests trampled under foot, widows, orphans and aged parents in loud mourning! Strangely enough, to our eternal shame, we seem dead to these horrors and miseries of wars. The sufferings and death of a single fellow-being often excite tender and active compassion, while we hear, without emotion, of thousands enduring every variety of woe in war. A single murder, in times of peace, starts a thrill of sensation while the countless murders of war are heard as an amusing tale. The execution even of a criminal sickens and shocks the mind, and philanthropy is labouring to substitute milder form of punishment for death, but benevolence has hardly made any effort to snatch from sudden and untimely death the countless victims leading on to the altar of war.

Substance: On reading the passage we get the idea that war is definitely devastating. War is nothing constructive, it is destructive. The ultimate result of war is that it desolates vast regions and destroys forests. Villages are turned into utter ruins and lush fields are left barren and changed into wasteland. Even human life is utterly destroyed. Scenes of desolation prevail everywhere—roads are strewn with the wounded and the dying, harvests are trampled and there is loud mourning of widows, orphans, and aged parents for the loss of their near and dear ones. Despite the rampant destructions caused by wars and the horrors and miseries that issue from them, humanity does not deter from the eternal shame. In times of peace a great deal of sensation is created by a single murder, whereas countless murders during war are relished as an amusing tale. The execution of a diehard criminal disgusts us and stirs us. Philanthropy labours to substitute milder form of death penalty, but benevolence does not in any way try to stop the sacrifice innumerous victims on the altar of war.

Comment: The passage is loosely structured as the key sentence occurs at the end. The piece is touching as the pathetic scenes attached to war are given graphically. It has a startling beginning with an interrogative sentence which is soon followed by a series of answers that uphold the devastations of war. The rampant destructions are alluded to with a series of exclamatory sentences. The use of 'Behold!' is poetic; in fact, it is reminiscent of Wordsworth, or for that mater it sounds biblical. The romanticism and religiosity associated with the word is lost when we are led to witness the utter desolation, ruin, and agony caused by war.

The simile used in the sentence is apt:

> Thousands in their vigour of life, blown up and scattered like chaff before the wind!

The figurative language makes the remark all the more telling because it makes the point poignant that despite war being devastating, it is a great pity that war, which leads to the murder of millions, is glorified. The passage has a sudden dramatic beginning with a short interrogative sentence:

> What is war?

This intensifies the curiosity in the mind of the reader to read further on. This adds a certain amount of poeticism to the style. The poeticism is further intensified by alliteration in the sentence soon following:

> Behold! vast *r*egions desolated, fo*r*ests *r*ent, villages in *r*uins, fields left ba*rr*en and waste!

Apart from the alliteration on the *r* sounds, there are other alliteration on the *v* and *sl* sounds in the sentence. Further on, there is assonance in the sentence:

> Strangel*y* *e*nough, to our *e*ternal shame, w*e* s*ee*m dead to th*e*se horrors and m*i*ser*ie*s of wars.

Example 6

Diligence and moderation (1) are the best steps, whereby to climb to any excellency. Nay, it is rare, if there be any other way. The heaven send not down their rain in floods, but by drops and dewy distillations (2). A man is neither good, nor rich, nor wise at once; yet creeping up these hills, he shall every day better his prospect, till at last he gains the top. Now he learns a virtue and then gives up a vice. Every something laid may in time make a stock (3) great. If a man does but save, he shall increase; and though when the grains are scattered, they be next to nothing, yet together they will swell (4) the heap. He that has the patience to small profits may quickly grow to thrive and purchase; they are easier to accomplish and come thicker. So he that from everything collects somewhat shall get a treasury of wisdom. And when all is done, this is the best way for a man. (166 words)

Central Idea: All great things of the world have been done by slow steps. Wisdom, too, cannot be attained by one jump but in a gradual process.

Word-notes: 1. Avoidance of extremes, 2. Coming in drops 3. Store; 4. Inflate.

Substance: All good things in life are to be attained by slow and diligent steps and not by one big jump. Thus goodness, wealth, and wisdom can be attained only bit by bit. Small savings make a large stock in course of time. This is as much true of the material gains as of spiritual acquisitions. Virtue, wisdom and all else are the results of patient labour. (66 words)

Comment: All good things of life are attained by slow steps and not by one big leap. Everything in nature works gradually. So also in the life of a man, he attains goodness, wealth, and wisdom only bit by bit. Small savings make up a large stock. The results of patient labour are virtue, wisdom, and all else.

By bringing in the archaic negative word '*nay*' the writer is emphatic about the fact that the only means of attaining excellency is by sheer diligence and that too by moderation. This fact is well-hammered with metaphorical reference of the heavens not sending down the rain in floods but by drops and distillations. The sentence is highly poetic not only because of the metaphor but also because of the melody created by the alliterations:

> The heavens sen*d* not *d*own their rain in floo*d*s, but by *d*rops and *d*ewy *d*istillations.

Not only is there alliteration on the *d* sounds but also on the *s* sounds and on the *n* sounds. The effect of a man rising to excellency step by step is well conveyed through the repetition of *nor* preceded by *neither* in the sentence:

> A man is *neither* good, nor rich, *nor* wise at once; yet creeping up these hills, he shall every day better his prospect, till at last he gains the top.

The passage is loose in structure as the key sentence occurs at the very outset:

> Diligence and moderation are the best steps, whereby to climb to any excellency.

Not only is the entire passage loosely structured but also the very sentence is loosely structured, as the main clause expressing the basic sentiment occurs at the very beginning, as though it begins with a bang and ends with a whimper. There is a magisterial tone in the passage, because the passage is rounded off with a sentence towards the end:

> *So* he that from everything collects somewhat shall get a treasury of wisdom.

The word *So* adds a conclusive note to the passage.

Though the author talks of 'a man' and continues with third person singular number 'he', the author actually generalizes the matter, as the theme dealt with in the piece is a universal truth, that it is only through diligence and moderation that one attains excellency. This moderation is wonderfully put across by using words like *climb* and *creeping* to finally reach the *top*.

The passage is reminiscent of biblical echoes in phrases like:

> If a man does but save...

and again:

And when all is done...

The word *creep* even brings to our mind Macbeth's use of the word in:

Tomorrow, and tomorrow, and tomorrow,
Creeps in this petty pace from day to day.

Thus the passage definitely has literary flavour. The author skilfully intersperses the passage with long sentences from time to time; these long sentences are rather copious. Despite the various beauties in the style, the author resorts to suppositions many a time with the word *if*.

Example 7

Of the validity of the modern demand for equality there is no doubt whatever. It has appeared in the form of the demand for equality between individuals, between classes, between nations. It has been at the root of every recent revolution and of most recent wars. Nor is it a demand which would be satisfied by the formal political equality of the nineteenth century. It is specifically a demand for economic equality—for equality of economic resources or equality of economic opportunity. This problem requires in the first instance, a positive and constructive rather than a negative and destructive programme. Our deliberate purposes should be to build up equality rather than to break down inequality. The process of equalisation can be achieved by gradual rather than by violent methods. Our first step should be to secure the distribution to all of what may, on a generous interpretation be called 'the necessaries of life': and since, in the area with which we are most likely to be concerned, this should not be difficult of attainment, the distribution of the necessaries of life may be supplemented by the distribution of many of the amenities and luxuries. Such a programme will create needs vast enough to make a full call on our resources.

Substance: There is a great force in the modern demand for equality—equality of classes, of nations, and of individuals. It is this which has led to wars. But rightly speaking, this equality should not be political but economic. It means the equal distribution of economic advantages and opportunities, of comforts and amenities of life, among people. Such equality can be achieved not by sudden revolution but by the development of the country's resources.

Comment: The keynote of the passage is struck at the very beginning where the writer puts forward the idea of modern demand for equality in every walk of life. The demand for true equality between man and man does not mean political equality. In the drive for equality a positive and constructive approach is required instead of a negative and destructive approach. In other words, the deliberate purposes should be to build up equality rather than to break down inequality. It implies the equal distribution of economic advantages and opportunities. This can be attained by a gradual process, not by a sudden revolution. This attainment is possible by the full development of the country's resources.

At times the writer resorts to rhetorical flourishes to beautify the style. In the sentence:

> It has appeared in the form of the demand for equality *between* individuals, *between* classes, *between* nations—

there is anaphora for the purpose of beautification in the style. Soon after, another rhetorical device has been used, where there is musicality caused by alliteration:

> It has been at the *r*oot of eve*r*y *r*ecent *r*evolution and most *r*ecent *wars*.

There is also assonance in the sentence following:

> *It is* specifically a demand for equal*ity* of econom*ic* resources or equal*ity* of econom*ic* opportun*ity*.

Further on there is another instance of alliteration in the expression:

> a posit*ive* and construct*ive* rather than a negat*ive* and destruct*ive* programme

The internal rhymes cause the effect of echo.

Example 8

I remember to have once seen a slave in a fortification in Flanders, who appeared no way touched with his situation. He was maimed, deformed, chained; obliged to toil from the appearance of day till nightfall and condemned to this for life; yet with all these circumstances of apparent wretchedness he sang, would have danced but that he wanted a leg, and appeared the merriest, happiest man of all the garrison. What a practical philosopher was there! A happy constitution supplied philosophy, and though seemingly destitute of wisdom, he was really wise. No reading or study had contributed to disenchant the fairy land around him. Everything furnished him, with an opportunity of mirth; and though some thought him from his insensibility a fool, he was such an 'idiot as philosophers might wish in vain to imitate'. They who, like him, can place themselves on that side of the world in which everything appears in a ridiculous or pleasing light, will find something in every occurrence to excite their good humour. The most calamitous events either to themselves or to others can bring no new affliction; the whole world to them a theatre in which comedies only are acted. All the bustle of heroism or the rants of ambition serve only to heighten the absurdity of the scene and make the humour more poignant. They feel, in short, as little anguish at their own distress or the complaints of others, as the undertaker, though dressed in black, feels sorrow at a funeral.

Substance: Once the writer met a mangled and chained slave in a fort in Flanders. Though the slave was condemned to lifelong toil, he never lost his cheerfulness of spirits. According to the writer, this slave is a type of the truly wise man, though people may consider him to be a fool. The source of the slave's happiness lies within him and not in the outward circumstances which are the very opposite of what is happy. The example of the slave is worthy of imitation by all. Those who take all unconcerned view of life, suffer from no misery. Life to them is a comedy; the noise and bustle of life only serve to excite their laughter. No calamity of life can affect the habitual cheerfulness of their mind.

Comment: The writer begins by recounting an event from his own life of once having seen a slave in a fort in Flanders. From sunrise to sunset he was compelled to labour lifelong. He was maimed, deformed, and chained in every way—he led a wretched life. Despite his miserable life he was full of cheerfulness all the time. From this incident the writer comes to the realization that persons like him do not suffer any new afflictions caused by the most calamitous events either to themselves or to others. The writer draws the conclusion that happiness depends on the mind and not on any external conditions. It is because of this the slave in the prison-house was cheerful, though to others his lot appeared very miserable.

As the writer is drawing upon his personal experience the passage strikes a subjective note. The asyndeton used to describe the condition of the slave seems to allude to the unending miseries in stock for the slave:

He [the slave] was maimed, deformed, chained.

The exclamatory sentence:

> What a practical philosopher was there!

seems to drive home the fact that the slave had been blessed with a practical philosophy of life.

The whole world being compared to a theatre is a beautiful metaphor (bearing a faint Shakespearean echo of 'All the world's stage'). For people blessed with such 'a happy constitution' comedies only are acted in the theatre. All the proclamations of heroism or rants of heroism serve only to heighten the absurdity of the situation and serves to make the humour more poignant. The word 'comedies' may be counted as a metonymy signifying the fun and frolic in human life. There is a tendency of the writer resorting to catalogue as is revealed in the sentence:

> He was maimed, deformed, chained...

The phrase 'in short' in the concluding sentence strikes a magisterial note, whereby the author's comment acts as a verdict:

> They feel, in short, as little anguish at their own distress or the complaints of others...

In other words, they are utterly indifferent to the sorrows and distresses of life. The author even takes the help of a simile in the concluding phrase:

> as the undertaker, though dressed in black, feels sorrow at a funeral. On the whole, the entire passage is written in a simple and lucid style.

Example 9

I am disposed; to agree with Captain Dolbey that the man who knows no fear exists only in the imagination of the lady novelist or those who fight their battles at the base. He who is conscious of fear ceases to be a hero. But the truth surely is that there would be no merit in being brave if you had no fear. The real victory of the hero is not over outward circumstance, but over himself. One of the bravest men of our time is a man who was born timid and nervous and suffered tortures of apprehension and who set himself to the deliberate conquest of his fears by challenging every danger that crossed his path and even going out of his way to meet the things he dreaded. By sheer will he beat down the enemy within and to the external world he seemed like a man who knew no fear. But the very essence of his heroism was that he had fought fear and won.

It is time we get rid of the notion that there is anything discreditable in fear. You might as well say that there is something discreditable in being tempted to tell a falsehood. The virtue is not in having no temptation to lie, but in being tempted to lie and yet telling the truth. And the more you are tempted, the more splendid is the resistance. Without temptation you may make a *plaster saint*, but not a human hero.

Substance: A man who knows no fear is a myth. People have a mistaken notion that a hero is one who knows no fear. Nothing can be more mistaken than this. True heroism lies in facing dangers and fears and conquering them. Besides, it means the conquest of one's inner enemies. To the outward world such a man appears free from fear; yet the fact remains that he faced fear and fought it. There is nothing disgraceful in knowing fear. Just as resistance to the temptation of telling a lie makes one a saint, so resistance to fear when it actually exists, raises a man to the full stature of a hero.

Comment: The passage is of a discursive nature where the author tries to prove his point that a true hero is he, who is not only free from fear but has conquered his enemies. The writer begins his argument from the premises by agreeing with Captain Dolbey that the man who knows no fear exists only in the imagination. To elucidate this fact he says that one who is conscious of fun ceases to be a hero. To strengthen his view point the author adds that there would be no merit in being brave if one had no fear; the real victory of the hero is not to hurdle over outward circumstances, but over himself. Thus the tussle is not outward but inward.

It sounds rather shocking when the author paradoxically enough states that one of the bravest men of our time is a man who was born timid and nervous and suffered various tortures of apprehension and who ultimately sets himself to the deliberate conquest of his fear by challenging the enemy that crossed his path and even going out of his way to meet the things he dreaded. The reality is that by sheer will only was he capable of beating down the enemy within, but to the world outside he emerged as the man who knew no fear. The actual fight was internal, not external. His heroism essentially lay in the fact that he had fought fear and ultimately emerged triumphant. After all, we may not be in a position to agree with the author because all that he expresses here is a very subjective viewpoint; this is evident from the presence of the first-person singular pronoun '*I*' at the very beginning of the passage. Nevertheless, the author has interspersed his piece with some short sentences like:

> He who is conscious of fear ceases to be a hero

in the midst of long sentences. Another short sentence:

> The real victory of the hero is not over outward circumstance,
> but over himself

may be considered the topic sentence of the passage, which comes somewhere in the middle of passage. Thus the extract has a mixed structure.

One noticeable feature of the passage is that it begins with first-person singular—'*I*', and finally shifts to second-person (singular/plural)—'*you*'. This shift in persons creates an effect—from particularity to generality and universalization. By bringing in second-person the author is capable of establishing a close rapport with the readers.

Example 10

The Germans, too had been an educated people, with western minds and hearts. Few nations had contributed more to our civilization in the past - in science above all - in modern times. They had worshipped science. To it they had sacrificed some of the basic human virtues - yet they had not gained the power to survive. Perhaps survival, in the last analysis, was fully as dependant on these virtues as on the power of arms - dependant on a perpetual balance of spiritual and material forces. The Germans had lost this balance. The temptation of scientific power had been too much for these citizens. With science, they felt, they could be supermen (1), they could rule the earth. Heedless of warning cries which arose both within and without their nation they had turned their backs on the deeper human values of their heritage (2). Instead of balancing science with other fields of wisdom, they had let it dominate them, turned it loose in war and conquest. In their search for materialistic power, they had set up science as their God and science had destroyed them.

In Germany, I learnt that if this civilization is to continue, modern man must direct the material power of his science by spiritual truths of his God. (210 words)

Central Idea: The case of the Germans proves beyond doubt that science without religion will destroy civilization.

Word-notes: 1. Higher man; 2. Things that are inherited.

Substance: The Germans had achieved great things in science in the past as well as in the present. They laid great emphasis on science and neglected the highest values of life. With science they dreamt dreams of world conquest. But they could not survive. The example of the Germans clearly proves that science must be regulated by religion, if human civilization is to survive. (63 words)

Critical Note: The passage gives an objective analysis of the downfall of the Germans in history. According to the author, despite their tremendous advancement in the field of science, particularly the power of arms, they failed to survive because they failed to mingle technical advancement with spiritual values. This, according to the author, is the key factor for any nation if it aspires to survive in history. In the ultimate analysis, the Germans failed to achieve this and, therefore, failed to survive.

The passage, apart from being an analysis from the point of view of history, presents an attitude of the author. He strongly believes in the parallelism between scientific advancement and spiritual uplifting and finds in Germany a case in point. However, his interpretation of things may not be without dispute and is likely to vary from person to person. However, the author has dealt with the subject with a balanced frame of mind without allowing his judgment to be tilted to either side.

Clarity of thought and lucidity of expression are the two main merits of the passage. It is easy to understand that the essay was written after World War II and hence it belongs to the category of modern prose.

Great things in science in the past as well as in the present have been achieved by the Germans. They had been an educated people blessed with western minds and spirits. At the cost of some basic human virtues they had worshipped science, they neglected the higher values of life. With science they dreamt of world conquest. Survival was dependent on the human values as well as on the power of arms. A perpetual balance must be struck between spiritual and material forces.The Germans failed to survive because they lost this balance.The temptation of scientific power had been too much for them.They suffered from the mistaken notion that with science they could be superhuman; they could thereby rule the world.

The Germans let science dominate them.They turned science loose in war and in conquest.The instance of the Germans already prove that science must be regulated by religion, if human civilization is to survive. The conclusion drawn by writer is that if this civilization is to continue, modern man must channelize the material power by the spiritual truths of his God is an absolutely personal view.

Example 11

The student should look forward to his examination not as a solemn ordeal which he is compelled to go through with the prospect of a degree, should he be successful, but as a means of showing his teacher and his fellows how he has profited by the work which he has done; those who pursue knowledge in this spirit and those, be it remarked, who examine in this spirit will look forward to examination with no apprehension; not perhaps with joy, for after all it is a bore to be examined and perhaps a still greater bore to examine, but it is a necessary step for the student in gaining self-assurance and the conviction of having profited by his exertions; and for the teacher, as a means of insuring that his instruction has not been profitless to his student. In this connexion I cannot refrain from remarking that that genius for competition which has overriden our nation of England appears to me to be misplaced. Far too much is thought of the top man; very likely the second, or even the tenth or it may be the fiftieth, has a firmer grasp of his subject, and in the long run would display more talent. Let us take comfort, however, in the thought, that the day of examinations for the sake of examinations, is approaching an end.

(Sir William Ramsay)

Substance: The writer is rather optimistic about the fact that the day of examinations merely for the sake of examinations is coming to an end.At present a great premium is set on examinations, but the days of examinations are coming to an end.The writer believes that examinations are basically the tests as to how far a student has profited by lectures of teachers. Examination should not be regarded as passports to degrees but as a means of giving an account by the student, of how he has profited by the instructions of his teacher.Thus regarded, examinations should have no terror for the student. Indeed there is nothing in the world more tedious than to examine and to be examined.The Englishmen have generally set an undue premium on examinations; the first successful candidate is regarded as the best: but in practical life, a student placed lower in the list may show real genius and attain success in life. Let us hope that the days of examinations may come to an end.

Comment: The passage has a didactic tone; there is sententious moralizing on the part of the author as he says that the student should look forward to his examination not as a solemn ordeal. A subjective note has been struck when the author steps in to express his own view that genius for competition has overridden the nation of England appears to him to be misplaced; he even goes to the extent of saying that only the top man is given thought to, though someone much below him in position may have firmer grasp on his subject. Moreover, he holds an optimistic view that the day is coming when examinations for the sake of examinations is approaching to an end. The most glaring defect in the author's style is the rather long sprawling sentence at the beginning of the passage.

Example 12

Now, to get great ideas we require great teachers. These teachers may be living persons with whom we come in daily contact; they may be dead and yet reach us through great books which they have given to the world. In whichever way it comes, the teaching required is that which guides to a large outlook. Yet after all it is only to a limited extent that the teacher, be he living or one who though dead yet speaks, can mould his students. There is no royal road to learning. The higher it is the harder is the toil of the spirit that is required for its attainment. But this toil brings with it happiness. As we advance along the path, we see more and more territory to traverse (1), new heights to scale, heights which are accessible only by patient labour, but the scaling of which promises us a new sense of possession. In all this there is much of the sweet in sad and sad in sweet. Yet the mere endeavour (2), even apart from the result, brings its reward. (180 words)

Central Idea: Though the teachers impart great ideas, it is after all by hard labour only that students can acquire learning. Their efforts may not always lead to success, yet the mere effort is something.

Word-notes: 1. Cover; 2. Attempt.

Substance: It is from the great teachers that we may get great and noble ideas. They may be dead or living. Their teachings enlarge our outlook on life. Yet, after all, the influence of those teachers is limited. It is on the hard toil of the learners that their progress depends. The path of progress is beset with difficulties. It may not be always possible to achieve success in this effort, yet the mere attempt has a great value. (78 words)

Critical Note: The focal point of the passage is the value of hard labour in the path of acquiring knowledge. The author strongly feels that whatever may be the knowledge we may gather from our teachers, living or dead, such knowledge must be supplemented by knowledge acquired through hard labour. There is no short cut way to learning.

The paragraph may be split up into two parts, one, the knowledge acquired from teachers and the other, the role of hard labour and toil in supplementing such knowledge. The changing over from one point to the other is natural and logical. The message that the author wants to convey is meant for common readers and this is comprehensible easily. The style and language is straight-forward and lucid with no unnecessary circumlocution. This is the hall mark of good prose.

Example 13

We think that, as civilization advances, poetry almost necessarily declines. Therefore, though we fervently admire those great works of imagination which have appeared in dark ages, we do not admire them the more because they have appeared in dark ages. On the contrary, we hold that the most wonderful and splendid proof of genius is a great poem produced in a civilized age. We cannot understand why those who believe in that most orthodox article of literary faith, that the earliest poets are generally the best, should wonder at the rule as if it were the exception. Surely the uniformity of the phenomenon indicates a corresponding uniformity in the cause.

The fact is, that common observers reason from the progress of the experimental science to that of imaginative arts. The improvement of the former is gradual and slow.

Ages are spent in collecting materials, ages more in separating and combining them. Even when a system has been formed, there is still something to add to, alter or reject. Every generation enjoys the use of a vast hoard bequeathed to it by antiquity, and transmits the hoard augmented by fresh acquisitions, to later ages. In these pursuits, therefore, the first speculators lie under the great disadvatages, and even when they fail, are entitled to praise. Their pupils with far inferior intellectual powers, speedily surpass them in actual attainments.

Substance: It is a truism of the author that poetry declines with the advance of civilization. There is nothing to wonder at, in the fact that great works of poetry were produced in the middle ages. On the other hand, the creation of a great work of poetic art in a civilized age, fills us with a sense of wonder. It bespeaks the supreme genius of the poet. The fact is that the progress of science follows laws which are diametrically opposite to those of arts. Science advances by slow and gradual steps. A long time is taken in collecting materials, and sifting them and discovering laws out of them. Hence the works of the pioneers in science are to be admired, even when they have failed. Inferior men of later ages might have excelled the great scientists of the past in actual performance, because they have the advantage of the accumulated knowledge of centuries.

Comment: The truism upheld by the author has been universalized when he brings in the plural pronoun *we* at the outset of the passage. The author seems to hold a rather prejudiced view of the advancement of science which he regards as something *slow* and *gradual*. Moreover, the author opines that men of science take a great deal of time in collecting materials, sifting them, and finally discovering laws out of them. Men of science who have failed in their work are entitled to praise and their pupils with inferior intellectual powers are capable of surpassing their mentors—such views put forth by the author sound rather prejudiced.

When the author comes to speak of poetry, he is full of adulation as he refers to it as 'the creation of great work of poetic art', 'fills us with a sense of wonder', it is the product of 'the supreme genius of the poet'. The epithets used reinforce this fact: '*great* work' and '*supreme* genius'. Despite all this, the author has rationally established the point that the methods of science and arts are diametrically opposite.

Example 14

Among the many who have enforced (1) the duty of giving, I am surprised there are none to inculcate (2) in ignominy (3) of receiving; to show that by every favour we accept, we, in some measure, forfeit (4) our native freedom; and that a state of continual dependence on the generosity of others is a life of gradual debasement (5).

Were men taught to despise the receiving of obligations with the same force of reasoning and declamation (6) that they are instructed to confer them, we might see every person in society filling up the requisite duties of his station with cheerful industry, neither relaxed by hope nor sullen (7) from disappointment.

Every favour a man receives in some measure, sinks him below his dignity; and, in proportion to the value of the benefit, or the frequency of its acceptance, he gives up so much of his natural independence. He, therefore, who thrives upon the unmerited (8) bounty of another, if he has any sensibility, suffers the worst of servitude (9) the shackled (10) slave may murmur without reproach, but the humble dependence is taxed with ingratitude upon every symptom (11) of discontent; the one may rave (12) round the walls of his cell, but the other lingers in all the silence of mental confinement (13). To increase his distress, every new obligation but adds to the former load, which kept the vigorous mind from rising; till at last, elastic (14) no longer, it shapes itself to constraint, put on habitual servility. (238 words)

Central idea: Dependence on others' charity degrades the character of man. The lot of an humble dependent is worse than that of slave.

Word-notes: 1.Emphasized; 2. Preach; 3. Disgrace; 4.Lose; 5. Degradation; 6. Eloquent speech; 7. Gloomy; 8. Undeserved; 9. Slavery; 10. Bound by chains; 11. Sign; 12.Cry like a mad man; 13. Inner restraint; 14. Supple.

Substance: Few people have ever pointed out the evil effect of receiving charity from others. Dependence on others' charity degrades the character of the dependent. The world would be a far better place if men were taught to hate receiving gifts from others. A man who always depends on the generosity of another gradually loses his native independence and self-respect. Nay, his state is even worse than that of a slave. A slave may vent his discontentment, without making himself liable to the charge of ungratefulness. But a hanger—one has to bide his time in inward smart (noun—a bodily or mental sharp pain; a stinging sensation—Concise Oxford Dictionary). Any expression of his discontent will be condemned as a mark of ingratitude. Thus, with every gift he receives, he loses the suppleness of his mind and becomes a hardened slave. (130 words)

Critical note: In the passage the author has raised an uncommon and unusual question regarding the undesirability of accepting favour from others. In his opinion, while the role of charity is propounded and praised as a social virtue and duty, the other side of the thing, that is the evil of accepting favour from others has seldom been brought to surface and criticized. The author then goes on to establish his point by offering various arguments. His main emphasis lies on the fact that a chronic receiver of charity loses his sense of independence and this makes him worse than a slave. What make his situation worse is that he is bound by a sense of obligation from which a slave is free.

The viewpoint of the author may be considered acceptable theoretically for the sake of argument. But for all practical purpose the situation as envisaged by the author, that is, a world free from parasites is not possible. Charity involves two sides, the giver and the receiver. If the receivers stop accepting charity which is otherwise considered a virtue, this virtue will be abolished from the society. Man may become totally self-centered. A situation like this may not be palatable to the author or to anybody. The views of the author, therefore, suffer from contradiction.

Despite the above shortcoming, the arguments have been presented in a logical manner. There is no ambiguity about what the author wants to say. His approach is straight-forward and the presentation is convincing.

Example 15

The man, who is perpetually hesitating which of the two things he will do first, will do neither. The man who resolves, but suffers his resolution to be changed by the first counter-suggestion of a friend,—who fluctuates from opinion to opinion, from plan to plan, and veers like a weathercock to every point of the compass, with every breath of caprice that blows,—can never accomplish anything great or useful. Instead of being progressive in anything, he will be at best stationary and more probably retrograde in all. It is only the man who first consults wisely, then resolves firmly, and then executes his purpose with inflexible perseverance, undismayed by those petty difficulties which daunt a weaker spirit,—that can advance to eminence in any line. Take your course wisely, but firmly; and having taken it, hold upon it with heroic resolution and the Alps and the Himalayas will sink before you.

Substance: Lack of steadiness or fixity of purpose leads to failure in life. The man who constantly flies from object to object can achieve nothing. Success depends upon the power of choosing the right course and then proceeding along it step by step, without being deterred by the difficulties that may crop up.

Comment: As the topic sentence occurs at the beginning of the paragraph, it may be regarded as a loosely constructed paragraph. The basic idea of the passage has been established at the outset: the man who first of all takes a wise decision and proceeds to work it out step by step is sure to achieve success in life. His success is such that the Alps and the Himalayas will sink before him. The two mountain ranges mentioned implicitly represent the height of impossibility; the concluding sentence:

> Take your course wisely, but firmly; and having taken it, hold upon it with heroic resolution and the Alps and the Himalayas will sink before you.

is an advice to the reader for attainment of success in life. Once the course is taken, it must be held upon with heroic resolution. The epithet *heroic* is apt because the person must be dauntless in spirit. There is an instance of listing: one can advance to eminence in any work of life by consulting wisely, then resolving firmly, and then finally executing his purpose with inflexible perseverance without being disheartened by petty difficulties which generally daunt a weaker spirit.

The simile 'veers like a weathercock', though the comparison may appear rather inane, is appropriate because the writer continues in the same vein to add 'with breath of caprice that blows'. There is alliteration in the sentence:

In*st*ead of being progressive in anything, he will be at be*st st*ationary... —where there is repetition of *st* combination.

Example 16

I remember to have once seen a slave in a fortification in Flanders, who appeared no way touched with his situation. He was maimed (1), deformed and chained; obliged to toil from the appearance of day till nightfall and condemned to this for life; yet with all these circumstances of apparent wretchedness he sang, would have danced but that he wanted a leg, and appeared the merriest, happiest man of all the garrison. What a practical philosopher was there! A happy constitution supplied philosophy, and though seemingly destitute of wisdom, he was really wise. No reading or study had contributed to disenchant (2) fairy land around him. Everything furnished him with an opportunity of mirth; and though some thought him from his insensibility a fool, he was such an 'idiot as philosophers might wish in vain to imitate'. They who, like him, can place themselves on that side of the world, in which everything appears in a ridiculous or pleasing light, will find something in every occurrence to excite their good humour. The most calamitous (3) events either to themselves or to others can bring no new affliction; the whole world is to them a theatre in which comedies only are acted. All the bustle of heroism or the rants (4) of ambition serve only to heighten the absurdity of the scene and make the humour more poignant (5). They feel, in short, as little anguish at their own distress or the complaints of others, as the undertaker (6), though dressed in black, feels sorrow at a funeral. (252 words)

Central Idea: Happiness depends on the mind and not on external conditions. Thus the slave in the prison-house was cheerful, though to others his lot appeared very miserable.

Word-notes: 1.Crippled; 5.Break the charm of; 3. Dangerous; 4. Talk wildly like a mad man; 5. Piercing, keen; 6. One who manages funeral.

Substance: Once the writer met a mangled and chained slave in a fort in Flanders. Though the slave was condemned to lifelong toil, he never lost his cheerfulness of spirits. According to the writer, the slave is a type of the truly wise man, though people may consider him to be a fool. The source of the slave's happiness lies within him and not in the outward circumstances which are the very opposite of what is happy. The example of the slave is worthy of imitation by all. Those who take an unconcerned view of life, suffer from no misery. Life to them is a comedy; the noise and bustle of life only serve to exciter their laughter. No calamity of life can affect the habitual cheerfulness of their mind.

Critical note: In this passage the author narrates his experience about a slave whose approach to life and thinking, apparently insensible and farcical, might serve as an object lesson to others. A lifelong prisoner and physically incapacitated, he never lost the cheerfulness of his mind and was totally indifferent towards the common joys and sorrows about himself as also others. The author feels that such indifference towards life raised him to the height of a real philosopher who is equally insouciant towards the world around him. The writer believes that happiness is something that does not depend on the things around them; rather it is something that makes its presence within one's own-self. As such these people suffer least in life.

The author feels that we have something to learn from this slave and we all should inculcate such an attitude within ourselves.

The passage beginning with 'I' establishes a nearness between the writer and the reader. Apparently he adopts the method of a story-teller but gradually plunges deep into the greater reality of life. He desires to create an awareness within us about what our approach towards life should be. He leads us to the verge of Stoicism.

The passage is autobiographical in nature and the message he wants to convey is incubated inside his memoir. The style is subjective, lucid and affords a smooth reading for the readers.

Example 17

If we should profit by our study, we must be careful not only to select proper books, but also to peruse them aright. The same book will affect the readers differently according to the purpose with which they read it. The butterfly sits, over the flower-bed gathering nothing; the spider collects poison from it; but the bee finds and stores up honey; so the object, for which you go to a book will determine the kind of fruit it will yield you. The same volume may be made to minister, to instruction or to rational amusement, or to a mere morbid love of excitement. The child takes off the lid of the tea-kettle for sport, the housewife for use—but James Watt for science, which ended in invention of steam-engine.

Substance: It is not merely the right selection of books but the way of reading them aright that can yield good results in study. The same book affects the different readers in different ways, according to their light and ability. Some may find a book instructive, while others will find it merely exciting.

Comment: The basic idea upheld in the passage is placed in the very opening sentence that if we are to benefit from our study, we must be judicious in our selection of books and are also expected to peruse them in a proper manner, the paragraph is of a loose nature. The main contention of the passage is that study of books yields results according to the manner of choosing them and reading them.

To illustrate this fact the writer speaks of a child who takes off the lid of a tea-kettle simply for the sake of sport, whereas the housewife commits the same act for a certain use, and James Watt too did take off the lid of the tea-kettle for the cause of science, which ultimately led to the invention of the steam-engine. In other words, the same act is committed by different persons with different purposes. The writer has chosen such an illustration in order to show that the same book will affect the readers differently according to the purpose they want to achieve they peruse the book. To support this point the writer pounces on another illustration: the butterfly sits on the flower-bed gleaning nothing; the spider collects poison by this very act; but the bee gathers and stores up honey in this act.

Thus each and every reader reads a book with an ulterior motive—the object for which one goes to a book will determine the kind of fruit it will yield to one. The same book will be capable of ministering, of imparting instruction, or offering rational amusement, or submitting to a mere morbid love of excitement.

The entire passage is written in a facile manner. There are no difficult words causing hindrance to our understanding of the passage. The illustrations that the writer goes in for are extremely mundane and utterly homely.

Example 18

Looked at in terms of space, the message of astronomy is at best one of *melancholy grandeur* (1) and oppressive vastness. Looked at in terms of time, it becomes one of almost endless possibility and hope. As denizens (2) of the universe, we may be living near its end rather than its beginning, for it seems likely that most of the universe had melted into radiation before we appeared on the scene. But as inhabitants of the earth, we are living at very beginning of time. We have come into being in the fresh glory of the dawn, and a day of almost unthinkable length stretches before us with unimaginable opportunities for accomplishment. Our descendants of the far-off ages, looking down this long vista (3) of time from the other end, will see our present age as the misty morning of the world's history; our contemporaries of today will appear as dim heroic figures who fought their way through jungles of ignorance, error and superstition to discover truth, to learn how to harness the forces of Nature, and to make a world worthy for mankind to live in. We are still too much engulfed (4) in the greyness of the morning mists to be able to imagine, however vaguely, how this world of ours will appear to those who will come after us and see it in the full light of the day. But by what light we have, we seem to discern (5) that the main message of astronomy is one of hope to the race and of the responsibility to the individual-of responsibility because we are drawing plans and laying foundations for a longer future than we can well imagine. (284 words)

Central Idea: The message of astronomy is at once sad and hopeful—sad because man occupies a little space in a vast universe; hopeful because man is still in the dawn of civilization and has endless possibilities.

Word-notes: 1. Sad glory; 2. Citizens; 3. Prospect; 4. Plunged; 5. Understand.

Substance: The study of astronomy fill us with a mingled feeling of melancholy and hope, —melancholy because of the consideration of the vastness of the universe as contrasted with the littleness of man and hope, because the earth we live in is quite young. Man is only in the dawn of human history and a boundless future lies ahead of him. Rich possibilities are before him. He has to conquer ignorance and superstition, discover truth and thus make the earth a better place to live in. Future generations of men will thus look upon the present generation as heroes who have carved out their civilization. Thus a great responsibility devolves upon the men of the present age, because they are the builders of the future of the world. (127 words)

Critical Note: The passage deals with human civilization and its existence and future against the backdrop of the universe and astronomy. Although our existence in the universe is of little significance which fact may cause gloom and melancholy to us, we have rays of hope if we consider our existence from the standpoint of human civilization. The author feels that on earth human civilization has just started and it has a long way to go. We are the pathfinders for our posterity and they will remember us for what we have done for them.

The author used contrasts like *melancholy grandeur, oppressive vastness* on the one hand and *endless possibility of hope* on the other. The passage concludes with a tone of optimism like *one of hope to the race*. The comparison of the present state of human civilization with *misty morning* is effective and creates a poetic sense in the minds of the readers. This imagery recurs in the passage a number of times like *morning mists and full light of day*.

All said and done, the message conveyed in the extract is ecumenical in nature bordering didacticism. The modern reader may not find the message of much relevance.

Example 19

It thrills one to read of the passion of loyalty which Florence Nightingale aroused everyone about her. A number of English gentlemen gathered around the hospital to do her bidding. Orderlies and attendants ran at her whisper. As for the patients, they almost worshipped her. Macdonald, who administered the fund *The Times* had raised for the service of the sick and wounded, draws a picture of this gentlewoman at Scutari—"As a slender form glides (1) quietly along each corridor, every poor fellow's face softens with gratitude at the sight of her. When all the medical officers have retired for the night , and silence and darkness settled down upon miles of prostrate (2) sick, she may be observed alone with a little lamp in her hand , making her solitary round." It is on this picture, the pitying women carrying her nurse's lamp through the long corridors where five thousand sick and wounded are lying—that our imagination loves to dwell. (161 words)

Central Idea: Florence Nightingale inspired all around her with a new faith. Wounded soldiers kissed her shadows she walked round the barracks at night, with a lamp in hand.

Word-notes: 1. Moves; 2. Lying down; bed-ridden.

Substance: The loyalty which Florence Nightingale inspired in every man who came in contact with her is admirable. Doctors, orderlies and attendants in the hospitals performed her bidding at her mere whisper. Patients almost worshipped her. As the slender woman quietly passed along the corridor of the hospital, the faces of the patients beamed with gratitude to her. The picture of this lady moving about in the hospital barracks with a lamp in hand, when doctors had retired at night, was one worthy of remembrance. (84 words)

Critical Note: It is obvious that it is an extract from the biography of Florence Nightingale. It highlights the popularity and acceptability of the great lady among the persons who came in contact with her. Popularly known as The Lady with the Lamp, the passage depicts this picture of Florence.

The style of the writer is lucid, simple and straight-forward as should happen in the case of a biography. The subject-matter being what it is, there is not much scope for logical arguments. The approach of the writer is direct and the massage is conveyed without ambiguity. The writer has taken the major portion of his writing from the description of the Lady given by MacDonald. The simple and direct approach to the subject may be said to be the main attraction of the passage.

Comment: The passage is of a descriptive nature as it gives a vivid picture of Florence Nightingale quietly gliding down the corridors tending the sick and wounded patients at Scutari. It is a tightly knit paragraph. The prose piece has a poetic flavour; this is so because of phrases like 'passion of loyalty', 'ran at her whisper'. At times there are alliterations in the sequence of words: '*f*ellow's *f*ace', 'a*l*one with a *l*itt*l*e *l*amp', '*p*icture, the *p*itying woman'. The writer is in the habit of using connective conjunction *and* evident from expressions such as: 'Orderlies *and* attendants', 'sick *and* wounded', 'silence *and* darkness'. In the concluding sentence there is internal rhyme: 'pity*ing*...carry*ing*... ly*ing*'; it is certainly a means of beautification of the passage on the whole. The passage upholds a romanticized picture of Florence Nightingale who inspired all around her with a faith. The wounded soldiers kissed her shadow as she walked round the barracks at night, with a lamp in her hand.

Example 20

In looking at our age, one is struck with one commanding (1) characteristic, that is , the tendency in all its movements to expansion, to diffusion (2), to universality. The tendency is directly opposed to the spirit of exclusiveness, restriction, narrowness, monopoly (3) which has prevailed in past ages. Human action is now freer, more unconfined. All goods, advantages, helps are more open to all. The privileged (4), petted individual is becoming less, and the human race is becoming more. The multitude is rising from the dust. Once we heard of the few, now of the many; one of the prerogatives (5) of a part, now of the rights of all. We are looking, as never before, through the disguises, envelopments of ranks and classes, to the common nature which is below them, and beginning to learn that every being who partakes of it has noble powers to cultivate, solemn duties to perform, inalienable rights to assert, a vast destiny to accomplish. The grand idea of humanity, of the importance of man as man is spreading silently, but surely. The idea that every human being should have the means of self-culture (6), of progress in knowledge and virtue, of health, comfort and happiness—this is slowly taking its place as the highest social truth. That the world was made for all; that no human being shall perish but through his own fault; that the great end of government is to *spread a shield over* (7) the rights of all—these propositions are growing into axioms (8), and the spirit of them is coming forth in all the departments of life. (271 words)

Central Idea: The present age is the age of democracy. The few have yielded place to the many and the government of every country cares more for the masses than the chosen few.

Word-notes: 1. Chief; 2.Extension; 3. Absolute possession; 4. Enjoying special rights; 5. Special rights; 6. Development of one's self; 7. Protect; 8. Self-evident truths.

Substance: The present age is marked by one striking quality—namely, its democratic tendency, its substitution of the few by the many. In the past there was a privileged class who had exclusive monopoly of the good things in life. But today all advantages have been thrown open to all without any distinction or rank. The worth and dignity of a man as man have been recognized today. It is admitted on all hands that every man has noble powers to cultivate, sacred duties to perform, and high purposes in life to fulfil. Knowledge, virtue, health and happiness are the lot of all men, and not the prerogatives of the few. The government of every country is prepared to protect the rights of the common man, providing facilities of self-realization for all. (131 words)

Critical Note: The passage brings out a contrasting picture of place man had earlier in the past and what place he is in today. Previously the society was governed by autocracy, dictatorship and feudalism and the common people were deprived of the various benefits to which they were entitled. The author feels that the time has changed. Today people are having their share of the benefits and advantages of society and the governments of the countries are also paying their attention to this.

It is clear that the message conveyed here has a socialistic bent which propagates the basic amenities for all in the society. The writer has conveyed this message quite clearly without any prevarication. It is not difficult also to imagine the writer's attitude which tilts in favour of socialism.

The passage may not be classified as a political writing as such because it speaks more about the social structure rather than any direct political leaning. The concept expressed is broad and generalized in nature. It narrates the evolution of society from a particular angle. In a sense, it is a blend of history and politics.

The passage is marked by clarity of thought and expression and the language is befitting to the subject. The writer's attitude is objective marked by absence of personal trait. We read the passage for what the writer has to say, and not for the picture of his personality. His style is masculine and approach straightforward. His attitude is not marked by any dogmatism.

Example 21

To men of any spirit the opposition of Nature constitutes a challenge which cannot be ignored. The sense of battle rouses a fierce joy in them that no mere adverse reasoning can ever destroy, and the very idea of impossibility is foreign to their nature. This spirit taught men to fly, regardless of the laws of gravity. It taught them to rush along the ground at speeds exceeding three miles—now almost four miles—in a minute. It taught them to jump down through thousands of feet of space aided by nothing better than something resembling a large umbrella.

The same spirit actuates mountain-climbers. No sooner do they perceive a peak than they must climb it. Although there are good scientific reasons for climbing mountains, they are not very strong ones; the *moral* reasons are far stronger. It is a noble thing to endeavour to surmount difficulties and to penetrate into realms where ordinary men dare not venture.

Substance: A courageous man is never daunted by the hostilites on Nature. He accepts Nature's challenge and overcomes it. 'Impossible' is a word that is unknown in his dictionary. It is this fierce spirit which has led men to speed-motoring, parachute-flight and mountaineering. It has led men to the distant ends of the earth. This spirit is more moral than physical.

Comment: The passage is structured loosely as the topic sentence occurs at the outset:

> To men of any spirit the opposition of Nature constitutes
> a challenge which cannot be ignored.

The rest of the passage endeavours to substantiate the fact that a man of courage feels called upon to accept the challenge of Nature, instead of yielding to her. It is this very spirit which has urged man to impossible deeds of valour. By virture of this dauntless spirit, man is capable of dangerous speed-motoring, parachute-flight, and mountaineering. Because of courage, man breaks away from his physical limitations and is capable of undertaking such risky adventures. In other words, nothing is impossible for man: all precarious feats can be achieved by man by his sheer dint of courage.

Man is not prepared to accept his surrounding Nature as he finds her. Man is prepared to face the challenges put forth by Nature—he overcomes all obstacles. The sense of battle rouses in man a fierce joy. The word 'Nature' being capitalized gives an indication that Nature has been personified as one who causes obstacles.

The very sentence contains an assonance of 'au' sound:

> To men *o*f any spirit *o*f *o*pposition *o*f Nature c*o*nstitutes a
> challenge which cann*o*t be ign*o*red.

This strain of assonance is further continued in the following sentence in words like: 'j*o*y', destr*o*y', '*o*f, 'im*po*ssibility', '*fo*reign'. There is an internal rhyme created in '*joy*...dest*roy*'. These rhetorical devices help to raise the prose passage to poetic heights at times.

Example 22

A great deal of the world's work is neither producing material things nor altering the things that Nature produces but doing services of one sort or another.

Thoughtless people are apt to think a brickmaker more of a producer than a clergyman. When a village carpenter makes a gate to keep cattle out of a field of wheat, he has something solid in his hand which he can claim for his own until the former pays him for it. But when a village boy makes a noise to keep the birds off, he has nothing to shew, though the noise is just as necessary as the gate. The postman does not make anything; he only delivers letters and parcels. The policeman does not make anything: and the soldier not only does not make things; he destroys them. The doctor makes pills sometimes; but that is not his real business, which is to tell you when you ought to take pills, and what pills to take, unless indeed he has the good sense to tell you not to take them at all, and you have the good sense to believe him when he is giving you good advice instead of bad. The lawyer does not make anything substantial, nor the clergyman, nor the member of Parliament, nor the domestic servant (though she sometimes breaks things), nor the Queen or King, nor an actor. When their work is done they have nothing in hand that can be weighed or measured; nothing that the maker can keep from others until she is paid for it. They are all in service: in domestic service like the housemaid, or in commercial service, like the shop assistant, or in Government service like the postman, or in State service like the King; and all of us who have full-size consciences consider ourselves in what some of us call the service of God.

And then, besides the persons who make the substantial things there must be persons to find out how they should be made. Beside the persons who do things there must be persons who know how they should be done, and decide when they should be done, and how much they should be done. In simple village life both the making or the doing and the thinking may be done by the same person when he is a blacksmith, carpenter or builder; but in big cities and highly civilized countries this is impossible: one set of people has to make and do whilst another set of people thinks and decides what, when, how much, and by whom.

Shaw: *Goods and Services* (*The Intelligent Woman's Guide to Socialism, 1928*)

Substance: In the given passage the author attempts to draw a distinction between the productive and the non-productive workers. In the former category may be included the village carpenter who makes a gate to ward off cattle from a field of wheat; in this regard the village boy who makes a noise to keep the birds off is also a productive worker, though he has nothing to show. Even the postman is a productive labourer, as much as the policeman and the soldier. The writer is keen enough to tell us that the soldier does not make things, but destroys them. In comparison to this class of workers, the doctor, the lawyer, the clergyman, and the member of Parliament are people who are non-productive because they do not make anything substantial. In the latter category the writer includes, the domestic service, the Queen or King, and the actor, since the work done by them does not show anything in hand that can be weighed or measured. Despite this categorization, they are all in service (what some consider the service of God).

Comment: The passage is loosely structured as the keynote of the passage has been struck at the very outset:

> A great deal of the world's work is neither producing material things nor altering the things that Nature produces but doing services of one sort or another.

The writer is out to make a general point in economic theory. In doing so, the writer does not in any way resort to confusing jargons from the realm of economics, thus he is able to easily reach out to his readers. The diction used by writer is absolutely clear and concrete. To establish his point, the writer refers to actual things and people, such as the village carpenter along with the gate he makes to keep the cattle out of a field of wheat. According to an economist of modern times this picture of the world's work presented by the author may appear rather over-simplified, but this is justified at this point in his presentation of general argument.

The writer is vigorous and emphatic in driving home his point as he keeps repeating:

> The postman *does not make*...The policeman *does not make*...the lawyer *does not make*...

It is more than clearly evident that the writer is prejudiced in his views about doctors when he remarks about pills:

> The doctor makes pills sometimes; but this is not his real business, which is to tell you when you ought to take pills, and what pills to take, unless indeed he has the good sense to tell you not to take them at all, and you have the good sense to believe him when he is giving you good advice instead of bad.

Apart from people who make the substantial things there are people who have the knowhow of the things made. They too, in a way, contribute to the making of a thing. This is especially evident in the city, whereas in the simple village life both the making (execution) and the thinking (conception) may be done by the same person, as the blacksmith, carpenter, or builder.

On the whole, the passage is of a discursive nature. The author tries to establish his point by his own eccentric way of reasoning.

Example 23

What is it that which first strikes us and strikes us at once in a man of education, and which among the educated men so instantly distinguishes the man of superior mind that 'we cannot stand under the same archway (1) during a shower of rain without finding him out?' Not the weight or novelty (2) of his remarks; not any unusual interest of facts communicated by him; for we may suppose both the one and the other precluded (3) by the shortness of our intercourse and the triviality of our subjects. The difference will be impressed and felt though the conversation should be confined to the state of weather or the pavement. Still less will it arise from any peculiarity of his words and phrases; for if he be, as we now assume, a well-educated man as well as a man of superior powers, he will not fail to follow the golden rule of Julius Caesar, and unless where new things necessitate new terms, he will avoid an unusual word as a rock. It must have been among the earliest lessons of his youth that a breach of this precept (4), at all times hazardous, becomes ridiculous in the topics of ordinary conversation. There remains but one other point of distinction possible; and this must be, and in fact is, the true cause of the impression made on us. It is the unpremeditated (5) and evidently habitual arrangement of his words, grounded on the habit of foreseeing in each integral part or (more plainly) in every sentence, the whole that he then intends to communicate; however irregular and desultory (6) his talk, there is *method in the fragments* (7). (273 words)

Central Idea: An educated man can be at once recognized by his power of conversation. It is not novelty or wealth of ideas, but the use of words that constitutes the chief excellence of his talks.

Word-notes: 1.Portico; 2. Newness; 3.Prevented; 4. Rule; 5. Natural; spontaneous; 6. Haphazard; 7. Underlying unity in the scattered portions.

Substance: The most striking feature of an educated man or a man of superior qualities of mind is his conversational power. Novelty or originality of remarks and the wealth of information given in talk are not his distinguishing qualities. Nor does his distinction lie in the peculiarity of words used. An educated man will always avoid an unfamiliar word, where a more familiar word would serve his purpose. Even though his conversation may be on a trivial subject, it will have an aroma of its own. Another great distinction lies in the construction of his sentences, in which every word is an organic part of the whole and arranged methodically so as to bring out fully the meaning he seeks to communicate. Even in his most casual talks he impresses us with this personal quality of his style. (137 words)

Critical Note: The passage deals with the true characteristic features of an educated man. According to the author, an educated man needs not parade his learning or knowledge or vocabulary in day-to-day life. The implication is that he knows that a show of his learning or language-power is not necessary in his daily life. Rather he knows that such exhibition would make him an object of ridicule to others. So he uses his vocabulary in a choosy manner and according to the situation. Despite this, the writer feels, it is not difficult to identify him from among the men of common frame of mind from his vocabulary and language. Another distinction lies in his construction of sentences that constitutes the excellent characteristic feature of his talk.

As observed above, the writer's point of discussion is singular; he is concerned with his own notion of an educated man or a man with a superior frame of mind. And his point of view is only the language used by him. This, despite being an uncommon approach, may be found to be acceptable and convincing.

The style is suited to the subject and the reference to the golden rule of Julius Caesar creates a sense of jerk and surprise in the minds of the readers although they get over this in no time. The arguments of the writer gather force and conviction because he does not deviate or digress from his arguments. He remains steady and constant to his arguments througho ut.

The writer's style is objective and clear. His personality is kept in the background. His observations are factual and scientific and detached from any emotional spark. By virtue of his objective attitude, his style is masculine. The sentence construction and choice of words are suited to the subject matter.

The passage has a dramatic beginning with an interrogative sentence at the outset. The question pertinently points out that an educated man can be at once recognized by the power of conversation. The author subsequently substantiates the fact that it is not novelty or wealth of ideas, but the use of words that constitutes the chief excellence of his talk. Though he talks of trivial subjects, there is a certain sparkle in his talk. His conversation is generally unpremeditated, and it is clearly habitual arrangement of his words. There is an amount of method in the fragments of his conversation because his conversation is firmly based on habitual arrangement of his words which reveals his foresight in each integral part or in every sentence. These qualities are what distinguishes an educated man from others.

Example 24

There are some books, when we close them, —one or two in the course of our life,—difficult as it may be to analyse or ascertain the cause, our minds seem to have made a great leap. A thousand obscure things receive light; a multitude of indefinite feelings are determined. Our intellect grasps and grapples (1) with all subjects with a capacity, a flexibility (2), and a vigour before unknown to us. It masters questions hitherto perplexing, which are not in touch or referred to in the volume just closed. What is the magic? It is the spirit of the supreme author, by a magnetic influence bending with our sympathizing intelligence that directs or inspires it? By that mysterious sensibility (3), we extend to questions which he has not treated with the same intellectual force which he has exercised over those which he has expounded (4). His genius for a time remains in us. 'Tis the same with human beings as with books. All of us encounter (5), at least once in our life, some individual who utters words that make us think for ever. There are men, whose phrases are oracles (6); who condense in a sentence the secrets of life; who blurt (7) out an aphorism (8) that forms a character or illustrate an existence. (211 words)

Central Idea: Great books, like great men, quicken our powers, so that we can understand things which baffled us so long.

Word-notes: 1. Try to overcome; 2. Elastic powers; 3. Capacity to feel; 4. Explained; 5. Meet; 6. Men or words full of wisdom; 7. Speak abruptly; 8. Proverb; pithy maxim.

Substance: There are some great but rare books which exercise a quickening influence over our mental powers. As we rise from a study of them, our intellect is so sharpened that we can easily understand the most difficult things and solve the most baffling problems. The fact is that the genius of the author stimulates our powers and perhaps leaves something of that genius within us. That is why our powers of understanding are so quickened. What is true of great books is also true of great men. All of us must have come across in our life some rare type of man, whose words set us deeply a-thinking, and whose short utterances have the soul of wisdom in them. Contact with such people is highly inspiring. (126 words)

Critical Note: The influence of great books on mankind has always been an accepted fact in our life. Similarly, on occasions, great persons come in our life whose messages leave a permanent impression on our minds and act as our guides in the paths of our lives. This is also an accepted fact. The above are the situations that form the subject of this passage.

According to the writer, great books and great men quicken our powers so that we can understand the things that baffled us so long. In reality this is very much possible and the arguments of the writer need not be disputed. His approach to his subject is direct without any digression. The arguments can be understood and appreciated by any sensible person. The effect could have been otherwise had he loaded his arguments with illustrations or references. Sometimes intentional omission of something like this adds force to the arguments. This is understandably so because the subject of the passage, instead of being controversial, is a sort of axiom.

As regards style, the sentences are at time lengthy creating a sense of jolt while one reads the passage. The arguments have been put forth with vigour and straightforwardness.

Example 25

Great books do not spring from something accidental in the great man who wrote them. They are the effluence (1) of their core (2), the expression of the life itself of the authors. And literature cannot be said to have served its purpose until it has been translated into the actual life of him who reads. It is the vast reservoir of true ideas and emotions. In the world deprived of literature, the broad, the noble, the generous tend to disappear and life would be correspondingly degraded, because the fallacious (3) idea and the petty emotion would never feel the upward pull of the ideas and emotions of genius. Only by conceiving a society without literature can it be clearly realized that the function of literature is to raise the plain towards the top level of the peaks. Literature exists so that where one man has lived finely, ten thousands may afterwards live finely. It is a means of life; it concerns the living essence. (162 words)

Central Idea: Literature, being the expression of the thoughts and emotions of great men, elevates and refines the mind of the readers. Without literature all good thoughts would disappear from the earth.

Word-notes: 1. Emanation; coming out; 2. Innermost part; 3. Wrong.

Substance: Great books are the very expression of the life of the authors and not the accidental products of their minds. Literature cannot be said to have discharged its function properly unless it is made a part of the life of the reader. It is the storehouse of the ideas and emotions of the authors. It elevates man to a higher level of existence. In a society without literature all great and noble ideas tend to disappear. Literature helps noble living, and thus its influence on life is deep. (88 words)

Critical Note: The role of literature in our life has been a subject-matter of discussion from time immemorial. According to the author, literature has to fulfil two conditions to attain greatness: first, it has to take its origin from the innermost core of the author's heart; second, it should occupy an integral part of the life of the reader. Great literature is not produced by fluke. It elevates the reader to the highest emotional level.

The argument of the author is an accepted fact not to be disputed at all. But what is remarkable about the passage is the manner in which the whole thing is presented. Here form gets the better of content. If clarity of thought, preciseness of expression, and lucidity of language are the qualities that make prose great, here is an example of that. The writer's approach to his subject is direct, totally devoid of any sort of pretension. To sum up, it is an extremely readable passage which, within its short framework, reflects all the qualities of ideal prose.

Example 26

There can be little question that the attainment of a federation of all humanity, together with a sufficient measure of social justice, to ensure health, education, and a rough equality of opportunity to most of the children born into the world, would mean such a release and increase of human energy as to open a new phase in human history. The enormous waste caused by military preparation and the mutual annoyance of competing great powers and the still more enormous waste due to underproductiveness of great masses of people, either because they are too wealthy for stimulus, or too poor for efficiency, would cease. There would be a vast increase in the supply of human necessities, a rise in the standard of life and in what is considered a necessity, a development of transport and every kind of convenience; and a multitude of people would be transferred from low-grade production to such higher work as art of all kinds, teaching, scientific work and the like. All over the world there would be a setting free of human capacity, such as has occurred hitherto only in small places and through precious limited phases of prosperity and security. Unless we are to suppose that spontaneous outbreaks of supermen have occurred in the past, it is reasonable to conclude that the Athens of Pericles, the *Florence of the Medici's*, Elizabethan England, the great deeds of Asoka, the *Tang and Ming periods in art*, are but samples of what a whole world of sustained security would yield continuously and cumulatively. Without supposing any change in human quality, but merely its release from the present system of inordinate waste, history justifies this expectation.

Substance: The establishment of a world federation, with a re-distribution of opportunities for health, education, and happiness equally for all, would undoubtedly bring about a new era in human history. This would save much of the wastage that is now caused by war and rivalry among nations and unequal distribution of wealth. The result would be an enormous increase in the supply of necessaries for life and a consequent rise in the standard of living. Besides, this would enable many, who in spite of their qualifications are at present engaged in ordinary work, to take up such skilled occupation as teaching, research and so on. This re-adjustment of social order and the means of production will bring in a golden age, parallels of which may be found in the age of Pericles in Athens, or the Elizabethan age in England, or the reign of Asoka in Indian history, or the period of the Tang and Ming dynasties in Chinese history. These are the periods of interest in human activity; and such periods will come to stay once for all, if a socialistic world order is established.

Comment: The passage is loosely structured as the topic sentence at the outset points to the fact that the establishment of a world federation will ultimately bring about the golden age of the world. This would result in the ending of present war and wastage of human energy. A notable feature of the style of the passage is that almost all the sentences comprising the passage are pretty long. Despite the long sentences the idea is put forward clearly.

At times the style rises to poetic heights, as when the writer uses the phrase—'*c*ontinuous*ly* and *c*umulative*ly*'—where there is alliteration and internal rhyme, thereby making it mellifluous. There is further alliteration in the concluding line where there is a cluster of '*st*' sounds in the phrase:

...sy*st*em of inordinate wa*st*e, hi*st*ory ju*st*ifies...

Example 27

Whenever we buy, or try to buy, cheap goods - goods offered at a price which, we know cannot be remunerative (1) for the labour involved in them-remember we are stealing somebody's labour. Don't let us *mince the matter* (2). I say in plain Saxon, stealing—taking from him the proper reward of his work and putting it into our own pocket. You know well-enough that the thing could not have been offered to you at that price, unless distress of some kind had forced the producer to part with it. You take advantage of this distress, and you force as much out of him as you can under the circumstances. The old barons of the middle ages used, in general, the thumb-screw (3) to extort property; we, moderns, use in preference, hunger, or domestic affliction; but the fact of extortion (4) remains precisely the same. Whether we force the man's property from him by pinching his stomach, or pinching his fingers, makes some difference anatomically; —morally, none whatsoever; we use a torture of some sort in order to make him give up his property; we use, indeed, the man's own anxieties , instead of the rack (5); and his immediate peril of starvation , instead of the pistol at the head; but otherwise we differ from a highway robber , merely in being less dexterous, more cowardly and more cruel. More cruel, I say, because the fierce baron and the redoubted (6) highwayman are reported to have robbed, at least by preference, only the rich; we steal habitually from the poor. We buy our liveries, and build our palaces, with money pilfered (7) out of children's and sick men's wages. (278 words)

Central Idea: Buying things at a cheap rate is a crime worse than robbery. A producer is compelled to sell his goods at a cheap price by the pressure of hunger and want. The buyer takes advantage of that; hence he is a greater culprit.

Word-notes: 1. Lucrative; profitable; 2. Minimize the thing; 3. An instrument of torture for squeezing the thumb; 4. Exacting money by force; 5. An instrument of punishment; 6. Dreaded; 7. Stolen.

Substance: Buying things at a cheap price means stealing the legitimate dues of the producer. It is only under pressure of hunger and poverty that the producer undersells his produces. Hence the buyer of cheap articles is no better that a highwaymen in the middle ages or the barons of the old who extorted money from their subjects by oppression. Nay, in a sense, he is even worse; for the highwaymen robbed the rich, while the buyer of cheap goods robs the poor producers. (83 words)

Critical Note: The theme of the passage may be termed as *financial exploitation of the poor.* But the writer deals with the subject from a novel angle. It is the exploitation where 'bargain' becomes the tool of exploitation for the buyer. By this act of bargaining, we deprive the seller of his legitimate share of profit and the result is exploitation. The writer compares the modern exploiters with those in the past and comes to the conclusion that we, the modern people are worse than the old barons and the highwaymen of the middle ages who used to rob only of the rich whereas we, the modern people, who are even worse than the barons and robbers, do not hesitate to exploit the poor who are left with no alternative but to sacrifice their profit. In other words, we take advantage of the distress sell.

The arguments put forth by the writer are debatable in more than one ways. The writer ideates a Utopian situation as if bargaining always takes away the legitimate profit of a seller. This means that he is selling his goods at a loss. But our common sense says that normally a trader or a businessman does not prefer such a situation. This may be true in exceptional cases, but that cannot be taken as a general rule. As such theory propounded by the writer may be true for the sake of argument, but in practical field, its cogency is rather limited.

Despite such shortcomings in his logic, it can be said to the credit of the writer that he is rather clear in his approach and his language is direct and to the point. The style is lucid and the writer has maintained an attitude of objectivity. However, he has maintained some sort of intimacy and closeness with the reader through the use of the words 'you' and 'we'.

Example 28

The family, like the house in which they live, needs to be kept in repair, lest some little rift (1) in walls should appear and let in the wind and rain. The happiness of a family depends very much on attention to little things. Order, comfort, regularity, cheerfulness, good taste, pleasant conversation - these are the ornaments of daily life, deprived of which it degenerates (2) into wearisome routine. There must be light in the dwelling, and brightness and pure spirits and cheerful smiles. Home is not usually the place of toil, but the place to which we return, and rest from our labours, in which parents and children meet together and pass a careless and joyful hour. To have nothing to say to others at such times, in any rank of life, is a very unfortunate temper of mind, and may perhaps be regarded as a serious fault; at any rate, it makes the house vacant and joyless. (156 words)

Central Idea: The happiness of domestic life depends upon attention to small things. Home is the place for rest, and children add to domestic happiness.

Word-notes: 1. Opening; 2. Sinks from excellence.

Substance: The happiness of a family depends upon close attention to small things. Peace, comfort, regularity, cheerfulness, good conversation— all these make for the supreme bliss of family life. Without these, life becomes dreary and cheerless. Home is the place to which men retire after toil of the day and spend the hour merrily in the company of children. To have no pleasant conversation at that time is to deprive the family life of its gaiety. Hence, like the house in which a man lives, family life too requires constant repair, so that nothing can destroy its beauty and comfort. (98 words)

Critical Note: The subject-matter of the passage is happiness in a family. In the opinion of the author, the happiness of domestic life depends upon attention to small things. Home is the place for rest, and children add to domestic happiness.

The message is simple and does not call for any dispute. The passage is marked by clarity and directness of expression. He establishes his belief by comparing a family life with a house. The comparison, although a bit conventional, is apt and suited to the theme. The style is lucid and his approach is detached and unemotional. However, there seems to be a didactic approach on the part of the author and this could not have been otherwise having regard to the theme of the passage. As such a tone of gravity and seriousness is maintained throughout. The word order and sentence construction are smooth without creating any jerkiness to the readers. If clarity is the objective in prose writing, this passage is a fine example.

Example 29

Literature is the written record of valuable thought, having other than a merely technical purpose. It is the preserved sum-total of the best ideas of the world's noblest men and women. It is the tale of 'the common humanity whose sorrowings and sinnings, whose hopes and joys and little triumphs constitute the great story which leads back and sets man face to face with the undiscoverable.' Of all existing occupations, therefore, none is better than that of good reading, wisely to be used. It is treasure laid up for heaven, for the mind endures when the body is scattered to dust. Literature is more real and more lasting than stocks and securities, statues and buildings. 'The world of imagination,' it has been observed, 'is not the world of abstraction and non-entity, as some conceive, but a world formed out of chaos by a sense of the beauty that is in man and the earth on which he dwells.' Every book we read may be made a rung in the ever-lengthening ladder by which we climb to knowledge and to that temperance and serenity of mind which, as it is the ripest fruit of wisdom, is also the sweetest. 'The riches of scholarship, the benignities of literature defy fortune and outlive calamity. They are beyond the reach of thief or moth or rust. As they cannot be inherited, so they cannot be alienated'. 'The grandest aim of imaginative art,' says Ruskin, 'is to give men noble grounds for noble emotion.' Literature is but one of the imaginative arts ; and it is that art, which presupposes a development of culture which has been aptly defined as an 'interest in the best things said and written in the world.' The best things are the remnant, the chosen few, the selected minority. There were nine sibylline; books, then three were thrown away, then again three, but the remaining ones were more valuable than the nine. 'Literature', says John Morley, 'consists of all the books—and they are not so many—where moral truth and human passion are touched with a certain largeness, sanity, and attraction of form.'

Substance: Literature is the expression of the best ideas of the greatest men and women of the world. It is the story of the joys and sorrows, hopes and triumphs of men, and brings us face to face with the great Unknown. Hence the study of good literature is the best occupation of men. Literature is more enduring than earthly possessions. The world of imagination is not full of airy nothings, as some people imagine; it is a solid world of reality carved out by the sense of beauty in man. Each good book, therefore, helps us to acquire knowledge and that perfect serenity of mind which is true wisdom. The enjoyment of good lierature therefore requires a culture, which has been defined as the interest in all the best thoughts and ideas of the world. Great literature, therefore, is very rare. In it moral truths and human passions are presented in a large and attractive form.

Comment: The passage is of a discursive nature where the author is out to establish the fact that literature is essentially the expression of best ideas of the great men of the world. Literature comprises the sorrows and sinnings, hopes and joys of human life. Study of literature ultimately gives not only wisdom but true peace of mind and happiness.

On the whole, the passage is written in simple and lucid style. The structure of the passage is of a mixed nature as the key sentence of the passage does not occur at the outset:

> It [literature] is the preserved sum-total of the best ideas of the world's noblest men and women.

What has been stated at the beginning has been substantiated in the sentence following in more concrete terms. For ornamentation the author resorts to polysyndeton in the sentence:

> It is the tale of the common humanity whose sorrowings and sinnings, whose hopes *and* joys *and* little triumphs constitute the great story...

—this figurative use of the connective conjunction '*and*' may be hinting at the unending list that constitutes the great story of literature. When talking about the fact that the riches of scholarship, the benignities of literature defy fortune and outline the various calamities a similar rhetorical device has been used—polysyndeton—as though there are other possibilities of calamities with the use of the alternative conjunction '*or*' in the sentence:

> They are beyond the reach of thief *or* moth *or* rust.

Example 30

I go into my library and all history unrolls (1) itself before me. I breathe the morning air of the world, while the scent of Eden's roses yet lingered (2) in it while it vibrated only to the world's first brood (3) of nightingales, and to the laugh of Eve. I see the Pyramids building. I hear the shoutings of the armies of Alexander; I feel the ground shake beneath the march of Cambyses. I sit as in a theatre; the stage is time, the play is the play of the world. What a spectacle it is! What kingly pomp, what processions file past, what cities burn to heaven, what crowds of captives are dragged at the chariot-wheels of the conquerors! I hear or cry 'Bravo!' when the great actors come on shaking the stage. I lift Homer, and I shout with Achilles in the trenches (4). The silence of the unpeopled Syrian plains, the outcomings of the patriarchs (5), Abraham and Ishmael, Isaac in the fields of eventide (6), Rebekah at the well, Jacob's guile, Easu's face reddened by desert sun heat, Joseph's funeral procession—all these things I find within the boards of my Old Testament. Oh, men and women, so far separated yet so near, so well-known , by what miraculous power do I know you all! (215 words)

Central Idea: The study of books in a library reveals before the reader the entire history of mankind in its various forms and such study acts as a link between the present and the past.

Word-notes: 1. Opens out; exposes; 2. Stayed about a place; 3. Young of an animal especially bird; 4. A long, narrow ditch; 5. A man who is the head of a family or tribe; 6. Evening; sunset.

Substance: When a man enters a library and looks at the books there, the whole history of the past lies fully displayed before his eyes. He remembers the dim days of creation when Adam and Eve lived in the Garden of Eden. The exploits of great heroes, the works of famous builders, authors and poets, the history of the Israelite people—all these are vividly brought before him by the books in the library. The past and the present seem to be linked up in a mysterious way by the study of books. (92 words)

Critical Note: Thematically the passage is about the study of books. The writer feels the past vibrating within himself as he glances through the pages of the books in a library. It is a real sensation for him. All the characters, mythical, historical, all the happenings of the past make their presence felt in his imagination.

Needless to say, the writer's treatment of the subject is romantic and hence subjective. He is totally lost in the world of books and has created a world of his own. The prose is marked throughout by touches which give way the writer's taste and temperament. He makes no attempt to keep his personal impressions to himself; he shows cleary that he is writing of things as if seen through his eyes. The effects on him are multifarious. Sometimes a sense of wonder engulfs him; sometimes he is engrossed in the past characters like Alexander, Achilles, Abraham, Ishmael, Isaac, Rebekah, Jacob and so on. The victories of the historical characters fill him with joy. The passage abounds in mythical and historical references and reasonably so, in order to give vent to his sensory faculty.

As far as the treatment of the subject is concerned, one may feel that the entire passage is written in a single breath. It has got a picturesque effect on the minds of the reader. He cannot help imagining things happening in front of his eyes, like a motion picture.

Example 31

Great books do not spring from something accidental in the great man who wrote them. They are the effluence of their core, the expression of the life itself of the authors. And literature cannot be said to have served its purpose until it has been translated into the actual life of him who reads. It is the vast reservoir of true ideas and emotions. In a world deprived of literature, the broad, the noble, the generous, would tend to disappear and life would be correspondingly degraded, because the fallacious idea and the petty emotion would never feel the upward pull of the ideas and emotions of genius. Only by conceiving a society without literature can it be clearly realized that the function of literature is to raise the plain towards the top level of the peaks. Literature exists so that where one man has lived finely ten thousands may afterwards live finely. It is a means of life it concerns the living essence.

(Arnold Bennet)

Substance: Great books are the very expressions of the life of the authors and not the accidental product of their minds. Literature cannot be said to have discharged its function properly unless it is made a part of the life of the reader. It is the storehouse of the ideas and emotions of the authors. It elevates man to a higher level of existence. In a society without literature all great and noble ideas tend to disappear. Literature helps noble living, and thus its influence on life is deep.

Comment: The author is of the view that literature, being the expression of the thoughts and emotions of great men, elevates and refines the mind of the readers. Great books are not written accidentally. They are the outflow of the authors' innermost feelings and the expression of the authors' life itself. The actual purpose of literature will be served only when literature can be translated into the actual life of the reader of literature. In the midst of the long sentences that make up the passage, the short pithy sentence attracts our attention:

> It [literature] is the vast reservoir of true ideas and emotions.

This sentence is very striking as it conveys the very essence of the whole passage. If the world were to deprived of literature, the breadth, the nobility, and the generosity in human life would disappear and life would become degraded. In a society devoid of literature, it is only literature that can help to raise the plain of life to its highest peaks. In fact, without literature all good thoughts would disappear from the earth.

Example 32

I am disposed to agree with captain Dolbey that the man who knows no fear exists only in the imagination of the lady novelist or those who fight their battles at the base. He who is conscious of fear ceases to be a hero. But the truth surely is that there would be no merit in being brave if you had no fear. The real victory of the hero is not over outward circumstances, but over himself. One of the bravest men of our time is a man who was born timid and nervous and suffered tortures of apprehension and who set himself to the deliberate conquest of his fears by challenging every danger that crossed his path and even going out of his way to meet the things he dreaded. By sheer will he beat down the enemy within and to the external world he seemed like a man who knew no fear. But the very essence of his heroism was that he had fought fear and won.

It is time that we get rid of the notion that there is anything discreditable in fear. You might as well say that there is something discreditable in being tempted to tell a falsehood. The virtue is not in having no temptation to lie, but in being tempted to lie and yet telling the truth. And the more you are tempted, the more splendid is the resistance. Without temptation you may make *a plaster saint* (1), but not a human hero. (249 words)

Central Idea: A true hero is he, who is not only free from fear but has conquered his inner enemies.

Word-notes: 1. Idol, but not a creature of flesh and blood.

Substance: A man who knows no fear is a myth. People have a mistaken notion that a hero is one who knows no fear. Nothing can be more fallacious than this. True heroism lies in facing dangers and fears, and conquering them. Besides, it means the conquest of one's inner enemies. To the outward world such a man appears free from fear; yet the fact remains that he faced fear and fought it. There is nothing disgraceful in knowing fear. Just as resistance to the temptation of telling a lie makes one a saint, so resistance to fear when it actually exists, raises a man to the full stature of a hero.

Critical Note: In this passage, the writer deals with the subject of fear, rather the lack of it, in human character that raises him to the level of a true hero. In his opinion, a man without fear does not exist. Fear is in-built in our mental constitution. What is really important is that one must conquer fear and win over the outward adversaries. So, the writer feels that there is nothing wrong if a person has fear in his mind. But the real test of heroism lies in conquering his fear within himself and this gets reflected in conquering the actual danger that lies ahead of him.

The writer approaches his subject from the psychological point of view. What is important for him is that the fear within must be conquered first. It may sound paradoxical, but it is true that fear is the basis of heroism. The treatment of the subject is novel and it takes us to the root of the concept of heroism.

The passage is a blend of subjective and objective writing, realism and impressionism. Here psychological analysis of character, while expressed in objective terms, is necessarily subjective in nature based in the writer's personal observation and deductions.

The approach of the writer is direct and the language is clear and straight-forward. By virtue of being partly objective, the views expressed by the writer are detached and unemotional. His emotions are kept below the surface. The writing is 'masculine' that is direct, emphatic and straight-forward. His prose style is traditional having the accepted patterns of sentence structure and choice of words.

Example 33

What is war ? Behold ! vast regions desolated, forests rent, villages in ruins, fields left barren and waste! Thousands in their vigour of life, blown up and scattered like chaff before the wind! Thousands again groaning in the agony of broken limbs! Beyond the scene of desolation, roads strewn with the wounded and the dying, harvests trampled under foot, widows, orphans and aged parents in loud mourning ! Stangely enough, to our eternal shame, we seem dead to these horrors and miseries of wars. The sufferings and death of a single fellow-being often excite tender and active compassion, while we hear, without emotion, of thousands enduring every variety of woe in war. A single murder, in times of peace, starts a thrill of sensation, while the countless murders of war are heard as an amusing tale. The execution even of a criminal sickens and shocks the mind, and philanthropy, is labouring to substitute milder form of punishment for death, but benevolence has hardly made any effort to snatch from sudden and untimely death the countless victims leading on to the altar of war.

Substance: On reading the passage we get the idea that war is definitely devastating. War is nothing constructive; it is destructive. The ultimate result of war is that it desolates vast regions and destroys forests, villages are turned into utter ruins and lush fields are left barren and changed into wasteland. Even human life is utterly destroyed. Scenes of desolation prevail everywhere—roads are strewn with the wounded and the dying, harvests are trampled, and there is loud mourning of widows, orphans and aged parents for the loss of their near and dear ones. Despite the rampant destructions caused by wars and the horrors and miseries that issue from them, humanity does not deter from the eternal shame. In times of peace a great deal of sensation is created by a single murder whereas countless murders during war are relished as an amusing tale. The execution of a diehard criminal disgusts us and stirs us. Philanthropy labours to substitute milder form of death penalty, but benevolence does not in any way try to stop the sacrifice of innumerous victims on the altar of war.

Comment: The passage is tightly structured as the key sentence occurs at the end. The piece is touching as the pathetic scenes attached to the war are given graphically. It has a startling beginning with an interrogative sentence which is soon followed by a series of answers that uphold the devastations of war. The rampant destructions are alluded to with a series of exclamatory sentences. The use of 'Behold!' is poetic; in fact, it is reminiscent of Wordsworth, or for that matter it sounds biblical. The romanticism and religiosity associated with the word is lost when we are led to witness the utter desolation, ruin, and agony caused by war.

The simile used in the sentence is apt:

> Thousands in their vigour of life, blown up and scattered
> like chaff before the wind!

The figurative language makes the remark all the more telling because, it makes the point more poignat, that despite war being devastating, it is a great pity that war, which leads to the murder of millions, is glorified. The passage has a sudden dramatic beginning with an interrogative sentence:

> What is war?

This intensifies the curiosity in the mind of the reader to read further on. This adds a certain amount of poeticism to the style. The poeticism is further intensified by alliteration in the sentence soon following:

> Behold! Vast *re*gions desolated, fo*re*sts *re*nt, villages in *ru*ins,
> fields left ba*rr*en and waste!

Apart from the alliteration on the *r* sounds, there are other alliterations on the *v* and *st* sounds in the sentence. Further on, there is assonance in the sentence:

> Strange*ly* *en*ough, to our *e*ternal shame, w*e* s*ee*m dead to
> th*ese* horrors and m*i*ser*i*es of wars.

Example 34

Education ought to teach us how to be in love always and what to be in love with. The great things of history have been done by the great lovers, by the saints and men of science and artists, and the problem of civilization is to give every man a chance of being a saint, a man of science, or an artist. But this problem cannot be attempted, much less solved, unless men desire to be saints, men of science and artists. And if they are to desire that continuously and consciously they must be taught what it means to be these things. We think of the man of science or the artist, if not of the saint, as a being with peculiar gifts, not as one who exercises, more precisely and incessantly perhaps, activities which we all ought to exercise. It is a commonplace now that art has ebbed away out of our ordinary life, out of all the things which we use, and that it is practised no longer by workmen, but only by a few painters and sculptors. That has happened because we no longer recognise the *aesthetic activity* as an activity of the spirit and common to all men. We do not know that when a man makes anything he ought to make it beautiful for the sake of doing so, and that when a man buys anything he ought to demand beauty in it, for the sake of that beauty. We think of beauty, if we think of it at all, as a mere source of pleasure, and therefore it means to us ornament added to things for which we can pay extra as we choose. But beauty is not an ornament to life, or to the things made by man. It is an essential part of both.

(Arthur Clutton-Brock)

Substance: The author is of the view that the purpose of education is ultimately to create in us an aesthetic sense. All great deeds in human history have been achieved by lovers of beauty. In fact, all saints, artists, and scientists have proved themselves to be lovers of beauty. We generally regard the artists and the scientists as somewhat rare and exceptional beings, who exercise activities which are not meant for the common man. It is a truism that aesthetic sensibility has slipped out of common life and that we do not demand beauty in all that is done. Beauty is generally regarded as an addition—something extraneous—something from without. It is not innate. Beauty is simply an ornament. But, truly speaking, beauty is an essential ingredient of life; every man should exercise a sense of beauty in all that he does and says.

Comment: The passage is loosely structured as the key sentence occurs at the outset:

> Education ought to teach us how to be in love always and what to be in love with.

To drive this point home, the author talks of men of science and artists and saints who are great lovers of beauty. Ultimately, the writer boils down to the fact that this sense of beauty has gone out of our lives. Beauty is not simply an ornament to life; it is an essential part of both life and man.

In everything a man does or says, there should be beauty. It is not only artists, saints, and scientists who are blessed with a sense of beauty, but this sense prevails in all men. It is through education that one inculcates this aesthetic sensibility. Now that art has ebbed away out of our ordinary life, we feel that it is practised only by a handful painters and artists. This is so because we are no longer capable of recognizing the aesthetic activity as an activity of the spirit and common to all men. The activity of aestheticism is not limited only to artists, painters, sculptors, scientists, and saints.

The tone of the entire passage is conversational. The very opening sentence seems the stress certain words so as to make the author's point poignant:

> Education ought to teach us *how* to be in love always and *what* to be in love with.

The sense of beauty is something that is inculcated in a man through education.

Within this short passage, quite a number of sentences begin with conjunctions—'*And*', '*But*'. This feature points to the fact that it is in the manner of a colloquy. The vocabulary used in the entire passage is rather simple. The author argues his point very rationally.

The writer of the passage is out to establish the fact that the main object of education is to rouse in each of us an aesthetic sensibility. All great things of the world have proceded from that aesthetic sensibility. The author is disheartened at the fact that this sense of beauty has now unfortunately disappeared from life.

The passage is loosely structured as the keynote is struck at the outset that the main object of education apart from all other things is to instill in each of us an aesthetic sensibility. After all, education should teach us how to be in love at all times and what to be in love with. The writer is sad that aesthetic activity is not recognized by us any longer. Aesthetic activity is an activity of the spirit which is common to all men. Even art has ebbed away out of our ordinary life; it is limited to the practice of a handful of painters and artists. Beauty should not considered merely as a source of pleasure and something that is ornamental. Beauty should not be regarded as an ornament to life or something added to the creation of man. Thus beauty is an essential element to both—to life, as well as the things made by man. The didactic note of the passage is evident from the abundant use of the word ought, moreover, the writer is in the habit of using conjunctions- *and*, *but*, *or*,—rampantly.

Example 35

The man who is perpetually hesitating which of the two things he will do first, will do neither. The man who resolves, but suffers his resolution to be changed by the first counter-suggestion of a friend, - who fluctuates (1) from opinion to opinion, from plan to plan, and veers (2) like a weathercock to every point of the compass, with every breath of caprice that blows,—can never accomplish anything great or useful. Instead of being progressive in anything, he will be at best stationary and more probably retrograde (3) in all. It is only the man who first consults wisely, then resolves firmly, and then executes his purpose with inflexible perseverance, undismayed (4) by those petty difficulties which daunt (5) a weaker spirit,—that can advance to eminence in any line. Take your course wisely, but firmly; and having taken it, hold upon it with heroic resolution and the Alps and the Himalayas will sink before you. (155 words)

Central Idea: The man who first of all takes a wise decision and proceeds to work it out step by step is sure to achieve success in life.

Word-notes: 1. Changes; 2. Changes direction; 3. Retreating; inverse; 4. Not afraid; 5. Terrify.

Substance: Lack of steadiness or fixity of purpose leads to failure in life. The man who constantly flies from object to object achieves nothing. Success depends upon the power of choosing the right course and then proceeding along it step by step, without being deterred by the difficulties that may crop up. (51 words)

Critical Note: Here the role assumed by the writer is one of preacher and teacher. He preaches and teaches the value of steadfastness in a man's character.Although the subject is rather commonplace and therefore may be said to suffer from lack of novelty, at times we need advice on such things that will act as an eye-opener for us. It is from this standpoint that the passage should be assessed.

The arguments enunciated by the writer are logical, clear, pragmatic and realistic. Being somewhat didactic, an objective tone is maintained throughout without betraying the personality and emotion of the writer. The prose style is 'masculine' i.e. direct, concrete and straight-forward.

The language is clear and free from any ambiguity or haziness.

Example 36

Asquith felt great reluctance (1) to express opinions on any subject upon which he did not know his own mind completely. For instance, in his youth he had been interested in philosophy, and he still possessed that respect for thought which only those who have drunk a fair draught (2) *at the springs of thought* (3), retain.Yet because he did not think his opinion on philosophical matters dependable, he was unwilling to discuss the fundamental problems of the universe or such meditative themes which require special knowledge. He would show you by a remark or two that he was even more aware of philosophy than most people who discuss it, but he would not presume to offer opinions. It was the same in literature. He discussed readily only those aspects of it of which he felt he had a thorough comprehension (4). Even there he would not talk more than he would listen. His object was to learn; he felt that all the students of literature, youth or old, must keep receptive mind (5) and not claim to have reached finality. He liked gossip (6) and semi-intellectual talk among friends, but he himself rarely contributed to such conversations anything but sound common sense. It was not humility so much as a sense of proportion and a sense of respect for truth, which is not attained without much discipline, that gave him the finely balanced attitude. (230 words)

Central Idea: Asquith did not express an opinion on a subject he did not know thoroughly. He was a good talker.

Word-notes: 1. Unwillingness; 2. Quantity drunk at a time; 3. Fountain of knowledge; 4. Understanding; 5. Mind that is ready to learn; 6. Idle talk.

Substance: Asquith was a perfect gentleman. He did not pass any opinion on a subject he did not know thoroughly. In his youth he had read philosophy deeply and knew the subject more thoroughly than many of the so-called philosophers. Yet he was careful enough not to express any opinion in a philosophical discussion. He was well-read in literature. But he was always more willing to receive than to give. He was a lover of talks but he always contributed to them sound common sense. This attitude of Asquith is the result of a sense of proportion and a respect for truth that he possessed. (104 words)

Critical Note: To convey his message on the value of self-restraint, the author has cited the example of Herbert Henry Asquith, the British statesman (1852-1928) who was otherwise known for his erudition, but never displayed his knowledge among the others. He was a true learner who always strived to gain knowledge from others and enrich himself. But whatever little he contributed during such discussions, his remarks sounded strong common sense. Thus he always maintained a sense of proportion.

The passage may either be an extract from his biography or it may be a part of an essay. Whatever it may be, the intention of the writer is clear. Taking Asquith as a model example, he wants his readers to learn some of the finer qualities which we need to possess.

The merit of the passage lies in its simplicity and lucidity of prose. There is no jolt in the sentence construction and the flow of words is smooth. The style is 'masculine' but it is untainted by any pomposity and crudeness. As far as the narrative is concerned, he has built up the image of the statesman with the help of small illustrations and drawing his observations from the same. His narrative style keeps the interest of the readers awake all through.

Example 37

It is of course true that we are all, in a sense, *slaves to our circumstances* (1). There are a few idle rich at one end of the scale and a few tramps (2) at the other who are so independent of circumstances that they can live what they call free life. They are not generally thought to be the most admirable specimens (3) of human kind. The rest of us have to earn our living, keep regular hours, do a long day's work and have only short holidays, be careful not to offend against custom and prejudice, show deference to employers and great many other people whom in our hearts we think to be our inferiors. The lot of some is undoubtedly much harder than that of others, and this inequality is one of the great social evils. Who cannot but sympathize with the poor man when he cries out that he is a wage-slave? It is a cry which *strikes a chord* (4) in a much wider circle than he seems to be aware of, for in a multitude of seemingly well-to-do homes, there is a sense of insecurity, the same sense of servitude (5), the same feeling of being involved in a round of meaningless toil for unappreciative masters. (207 words)

Central Idea: Except only a few idle rich and vagabonds, the majority of people are wage-earners. Their lot is very hard.

Word-notes: 1. Subject to the conditions of life; 2. Vagabonds; 3. Samples; 4. Echoes; 5. Slavery; 6. That cannot appreciate services.

Substance: It is only a few idle rich and vagabonds that can live a life of independence. The rest of the people are condemned to live a life of hard labour and servitude. This inequality of lot is the worst feature of the society. The cries of the toiling masses find a ready echo in the hearts of many so-called rich, who, too, in their turn have to feel bitterly a sense of insecurity and ingratitude from their masters. (78 words)

Critical Note: The passage deals the perennial socio-economic problem, —the problem of the haves and have-nots and also the position of those who belong to in between. The author rightly equates the idle rich with those who have nothing to lose. Both the classes belong to the two different sides of the same scale though from the economic point of view their positions are poles apart. In between, there is the working class or the middle class who are to earn their livelihood with great toil and labour. The voice of protest from this working class is heard by the so-called well-to-do class, but they are also helpless being placed in the same vicious circle.

The author has highlighted the major economic problem with utmost clarity of thought. His arguments have withstood the test of time and the situation he has focused is valid even today, particularly in the third world countries. The author has maintained objectivity and detached attitude throughout his writing and his observations are quite balanced and unbiased. His subject being the global socio-economic problem, there is little scope of being personal with the readers.

The sentence construction and word arrangement, though smooth by and large, suffers from certain jerks towards the end of the passage. His treatment of the subject is factual and realistic.

Example 38

Everything in nature except man acts as it does, because it is its nature so to act. It is, therefore, pointless to argue whether it is right to act as it does, pointless to exhort (1) it act differently. We do not say of a stone that it ought to go uphill (2), or blame as tiger for tearing its prey. When, however, we consider a human being, we can say not only 'this is what he is like', but also, 'that is what he ought to be like'. Man, in other words, and man alone can be judged morally. What is the reason for this distinction between man and nature? It is to be found in the fact that man has a sense of right and wrong, so that, whatever he may in fact do, we recognize that he ought to do what is right and eschew (3), what is wrong. Man is thus set apart from everything in nature by virtue of the fact that he is a free moral agent. (170 words)

Central Idea: Man is distinguished from lower animals in that he possesses a moral sense.

Word-notes: 1. Urge; 2. Up a hill; 3. Avoid.

Substance: Man is distinguished from all other objects of nature in that he is a free moral agent and has a sense of right and wrong. All other things—animate or inanimate—act in a peculiar way because it is their nature to act so. But in all his actions man is guided by a moral sense. (55)

Critical Note: In this passage, the writer draws a distinction between man and other objects (both animate and inanimate) from the point of view of their nature. His argument is that in case of other objects, we take their behaviour for granted accepting the fact of their nature. But in case of human beings, the moral sense becomes the guiding principle in judging the righteousness or otherwise of his actions. The arguments put forth by the writer are logical. His logic of distinguishing man and other objects from the view point of morality may be considered justified because, apart from other things like intellect and intelligence, morality is the prime distinguishing factor. The writer's treatment of the subject is objective and unemotional. His approach is direct and logic straight-forward. The prose style is traditional and spontaneous without any jerk. The last sentence of the passage is the final summing up of his arguments and makes the passage a complete thesis.

Example 39

Her image accompanied me even in places the most hostile to romance. On Saturday evenings when my aunt went marketing I had to carry some of the parcels. We walked through the flaring streets, jostled by drunken men and bargaining women, amid the curses of labourers, the shrill litanies of shop-boys who stood on guard by the barrels of pigs' cheeks, the nasal chanting of street-singers, who sang a *come-all-you* about O'Donovan Rossa, or a ballad about the troubles in our native land. These noises converged in a single sensation of life for me: I imagined that I bore my chalice safely through a throng of foes. Her name sprang to my lips at moments in strange prayers and praises which I myself did not understand. My eyes were often full of tears (I could not tell why) and at times a flood from my heart seemed to pour itself out into my bosom. I thought little of the future. I did not know whether I would ever speak to her or not or, if I spoke to her, how I could tell her of my confused adoration. But my body was like a harp and her words and gestures were like fingers running upon the wires.

James Joyce: *Araby* (from *Dubliners*)

Substance: This passage is a fairly complex passage about a young boy falling in love. The paragraph is loosely structured. In this passage the diction and rhythm, especially important for the tone, produce a nice balance between romantic and matter-of-fact. Such evocative words as *romance*, *sensation*, *strange*, *bosom*, even *harp*, echo the language of sentiment. Along with these evocative words, another group of words adds religious heightening to the emotions described: *image*, *litanies*, *chanting*, *chalice*, *prayers*, *praises*, *adoration*. The parallel between religious feelings and the young boy's most intense personal emotion is suggested.

Comment: Associated with this romanticism and elevated diction, the rhythm of almost all the sentences is lyrical, like that of a series of very short poems. And yet the tone of the whole passage is not purely rhapsodic, as it would be if there were not other elements involved. Against the romantic diction is posed another group of words: *curses*, *pigs' cheeks*, *nasal*, perhaps even *the future*. At least one sentence is distinctly prosaic:

> I thought little of the future.

Although the individual sentences may sound like lyrics, the paragraph is definitely not a poem. Read together, the sentences often begin abruptly, and there are more breaks, more separate sentences, than there would be in an emotional outburst. After all, the feeling is controlled and modified; it is the tone of a mature man, certainly not that of an adolescent boy. Moreover, the tone is that of reminiscence, not of pure ecstasy.

There is a subjective note struck in the passage, as there is a first-person narrative account being given. The similes resorted to in the concluding sentence—'my body was like a harp' and 'her words and gestures were like fingers running upon the wires'—is full of romantic effusion.

The passage has a dramatic beginning:

> Her image accompanied me even in places the most hostile
> to romance.

There is a great deal of suspense created at the very outset. We are set to wondering as to whom the possessive adjective '*her*' refers to; similar suspense is created by the personal pronoun '*me*'. The phrase 'in places the most hostile to romance' acts as a backdrop for the setting of the passage.

Moreover, a narrative strain runs all through the passage. The narrative has touches of particularization when details are included, like 'Saturday evenings'. The epithets tagged to the substantives are effective as they add to the hostile atmosphere: '*flaring* streets', '*drunken* men', and '*bargining* women', '*shrill* litanies of shop-boys', '*nasal* chanting of street-singers', 'noises converged in a *single* sensation of life'. Finally, all these lead to the '*confused* adoration' for the beloved. The climactic point comes at the end of the passage with the similes: 'my body was like a harp' and 'her words and gestures were like fingers running upon the wires'.

The parentheses: '(I could not tell why)'—helps the narrator to establish a close rapport with the reader, as though confiding with the reader.

Example 40

The idea that education should cover all useful fields of equipment (1) is futile and erroneous. The limitations of time and immaturity should be kept in mind, and more time should be spent on evolving the capacity to acquire knowledge, and to think aright than on substantial equipment straightway. The pressure of too many subjects is not a good thing for the young and we must see to it that their capacity to think aright can be developed and correct methods of work can be implanted. To give an example, I would point out that history cannot be understood by boys and girls who have not seen or experienced much of life and its problems. The brain is a machine which should be properly assembled and adjusted during youth. Once this is done, it will take care of itself and there is plenty of time for acquiring information in all branches. The stress during youth should be on training, on creating a habit of correct observation, of scientific curiosity, and of thinking aright and not on cramming (2) the brain with information. (180 words)

Central Idea: Education does not mean filling the brain of youths with information but development of the power of observation, scientific curiosity and correct thinking.

Word-notes: 1. Outfitting; 2. Fill overful.

Substance: It is wrong to suppose that education should impart knowledge on a variety of subjects. The brain of youths is immature and the pressure of too many subjects is bound to be harmful. The purpose of education is, therefore, to train the mind, to develop the powers of accurate observation, correct thinking and a curiosity for all things. Diffusion of knowledge is of the least importance in education. (68 words)

Critical Note: The theme of the passage relates to the method of education among the youths. The logic proffered is that the brain of the youths should not be crammed with bookish knowledge; instead, during this period their minds should be made to develop the power of observation, correct thinking and an all round curiosity. As a matter of fact, the logic of the author is quite valid and acceptable. Such inadequacy of education system is all the more palpable in the present day also. But on a deeper reading of the passage, one cannot help observing that the views expressed are too generalized rather than specific. The author is silent about the specific steps or methods to be adopted for 'creating a habit of correct observation, of scientific curiosity, and of thinking aright'. Some concrete suggestions could have made his logic sounder, acceptable and pragmatic.

From the view point of the treatment of his subject, it can be said that objectivity is maintained in the writing, such objectivity being the outcome of the writer's minute observation of his day's education system and its impact on the youths and the conclusions drawn from such observations. The language is simple and can be understood easily. As such clarity is maintained throughout.

Example 41

Of the validity of the modern demand for equality there is no doubt whatever. It has appeared in the form of the demand for equality between individuals, between classes, between nations. It has been at the root of every recent revolution and of most recent wars. Nor it is a demand which would be satisfied by the formal political equality of the nineteenth century. It is specifically a demand for economic equality—for equality of economic resources or equality of economic opportunity. This problem requires, in the first instance, a positive and constructive (1) rather than a negative (2) and destructive programme. Our deliberate purpose should be to build up equality rather than to break down inequality. The process of equalization can be achieved by gradual rather than by violent methods. Our first step should be secure the distribution to all of what may, on a generous interpretation (3), be called the necessaries of life: and since, in the area with which we are most likely to be concerned, this should not be difficult of attainment, the distribution of the necessaries of life may be supplemented by the distribution of many of the amenities (4) and luxuries. Such a programme will create needs vast enough to make a full call on our resources. (208 words)

Central idea: True equality between man and man does not mean political equality. It means an equal distribution of economic advantages and opportunities. This cannot be attained by a sudden revolution but by the full development of the country's resources.

Word-notes: 1. Creative; 2. Destructive; 3. Explanation; 4. Pleasant ways.

Substance: There is a great force in the modern demand for equality - equality of classes, of nations and of individuals. It is this which has led to wars. But rightly speaking, this equality should not be political but economic. It means the equal distribution of economic advantages and opportunities, of comforts and amenities of life, among all people. Such equality can be achieved not by sudden revolution but by the development of the country's resources. (74 words)

Critical Note: The theme of the passage is equality. The author believes, and rightly, that equality does not merely imply political equality; it is the economic equality i.e. the equal distribution of economic resources among people that really matters. Further, he is not in favour any violent measure in bringing equality. Such equality is to be built up gradually rather than violently. His observation is: 'Our deliberate purpose should be to build up equality rather than to break down inequality'. The writer has highlighted the true problem of economics that lay behind all the past wars and revolutions. The theory propounded by the writer has got a socialistic tilt and he has established his viewpoint accordingly with conviction. As such the viewpoint of the writer is very much practical and pragmatic.

The detachment of his attitude is felt throughout and his views are based on close study of the history and politics although no specific reference is given in the passage.

His style is simple and choice of words is in keeping with his subject. The true merit of his style lies in its compactness and clarity of thought and expression.

Example 42

To men of any spirit the opposition of Nature constitutes a challenge which cannot be ignored (1). The sense of battle rouses a fierce joy in them that no mere adverse (2) reasoning can ever destroy, and the very idea of impossibility is foreign to their nature. This spirit taught men to fly, regardless of the laws of gravity (3). It taught them to rush along the ground at speeds exceeding three miles—now almost four miles—in a minute. It taught them to jump down through thousands of feet of space aided by nothing better than something resembling a large umbrella.

The same spirit actuates mountain climbers. No sooner do they perceive a peak than they must climb it. Although there are good scientific reasons for climbing mountains, they are not very strong ones; the *moral* reasons are far stronger. It is a noble thing to endeavour to surmount (4) difficulties and to penetrate into realms where ordinary men dare not venture. (159 words)

Central idea: A man of courage feels called upon to accept the challenge of Nature, instead of yielding to her. It is this spirit which has led men to impossible deeds of valour.

Word-notes: 1.Neglected; 2. Contrary; hostile; 3.The scientific law of gravitation; 4. Overcome.

Substance: A courageous man is never daunted by the hostilities of Nature. He accepts Nature's challenge and overcomes it. It is this fierce spirit which has led men to speed-motoring, parachute flight and mountaineering. It has led men to the distant ends of the earth.This spirit is more moral than physical. (52 words)

Critical Note: Man's indomitable fighting spirit, his quest for adventure, his defiance of the laws of Nature, —these are the theme of the passage. But, the writer feels, such courage is supported by great moral strength which is the strongest motivation for him. The writer has arranged his logic step by step by illustrating various adventurous triumphs achieved by man through ages and has drawn his conclusion accordingly.

The prose style constitutes simple words and well-constructed sentences. He is traditional and conservative in his style. His approach is direct and unambiguous. However, an undercurrent of his personal emotion pervades the whole passage. As readers, we cannot help feeling that the author also feels pride in the adventurous and moral triumphs of man. Although, on the face of it, the writing appears to be objective, the subdued personal sentiment of the author makes the writing a blend of something personal and impersonal.

Example 43

We cannot doubt that if men lived the kind of life which all great religious teachers urged them to live, the world would be much better and happier, and at least a more civilized place than it is or ever has been. Unfortunately their teachings have usually been found to be too difficult for people to follow, though that is no reason why they should not try to follow them.

All great religious teachers of mankind have insisted on (1) this: that men ought not to live for themselves alone. We ought not, they have said, to spend all our time and energy in getting just what we want for ourselves, power and money and importance in the world; we ought to serve something greater than ourselves, whether a god or a cause or our fellow-men. It is by serving this something greater that man will forget themselves and so achieve happiness. This or something like this is what the great religions have taught. (163 words)

Central idea: The noble ideals taught by the great religious teachers of the world, if rightly followed, would turn this earth into a paradise.

Word-notes: 1. Emphasized.

Substance: All great religious teachers of the world have taught men to live not for themselves alone, to get over the selfish love of power and wealth and to live a life of noble ideals. Unfortunately, men have found it difficult to follow these ideals. There is no denying the fact that the salvation of mankind lies in following these religious teachings and in nothing else. (65 words)

Critical Note: The noble ideals taught by the great religious teachers of the world, if rightly followed, would turn this earth into a paradise. But unfortunately their great teachings are being ignored by men and the earthly paradise remains elusive. This is a didactic theme and the author has also assumed his role accordingly. He reiterates the teachings of all great religious teachers and regrets that men have failed to translate such teachings into action.

This perennial contradiction in human behaviour has been aptly enunciated by the author in the above passage. Such contradiction had been there in the past, it is there at present and it will remain in future. Since the passage is didactic in nature, it is assumed to be meant for the common readers and accordingly the writer has adopted a style that is clear, transparent and logical. It may not be proper to term the writing as 'objective' in the true sense since the presence of the writer is felt in the background.

Example 44

If we should profit by our study, we must be careful not only to select proper books, but also to peruse them aright. The same books will affect the readers differently according to the purpose with which they read it. The butterfly sits over the flower-bed gathering nothing; the spider collects poison from it; but the bee finds and stores up honey; so the object for which you go to a book will determine the kind of fruit it will yield you. The same volume may be to minister (1) to instruction or to rational (2) amusement, or to a mere morbid (3) love of excitement. The child takes off the lid of the tea-kettle for sport, the housewife for use—but James Watt, for science, which ended in invention of steam-engine. (129 words)

Central idea: Study of books yields results according to the manner of choosing them and reading them.

Word-notes: 1.Give; 2.Reasonable; 3. Unhealthy.

Substance: It is not merely the right selection of books but the way of reading them aright that can yield good results in study. The same book affects the different readers in different ways, according to their light and ability. Some may find a book instructive, while others will find it merely exciting. (52 words)

Critical Note: The theme of the passage is proper selection of books and reading them in right earnest. It is possible that the writing has been intended for young readers or students. May be it was a lecture delivered to the learners. Whatever it may be, it is a piece of advice for the youth. This is evident from the fact that the writer has drawn a number of illustrations to drive home his point. The logic of the writer is cohesive, not to be disputed. His arguments are forceful and straightforward.

The writer's view point is clear and unambiguous. Therefore, his approach is direct. The sentence construction and style is modern but somehow conventional. The theme having a didactic note, his approach is serious and objective.

Example 45

Thought and speech are inseparable from each other. Matter and expression are parts of one: style is a thinking out into language. This is what is called *literature*; not *things*, not the verbal symbol of things; not, on the other words, mere *words*; but thoughts expressed in language. Call to mind the meaning of the Greek word which expresses the special prerogative of man over the feeble (1) intelligence of inferior animals. It is called *Logos*: what does *Logos* mean? It stands for both *reason* and for *speech*, and it is difficult to say which it means more properly. It means both at once: why? because really they cannot be divided because they are in a sense one. When we can separate light and illumination, life and motion, the convex (2) and the concave (3) of a curve, then will it be possible for thought to tread speech under the foot, and to hope to do without it—then will it be conceivable that the vigorous and fertile intellect should renounce its own double, its instrument for expression, and the channel of its speculations and emotions.

There are some critics, who consider fine writing to be *an addition from without* to the matter treated of—a sort of ornament super induced (4), or a luxury indulged in, by those who have time and inclination for such vanities. They speak as if *one* man could do the thought, and *another* the style. With them 'fine writing' is a trick and a trade, and language is but the hired servant of reason. But can we really think that Homer, or Pinder, or Shakespeare, or Walter Scott, were accustomed to aim at diction (5) for its own sake, instead of being inspired with their subject, and pouring forth beautiful words because they had beautiful thoughts? The elocution (6) of a great intellect is great: his language expresses, not only his great thoughts, but his great self. (317 words)

Central idea: Thought and expression are indissolubly linked up. A fine thought must necessarily find expression in noble words.

Word-notes: 1. Weak; 2. Curve like the outside of a circle; 3. Opposite of convex; 4. Imposed from outside; 5. Language; choice of words in speech or writing; 6. Eloquence.

Substance: Thought and expression are inseparably connected. Literature means thoughts expressed in language, and the absence of either cannot make literature. The Greek word 'Logos', which means both reason and speech, points out how the two are inalienable and essentially one and the same thing. A vigorous intellect must needs inevitably find out its medium of expression. Some people are apt to think that fine writing is something external to the great writers—a sort of luxury indulged in at leisure. Nothing can be more erroneous than this. Homer, Shakespeare or Walter Scott wrote because their inspired thoughts must need find expression in beautiful words. It is the inner law of their minds that drove them to writing. Their writings are the expression of their great selves. (126 words)

Critical Note: The theme of the passage is the relationship between thought and its expression in literature. According to the author, the two elements are inseparable. Literature, according to the writer, is 'thoughts expressed in language'. The author, at the same time, warns the reader that good writing or good language should not be misconstrued as mere ornamentation. It is an inevitable expression of inspired thoughts. He establishes his point from the Greek word *Logos* that means reason and speech at the same time.

The logic proffered by the writer does not call for any dispute. He has established his point by comparisons and contrasts and also by illustrating great literary figures.

The construction of sentences is at times long and complicated and this takes away the smooth flow of reading; it creates jolting effects in the minds of the readers. This could have been avoided. As for choice of words, common and simple words have been used.

The author maintains an attitude of detachment and his personality, emotions and sentiments remain veiled which is one of the main criteria of objective writing.

Example 46

Literature is one of the instruments, and one of the most powerful instruments, for forming character, for giving us men and women armed with reason, braced (1) by knowledge, clothed with steadfastness and courage, and inspired by that public spirit and public virtue, of which it has been well said that they are the brightest ornaments of the mind of man. Bacon is right, as he generally is, when he bids us read not to contradict and refute but to weigh (2) and consider. In the times before us that promise and threaten deep political, economical and social controversy (3), what we need to do is to induce our people to weigh and consider. We want them to cultivate energy without impatience, activity without restlessness, inflexibility (4) without ill humour. I am not going to preach to you any artificial stoicism (5); I am going to preach to you any indifference to money, or to the pleasures of social intercourse, or to the esteem and good will of our neighbours, or to any other of the consolations and the necessities of life. But after all, the thing that matters most, both for happiness and for duty, is that we should habitually live with wise thoughts and right feelings. Literature helps us more than other studies to this most blessed companionship of wise thoughts and right feelings, and so we have taken this opportunity of earnestly commending it to your interest and care. (237 words)

Central idea: Literature forms our character by imbibing us with noble qualities. It brings us into touch with great minds and thus makes for happiness.

Word-notes: 1. Strengthened; 2. Judge; 3. Debate; 4. Rigidity; 5. Self-control; austerity.

Substance: Literature forms our character, by informing the mind with reason, knowledge, courage and public virtues, which are the very ornaments of character. This purpose of the study of literature, as Bacon has rightly said, is not to refute the argument of others but to acquire the power of thinking and understanding. In the times that lie ahead of us—a period of political controversy—this habit of thinking and weighing is absolutely necessary. Therefore, men should cultivate energy, activity and steadfastness. This does not mean that we are to be indifferent to wealth or the pleasures of social intercourse or other necessaries of life. But the best way of becoming happy and dutiful is to study literature, to imbibe the great thoughts and feelings of great authors. Hence the writer recommends the study of literature to all of us. (139 words)

Critical Note: Whether we should study literature or not, and if yes, what benefit we derive from it—this forms the subject-matter of the passage. The author feels, and rightly, that study of literature broadens our mind, forms our character and keeps the power of judgement alive. The author, however, is silent about the pleasing and entertaining aspects of literature, presumably because these do not fit into the subject-matter of his treatise. However, this does not take away the merits of the writing.

The author's approach to the subject is somewhat didactic and moral. The arguments have been put forth forcefully with authority. He reinforces his arguments with the example of Bacon. Further, he bases his arguments in relation to the 'deep political, economical and social controversy' which adds a new dimension to his findings.

The passage is marked by clarity of thought and expression. The sentences are, at times, long but that does not pose any problem for the common readers. This is because the writer's approach is direct and emphatic. The writer adopts the traditional and conventional style of writing.

The writer of the passage observes that literature forms our character, by informing the mind with reason, knowledge, courage and public virtues, which are the very ornaments of character. This purpose of the study of literature, as Bacon has rightly said, is not to refute the argument of others but to acquire the power of thinking and understanding. In the times that lie ahead of us—a period of political controversy—this habit of thinking and weighing is absolutely necessary. Therefore men should cultivate energy, activity and steadfastness. This does not mean that we are to be indifferent to wealth or the pleasure of social intercourse or other necessaries of life. But the best way of becoming happy and dutiful is to study literature, to imbibe the great thoughts and feelings of great authors. Hence the writer recommends the study of literature to all of us.

According to the author of the passage, literature helps to form our character by imbuing us with noble qualities. Literature brings us into touch with great minds and thus makes room for happiness. In order to assert his views strongly, the author is repetitive in his expressions as is noticeable at the outset of the passage by stating that 'Literature is one of instruments' and harps on the same fact in the next phrase 'one of the most powerful instruments'. Soon after, the author keeps repeating the phrase 'I am not going to preach to you any...'. The passage sounds like a colloquy. There is a note of subjectivity when the author himself enters the passage in person: '*I*' is resorted to put across his views. The habit of repetition is noticeable further in the author's use of the phrase '*or to*' as many as three times in quick succession.

A magisterial note has been struck with authors use of the phrase '*but after all*' towards the end of the passage; it seems to add a conclusive note to all that has been said. Nevertheless, the passage is remarkable for its lucidity of style.

Example 47

Literature is the written record of valuable thought , having other than a merely technical purpose. It is the preserved sum-total of the best ideas of the world's noblest men and women. It is the tale of 'the common humanity whose sorrowings and sinnings, whose hopes and joys and little triumphs constitute the great story which leads back and sets man face to face with the undiscoverable'. Of all existing occupations, therefore, none is better than that of good reading, wisely to be used. It is treasure laid up for heaven, for the mind endures when the body is scattered to dust. Literature is more real and lasting than stocks and securities and buildings. 'The world of imagination', it has been observed, is not the world of abstraction (1) and non-entity (2), as some conceive, but a world formed out of chaos (3) by a sense of beauty that is in man and the earth on which he dwells. Every book we read may be a rung in the ever-lightening ladder by which we climb to knowledge and to that temper and serenity of mind which, as it is the ripest fruit of wisdom, is also the sweetest. The riches of scholarship, benignities (4) of literature defy fortune and outlive calamity. They are beyond the reach of thief or moth or rust. As they cannot be inherited, so they cannot be alienated (5).' 'The grandest aim of imaginative art', says, Ruskin, 'is to give noble grounds for noble emotion.' Literature is but one of the imaginative arts; and it is that art which presupposes a development of culture which has been aptly defined as an 'interest in the best things said and written in the world.' The best things are the remnant (6), the chosen few, the selected minority. There are nine sibylline (7) books, then three were thrown away again, then again three, but the remaining ones were more valuables than the nine. 'Literature', says John Morley, 'consists of all the books—and they are not so many—where moral truth and human passion are touched with a certain largeness, sanity, and attraction of form. (356 words)

Central idea: Literature is the store-house of best ideas of the great men of the world. Study in literature, therefore, gives not only wisdom but true peace and happiness.

Word-notes: 1. Idea; 2. Unimportant thing; 3. Disorderly form of things; 4. Gifts; 5. Estranged; 6. Relic; 7. Collections of oracles belonging to ancient Roman State and often consulted magistrates for guidance; oracular; prophetic.

Substance: Literature is the expression of the best ideas of the greatest men and women of the world. It is the story of the joys and sorrows, hopes and triumphs of men, and brings us face to face with the great Unknown. Hence the study of good literature is the best occupation of men. Literature is more enduring than earthly possessions. The world of imagination is not full of airy nothings, as some people imagine; it is the solid world of reality carved out by the sense of beauty in man. Each good book, therefore, helps us to acquire knowledge and that perfect serenity of mind which is true wisdom. The enjoyment of good literature, therefore, requires a culture, which has been defined as the interest in all the best thoughts and ideas of the world. Great literature, therefore, is very rare. In it moral truths and human passions are presented in a large and attractive form. (155 words)

Critical Note: The theme of the passage is the study of literature. Literature is considered as the store-house of the best thoughts and ideas of man and is therefore, more valuable that materialistic things. To establish his view point, which is not to be contradicted, the author has taken resort to comparisons and contrasts, illustrations from the past and also observations from scholars.

The passage which is considerably long contains only one idea, as indicated above, that is, why we should study literature. To establish his point, the author has used as many as 356 words. Thus his treatment is pompous and flamboyant. Obviously, the prose style is not of modern age; rather it belongs to the late nineteenth century or early twentieth century. The sentences are long and complex posing occasional jolts to the modern readers. The prose is, therefore, definitely traditional rather than modern. The author's approach, however, is objective, marked by the absence of the author's personality.

—o—

CHAPTER IV

Substance & Critical Appreciation (Poetry) Examples worked out

Example 1

Tell me not, in mournful numbers,
        Life is but an empty dream!
For the soul is dead that slumbers,
        And things are not what they seem.

Life is real! Life is earnest!
        And the grave is not its goal;
"Dust thou art, to dust returnest,"
        Was not spoken of the soul.

Not enjoyment and not sorrow,
        Is our destined end or way;
But to act, that each tomorrow
        Finds us farther than to-day.

Art is long, and Time is fleeting,
        And our hearts, though stout and brave,
Still, like muffled drums, are beating
        Funeral marches to the grave.

(*A Psalm of Life* Extract: H.W. Longfellow)

Substance: The poet is not of the view that life is a meaningless dream devoid of any substance. He, who spends his life aimlessly, is already dead. Life is real; so it should not be treated lightly. It should be remembered that death is not the end of life. The soul does not turn into dust with the physical death. Our way of living should not be aimed at enjoyment or mourning. The aim of life should be to act wisely in such a way as to make our future better than the present. The work assigned to us is too demanding as well as time-consuming. But time passes quickly leaving us bewildered. Under such circumstances, our hearts although strong and brave, are beating funeral marches to the grave like the drums covered with cloth.

Critical Note: The poet's mission in this poem is to instruct and guide, to stir and vivify, to inspire and energize. He wants to give expression to the nation's energetic approach to life.The poem teaches basic values and lays the foundation for a good ethical life. Since the poem aims to teach, it is called a didactic poem. According to the poet, acting at the present moment is the principal success formula in life:

> But to act, that each tomorrow
> Finds us further than to-day.

The poem has a solemn title—*A Psalm of Life*. Psalm is a sacred song. This suggests the solemnity of the theme. In the subsequent part of the poem, the poet, following the Christian tradition talks about faith in God as well as love for one's neighbour.

The whole poem is a collection of moral principles to be followed by people. These principles, as indicated in the above stanzas, are as follows:

- Life has a serious mission.
- Life does not end with death.
- We have a destiny irrespective of our joys and sorrows.
- Time is too short for our long mission.

The poem is a musical lyric. Such poetry has wide range as it touches the various aspects of experience including the broad interests of our common humanity, the lyric of patriotism, the religious emotion. The poet is only the messenger of whole humanity voicing the general principles of morality.

The poet uses a direct style. The words are simple but memorable. They are meant to teach how to live. The poem appears simple but it presents a universal theme, applicable at all times.

There are a number of figures of speech. We have simile when our hearts are compared to *muffled drums*. Here is an example of metaphor: *Life is but an empty dream…Art is long and time is fleeting…*

The poem is presented in memorable verses, having a regular rhyming pattern. Each stanza has four lines. In every stanza the first line rhymes with the third and the second line rhymes with the fourth. In other words, the poem is made up of quatrains in alternately rhyming couplets. Many stanzas have become so memorable that they are extensively quoted. The poem is enjoyable because of its swift rhythm and rhyming pattern.

Example 2

Batter my heart, three person'd God; for, you
As yet but knocke, breathe, shine, and seeke to mend;
That I may rise, and, o'erthrow mee, 'and bend
Your force, to breake, blowe, burn and make me new.
I, like an usurpt towne, to' another due,
Labour to' admit you, but Oh, to no end,
Reason your viceroy in mee, mee should defend,
But is captiv'd, and proves weake or untrue.
Yet dearely' I love you, 'and would be loved faine,
But am betroth'd unto your enemie:
Divorce mee, 'untie, or breake that knot againe,
Take mee to you, imprison mee, for I
Except you' enthrall mee, never shall be free,
Not ever chast, except you ravish mee.

(John Donne)

Substance: In this sonnet the poet is trying to grapple with a complex and disruptive experience. The sonnet is centred on a personal experience. There is an extremely complex interplay between the arrangement of his experience and the shape of his conventional form of the sonnet. The first four lines make a clear paragraph, saying 'be stronger with me.' The next four lines are another unit, consisting of the extended metaphor of the 'usurp'd town'. The final six lines make a unit, mixing the language of love and war, and asking God to rescue him from the devil and take over control of him. There is a break after the first two of these lines, however, for they continue the explanation of his position, which had started in the previous unit at line five; whereas the final four lines are his request.

Comment: This is the way in which the experience comes to us: these are the groups in which we read the poem. They are not sharply divided, as different factors link or separate the parts. In the concluding lines of the poem, the poet is using two paradoxes: unless (except) you enthrall (imprison) me, I shall never be free, and, unless you ravish me, I shall never be chaste. The paradoxes rest in the seemingly contradictory words *enthrall* and *free*, *chaste* and *ravish*. The line has meaning because he is asking *God* to *stake* possession of his soul to give him *true* freedom and *true* chastity, by taking away his imperfect, earthly versions of these things.

The words *enthrall* and *ravish* are ambiguous: *enthrall* means 'put me in your thrall, enslave' and also 'fill *with delight*, enrapture'; *ravish* means 'rape, take by force, despoil' and even 'fill with pleasure, enrapture'. Thus these words also present a request which is not paradoxical. The poet will never be free and chaste, unless God fills him with delight.

This ambiguity enables the poet to express precisely what he desires. God should forcefully take over complete control of him, destroy his independent self, but through this destruction, this self-abnegation, he will be gloriously enraptured by God, fulfilled in God.

In this poem the poet uses sexual imagery to speak of religion. The connexion between the two subjects is so basic and so traditional that his method would hardly call for comment if it were not for the extraordinary intensity with which he pursues it. Both the intensity and the fusion of one area of experience with another are in perfect keeping with what we know of his life and opinions in general.

The violence of the sentiment is faithfully served by technique of the poem, which illustrates the way in which many poets do not state their theme so much as enact it, the battering which the poet asks God for is felt throughout the poem; and heard too: it is a very noisy poem. We come across genuine examples of onomatopoeia, especially through words like: *batter*, *knocke*, *breake*, *blowe*, *knot*, and *enthrall*. When it is not the sound it is the rhythm: the simile of the siege is comparatively quiet, except for a clattering effect of the *t* sounds, but the rhythm accurately represents the chopping and changing of battle. The first four lines act out their meaning with both rhythm and sound. The poem works through to a peaceful ending and in this case the sudden tranquility is very much like the aftermath of sexual strife, in sound as well as meaning.

The poem includes two devices. The first device is that of the catalogue or list:

> ...for 'you
> As yet but knocke, breathe, shine, and seeke to mend;
> That I may rise, and stand, o'erthrow mee me new.
> Divorce mee, 'untie, or breake that knot againe,
> Take mee to you, imprison mee...

The effect of the technique is that it conveys the idea of a series of demolishing blows. The other device is seen in the sixth line—the use of the exclamatory word *Oh*. The exclamation is integrally connected with the rhythm and the intention of the rhythm. The exclamation is capable of inducing an emotion.

The poem as a whole demonstrates the poet's deft handling of meter. He keeps to the iambic pentameter norm which is a traditional element in the English sonnet but he treats it as a basis or a starting point from which he continually departs for good poetic reasons of his own. In fact only four of the lines are regular, and one of these, the second, depends on violent elision for its regularity:

But am betroth'd unto your enemie:
Divorce mee, 'untie, or breake that knot againe,
... ...
Except you' enthrall mee, never shall be free,
Nor ever chaste, except you ravish mee.

The other lines display almost every possible variation of the imabic pattern. There is the trochaic foot:

Batter my heart...
But is captiv'd...
Take mee to you...

There is the strategically placed elision:

O'erthrow mee, 'and bend...
Labour to'admit you...
Yet dearly' I love you...

And most characteristically of these, there is the foot which is neither iambic not trochaic for both syllables bear an equal stress—spondee:

As yet but knocke, breathe, shine and seek to mend...
Your force, to breake, blowe, burn and make me new

The sonnet comprises an octave of Petrarchan type and a sestet of Shakespearean type, having a rhyme scheme *abba abba cdcdee.*

Example 3

They hanged him on clement morning, swung
between the falling sunlight and the women's
breathing, like a black apostrophe to pain.
All morning while the children hushed
their hop-scotch joy and the cane kept growing
he hung there, sweet and low.

At least that's how
they tell it. It was long ago
and what can we recall of a dead slave or two
except that when we punctuate our island tale
they swing like sighs across the brutal
sentences, and anger pauses
till they pass away.

Substance: In the opening stanza the poet poignantly places the execution in its mundane setting. He leaves no doubt, however, about the strong emotions it arouses. In the middle of the restrained description of the simple way the people show their respect for this man, the poet uncompromisingly forces us to recognize the brutality of the situation. The man hangs, 'like a black apostrophe to pain'—the simile used here is striking.

Comment: The opening stanza conveys both the brutality and the strange dignity of the scene. The poet wonderfully faces the two things—brutality and strange dignity—in the irony of its final line:

he hung there like, sweet and low.

The soothing words *sweet and low* taken from a smooth flowing poem by Tennyson, are so inappropriate as a description of the mood evoked by a hanging man that we read them ironically, and become more aware of the actual situation. On another level, however, we take the words without irony. In fact, the words give a strange muted dignity to the brutal scene.

This mixture is also present in the very first line of the stanza, where the word *clement* is broadly ironic, coming after *hanged*, the wonder as to how a morning on which a man is hanged be a *clement*, merciful morning. The irony conveys the lack of humanity of the people who hang the man; but as we read on, the word takes on a further meaning is where *clement*, with its mild, benevolent sunshine—'falling sunlight', where human executioners are merciless; it is ironic that nature should show restraint, as though it felt for the condemned man.

In the second stanza the poet moves away from this past, using plain unemotional words to place it at a distance:

At least that's how
they tell it. It was long ago
and what can we recall

But he shows the tie of such disregard for human suffering, even if it took place in the past. He leads straight on:

and what can we recall of a dead slave or two,

the inhumanity of the last words jerks us back to the reality of the suffering. Their irony is both an exposure of the callous disregard the executioners had for a human being, and an assertion of the humanity of the victim. It is also an indictment of our own tendency to forget the past and gloss over its sufferings.

Having brought this suffering emotional tone back into his poem, the poet ends with a forceful description of the real emotions with which the slaves are to be remembered:

they swing like sighs across the brutal
sentences, and anger pauses
till they pass away.

This poem proves the fact that irony need not always be amusing or unemotional. Irony is the very measure of this poem's intensity.

Example 4

In childhood's pride I said to Thee:
"O Thou, who mad'st me ofThy breath,
Speak, Master, and reveal to me
Thine inmost laws of life and death.

"Give me to drink each joy and pain
Which Thine eternal hand can mete,
For my insatiate soul can drain
Earth's utmost bitter, utmost sweet.

"Spare me no bliss, no pang of strife,
Withhold no gift or grief I crave,
The intricate lore of love and life
And mystic knowledge of the grave."

Lord, Thou didst answer stern and low:
"Child, I will hearken to thy prayer,
And thy unconquered soul shall know
All passionate rapture and despair.

(*The Soul's Prayer* Extract: Sarojini Naidu)

Substance: In the innocence of her childhood, the poet prayed to God, who had created her by breathing His life into her, to reveal the innermost mysteries of life and death. She prayed for the grace to accept every joy and sorrow which had come to her from His everlasting will. Her soul, ever unsatisfied would accept the failure or success on earth, as coming from His hand. The poet desired her Creator to spare her no happiness nor any pain or struggle or grief. She wanted to know the complex mysteries of love and life as well as the mysterious knowledge of death. God gave His answer frankly revealing the mysteries of knowledge. God said that He would answer her prayer and her innocent soul would come to know about the deepest joy and despair.

Critical Note: The mysteries of life and death are best revealed in the innocent period of childhood. Like a child, the poet prayed to God to reveal the 'inmost laws of life and death'. The child's request was soon granted. God replied to her revealing the mysteries of knowledge to her. This is the theme of the extract from the poem.

The poet brings out the universal religious principle of salvation through suffering. In order to achieve peace and salvation Divine Love has to consume our desires like fire. Through this poem, the poet tries to understand the innermost laws of life and death. The poet speaks like a mystic. She enters the inner circle of the Divine and pours out her feelings and desires. She has reached a mystic state where she surrenders herself to Divine Providence.

In this poem, the poet gives vent to self-expression. The poem comes under the category of lyrical poetry. The lyrical poem is restricted to the simple form of poetry in which the poet is restricted to the simple form of poetry, in which the poet is mainly occupied with her own thoughts and feelings.

The simplicity of language and lucidity of expression catch the reader's attention. The form of the dialogue between the human soul and Divine Soul lends a novel charm to the lyric. The flow of lines is smooth. Each stanza has four lines, in which the first and the third lines rhyme. Similarly, the second and the fourth lines rhyme.

The choice of words and phrases is in keeping with the solemn subject. The use of the pronoun 'Thou' and its other forms seem apt in a poem which includes a dialogue between God and man. The poem is a superb blend of archaic and colloquial expressions.

Archaic words:

In childhood's pride I said to Thee
"*O Thou*, who mad'st me of Thy breath,

Colloquial expressions:

Speak, Master, and reveal to me
Thine inmost laws of life and death.

Example 5

I wander thro' each charter'd street,
Near where the charter'd Thames does flow,
And mark in every face I meet
Marks of weakness, marks of woe.

In every cry of every Man,
In every Infant's cry of fear,
In every voice, in every ban,
The mind-forg'd manacles I hear.

How the Chimney-sweeper's cry
Every black'ning Church appalls;
And the hapless Soldier's sigh
Runs in blood down Palace walks.

But most thro' midnight streets I hear
How the youthful Harlot's curse
Blasts the new born Infant's tear,
And blights with plagues the Marriage hearse.

(William Blake)

Substance: When two words rhyme in a poem, they are brought into relationship: we are made to feel some kind of connexion between them, the poem opens thus:

I wander thro' each charter'd street,
Near where the charter'd Thames does flow,
And mark in every face I meet
Marks of weakness, marks of woe.

The rhymes bring *street* and *meet* into association, reinforcing the sense of numerous chance of outdoor encounters. The link between *flow* and *woe* suggests that it is not only the river that flows: there is a flowing movement of the sad-faced people through the streets. The mere fact of being rhyme-words gives greater prominence to these four words. The rhymes also increase our consciousness of the line ending, and so reinforce the metrical pattern. The rhyme at the end of a sentence gives a sense of finality and completeness.

Comment: The poem is made up of four quatrains of alternately rhyming couplets. All the rhymes are masculine. The poem has a heavy insistent rhythm, which is reinforced by the use of repetition, like *mark*, *Marks*, *marks* (all heavily stressed) in the opening stanza. The rhythm not only suggests the dead mechanical movements of the people in the streets of London, but also has an ominous ring, a hint of prophetic doom.

The poem gives us the poet's vision of London in this time, in the early phases of the Industrial Revolution. The streets through which the poet wanders are *charter'd* (in line 1): that is, they are privileged, given special rights by a royal charter (as most English cities are). This is ironical. This is ironical, for, while certain citizens of London may enjoy privileges, this is not the case with the people in the streets that the poet is observing. The poet underlines the irony by saying that the River Thames too is chartered. But a charter is also a written contract, especially for the conveyance of landed property, so the poet is also saying that London is a mass of private property, tied up in legal contracts. In contrast to the charters are the *faces* (in line 3) of the people—a word with which the poet insists on using for their humanity. In every face the poet marks ('observes') marks ('signs') of weakness and sorrow.

In the second stanza the universality of these signs is emphasized by the insistent repetitions: *In every... every... In every... In every... in every.* The insistent repetition of the poem underlines the dirge-like or wailing quality and the wide-spread degradation. The word *ban* (in line 7) can mean both 'a curse, imprecation' and 'an official prohibition, interdict'. In and through the marks of weakness and of woe the poet hears the *mind-forg'd menacles* (in line 8), an expression which is highlighted at the centre of the line by its three successive stressed syllables. People are in chains, but in chains of their own creation, forged by their minds. External authorities (the church and the palace of the following stanza) bind and oppress people, but people contribute to their own servitude by internalizing the commands of authority. True freedom, the poet implies, begins with the internal freedom of the individual, the liberation of the self. It cannot admit enlightenment or humanity.

The third stanza deals with the evil effects of established institutions, both religious (*the church*) and secular (*the palace*). The chimney-sweeper (in line 9) refers to the common practice of employing small children to climb up inside chimneys to clean them: little boys were cheaper than long brushes. For a century there was an outcry against this barbarous practice, but it was not finally stamped out until 1875. The cry of the chimney-sweeper discomfits or dismays (appeals of) the church, because it calls attention to the discrepancy between the church's teachings and the reality around it. The church is turning black (black'ning) because, like all buildings in industrial England, it is coated with soot from the chimney smoke: the church cannot escape the blight put on everything by industrialism; there is also a suggestion that the church is morally corrupt. The secular authority, the palace is responsible for wars, which claim the blood of the unfortunate (*hapless*) soldier.

Worst of all is sexual corruption. In the final stanza the poet hears the curse of the young prostitute, that is, one for whom sex has become a commodity to be sold on the market. The verb *to blast* (in line 15) could mean 'to blight, to sap the beauty or promise of', but it also had a stronger meaning, 'to strike with the wrath of heaven'. The infant whose tear is thus blasted may be that of a woman whose husband has made use of the prostitute: in a society where the institutionalized forms of sexual behaviour are marriage and prostitution, the latter may have a baleful effect on the children of marriage. But the infant may equally well be that of the prostitute herself: in an age lacking effective birth-control techniques, a prostitute was likely to have unwanted children, and to curse them. The baleful effects of prostitution on marriage are evoked in the final line of the poem: the *plagues* can be infectious diseases, or more generally afflictions and calamities; but the word also meant 'a variation of divine anger or justice, punishment by God'. The final word in the line, *hearse*, is unexpected and startling: the coach in which the married couple ride is suddenly turned into a funeral-carriage; or their marriage-bed is turned into a coffin. (The word *hearse* means 'a carriage constructed for carrying the coffin at a funeral', but formerly also meant 'bier, coffin, tomb, grave'.) It is an unexpected connection of *marriage* with *hearse* that gives the line its remarkable shock-effect.

The poet in the poem decries the three great evils of society—callousness of society as exemplified by the chimney sweeper's miserable life, the adversity of war as expressed in the case of the soldier, and lust represented in the malpractice of harlotry that looms large as a threat to the purity of marriage and the happiness of the offspring. The child chimney sweeper, the soldier, and the harlot are the various types of people oppressed—typical victims of a system based not on brotherhood but on fear. Each in his (or her) own way shows up the shams on which society thrives. The chimney sweeper's wretched life is supported by the churches, the soldier's death is demanded by he court, and the harlot's calling is found on her by the marriage laws. The contrasts between the truth and pretence, between natural happiness and unnatural repression are stressed by the poet in these three examples. It portrays the corruption of society. In fact, it is the corruption of civilization by the power of reason whose self-imposed manacles have restricted every spontaneous joy. The street cries of chimney-sweepers loudly accuse the church and the death sighs of the soldier stain the State. Love itself—the fundamental human virtue—is negated and this negation degenerates the holy marriage-bed—the very institution basic to society—into a blighted hearse. *Marriage hearse* is a shocking collocation, which signifies 'marriage-bed'. It is blighted by the young harlot's curse, and, therefore, it is a hearse.

The poem consists of alternate lines rhyming in five quatrains. It describes, with a fine economy of language and association, the degradation of contemporary life in the city, taking in disease and poverty and particularly the marks of weakness, marks of woe. The repetition of words like *mark* and *every* is noticeable. The insistent repetition of the phrase *In every* underlines the dirge-like or wailing quality and the widespread degradation. These words and others chime throughout the poem, uniting it while at the same time suggesting the repetitive quality of life in the city. The deseription of the city amounts to a virtual catalogue of the qualities we generally associate with experience: 'weakness' and'woe', the 'cry of fear', the 'black'ning' of the church, the savage insistence on the otherwise hidden relation between the plight of the prostitute and the terrifying 'marriage hearse'. In this world, we notice, no real purposes are possible, even for the 'wandering' narrator.

In the poem the poet gives his personal view of the 'chartered liberty' on the countrymen prided themselves, and exposes the indisputable, ugly facts. The poem attacks three great evils of society—cruelty as seen in the chimney-sweepers' wretched condition, war as represented by the soldier, and lust represented in the harlot who is a threat to the purity of marriage and the happiness of children. The child chimney-sweeper, the soldier, and the harlot are the poet's types of the oppressed—characteristic victims of a system based not on brotherhood but on fear. Each in his own way shows up the shams on which society thrives. The chimney-sweepers' condemned life is supported by the churches; the soldier's death is demanded by the court; and the harlot's calling is faced on her by the marriage-laws. The contrasts between truth and presence, between natural happiness and unnatural repression, are stressed in the poem in these three instances.

The extent of human degradation is most fully conveyed in the second verse. In the third stanza the poet illustrates the social evils through the lot of the chimney-sweeper and the soldier which are condoned by the church. The concluding stanza returns to the theme of disease and even equates the marriage bed with a hearse. The concluding line of the poem:

And blights with plagues the Marriage hearse

contains a superb paradox, for hearses are used at funerals, not weddings. It seems to signify the horrors that the child will inherit in an evil world, as well as the curse of venereal disease. In fact, the harlot's 'curse' may be a reference to venereal disease. The curse has a two-fold significance: first, it shows that the new-born child will have no future in the world, being an illegitimate child, and second, the curse will call down a plague on the hearse (or coffin, or dead body) or married love. The implications behind the line are the consequences of loveless marriage. An unhappy husband goes to seek diversion in the arms of a young prostitute. The prostitute gives birth to a child. She then curses the man's unhappy marriage as being responsible for her misery.

The repetition in the poem serves certain functions: the repetition of *every*, which hammers through the poem like the dull boot of totalitarianism; again the repetition of *charter'd*, which brings within itself two virtually opposing meanings, 'charter'd' as 'freed' and 'charter'd' as 'constrained'; the repetition in two different stanzas of 'Infant' which emphasizes in the first instance the child's teror and bewilderment at the world in which it finds itself, and in the second establishes with fightening force the source of this bewilderment in the confusion of love and sex, life and death.

The poem is remarkable for its auditory and visual power, we have in the poem cries, voices, and bans. 'Bans' may be regarded in double sense, 'bans' as prohibitions, and bans as the words read out in Church to permit marriage. All these sounds relate to the general scenario of the poem, to the poet's everyday walk through the streets of the city. Apart from hearing, the poet is also engaged in seeing: he sees—and 'marks', in the doubled sense of 'noticing', or 'remarking upon' and of 'marking down on paper'—the faces, and he sees also a terrible vision, which is of the churches dripping with darkness, the palaces soaked in blood.

The poem deals in opposites brought together, which is evident in the final lines, where 'blasts the new-born Infant's tear' is coupled with 'blights with plagues the Marriage hearse'. The poet may be indicting the practice of whoredom, or may be bringing into breathtakingly close conjunction the stifling nature of conventional marriage and the victimisation which attends the lot of harlot.

Example 6

As a fond mother, when the day is o'er,
Leads by the hand her little child to bed,
Half willing, half reluctant to be led,
And leave his broken playthings on the floor,
Still gazing at them through the open door,
Nor wholly reassured and comforted
By promises of others in their stead,
Which, though more splendid, may not please him more;
So Nature deals with us, and takes away
Our playthings one by one, and by the hand
Leads us to rest so gently, that we go
Scarce knowing if we wish to go or stay,
Being too full of sleep to understand
How far the unknown transcends the what we know.

(*Nature*: H.W. Longfellow)

Substance: In this sonnet a mother and her child have been compared with nature and man. Though it is time to go to bed, the child is unwilling to leave his playthings. So the mother promises to give it more splendid playthings and thus persuades it to go to bed. The poet sees a similar relationship between mother nature and man who is her child. Man's life on earth has been conceived as a long journey whose final destination is the world beyond the grave. We, men are unwilling to move towards this destination as we are too fond of our earthly possession, just as a child is unwilling to leave its dear playthings and go to bed. Our journey through life under the affectionate guidance of nature has been described metaphorically in the last six lines of the poem. Thus playthings refer to all our earthly possessions for which we feel such a fond attachment. As we grow in years, we inevitably come nearer and nearer to our final destination even though we wish to stay here on earth for ever.

Critical Note: It is a fine sonnet in which one of the profoundest truths of man's life has been presented through a beautiful comparison. Nature has been compared to a mother while man has been compared to a child.

The first eight lines of the poem describe how the unwilling child is gently being led by its mother to bed. This part of the poem clearly shows the poet's power of observation and his descriptive skill. His presentation of the scene is quite realistic, and we can see the child gazing at the playthings through the open door.

In the next six lines of the poem, man's journey through life has been metaphorically described. Nature here is conceived as a friend, philosopher, and guide to man. So these lines may remind the reader of Wordsworth's concept of nature. The real beauty of the poem lies in the metaphorical representation of man's journey through life under the affectionate guidance of nature. Some words and expressions in the latter part of the poem have been used metaphorically. Thus 'playthings' refer to man's earthly possessions. The expression 'too full of sleep' refers to man's ignorance of true aim and purpose of life. The 'unknown' is our eternal home beyond the grave. The familiar world in which we live is referred to as 'what we know'.

The sonnet is written in iambic pentameter. The rhyme scheme is: *a b b a, a b b a* and *c d e* and *c d e*. The sonnet is a long drawn comparison. The octave or the first eight lines of the poem contain one component part of the comparison. The sestet or the last six lines contain the other part. Thus there is a clear demarcation between octave and the sestet. It is a sonnet of Petrarchan variety.

Example 7

Beside yon straggling fence that skirts the way
With blossom'd furze unprofitably gay,
There, in his mansion, skill'd to rule,
The village master taught his little school;
A man severe he was, and stern to view,
I knew him well, and every truant knew;
Well had the boding tremblers learn'd to trace
The days disasters in his morning face;
Full well they laugh'd with counterfeited glee,
At all his jokes, for many a joke had he:
Full well the busy whisper, circling round,

Convey'd the dismal tidings when he frown'd:
Yet he was kind; or if severe in aught,
The love he bore to learning was in fault.
The village all declar'd how much he knew;
'Twas certain he could write, and cipher too:
Lands he could measure, terms and tides presage,
And e'en the story ran that he could gauge.
In arguing too, the parson own'd his skill,
For e'en though vanquish'd he could argue still;
While words of learned length and thund'ring sound
Amazed the gazing rustics rang'd around;
And still they gaz'd and still the wonder grew,
That one small head could carry all he knew.
But past is all his fame. The very spot
Where many a time he triumph'd is forgot.

(*The Village Schoolmaster:* Oliver Goldsmith)

Substance: The school is located by the side of the border made of an irregular row of shrubs growing wildly. The path to the school passes along the border. The prickly evergreen bush has small yellow flowers but there is no one to appreciate their beauty. There the village school master—an able administrator—teaches the noisy little school.

The school master is the most learned member in a village community. He inspires the pupils as well as the village folk. In the school he is a man of strict discipline and stern appearance. His displeasure is depicted on his face, which makes his pupils behave in a proper manner. They pretend to laugh at his jokes in order to keep him happy.

In spite of his stern appearance, he loves his pupils, wishes their welfare. The teacher, besides his knowledge, is a good debater. The villagers crowd around him to listen to his words. They wonder how his head contains so much knowledge.

Critical Note: The poem has a rural background. It depicts objects, people and manners in a village in the eighteenth century. The school is small—a little school. The teacher is the most learned man in the village. He can argue, calculate and predict. The villagers gather around him wondering about the volume and depth of his knowledge.

The poet has excelled in using the narrative skills. He gives exactly the location of the school. It is "Beside yon straggling fence that skirts the way". Then he uses the description of the school, a *noisy mansion*. He maintains realism which contributes to visualize the condition of the school. The way the pupils behave in a classroom is depicted with minute details.

The teacher's argumentative skills and perseverance in the face of defeat are narrated in a simple language.

The poet is sympathetic towards the teacher.The teacher's appearance, strictness, learning and kindness are referred to using humour in order to maintain the interest of the readers.The pupils laughed with *counterfeited glee* at the jokes shared by the teacher.

When the teacher frowned, the children sensed the danger and conveyed the dismal tidings to all the pupils. The truant children were afraid of him.

The poet uses words spontaneously to express his feelings of understanding and appreciation for his native village.The school is fondly remembered as a *noisy mansion*, where the teacher was skilled to rule.The pupils were frightened of the teacher. By suitable words and expressions, the author succeeds in his objective of describing his village and its pupil.

As regards rhyming pattern, the poet has used a couplet pattern that is, a pair of rhymed lines.

Example 8

A gang of labourers on the piled wet timber
That shines blood-red beside the railway siding
Seem to be making out of the blue of the morning
Something faery and fine, the shuttles sliding.

The red-gold spools of their hands and their faces swinging
Hither and thither across the high crystalline frame
Of day: trolls at the cave of ringing cerulean mining
And laughing with labour, living their work like a game.

Substance: In this poem, the poet is recreating an image of some men he has seen at work.The run-on lines enhance the activity of the men, but also the feeling of enchantment that the poet creates through his language and the metaphor of the *trolls*.

Comment: The long noun phrase of the opening two lines provides us with much concentrated description. While some of the modifiers are factual—*piled, wet, railway*, the poet's use of *blood-red* and the verb *shines* begins to lift the vision of a *gang of labourers* beyond the everyday. We are driven on towards the end of the stanza where the literal becomes figurative: the everyday work is transformed into something *faery and fine* (in line 4). The soft fricatives are unexpected in a poem about railway workers, yet the poet has prepared us for this transformation by his use of the verb *Seem* (in line 3) with its connotations of mystery and uncertainty.

Although the two stanzas are divided by an end-stopped line, the final image of the *shuttles* in the first stanza is developed in the second where the workers' hands become *spools* (in lines 4-5). The connotations of weaving build upon the suggestion that they are *making.../something faery and fine.* Traditional images of the coarseness of labouring have been replaced with a sense of creativity. This is enhanced by the poet's concentration on rich colours that intensify the other-worldly atmosphere—*blood-red, red-gold, crystalline, cerulean.*

The present participle *swinging* and the adverbial *hither and thither* (in lines 5-6) draw attention to the movements of the men. Framed against the sky, they are reduced to their parts—*hands* and *faces*—almost like elements of a machine. The final lines, like the first, are made up of a complex noun phrase that makes explicit the comparison between the men and the fairy world. The soft repeated lateral sounds—'*l*aughing', '*l*abour', '*l*iving', '*l*ike'—like the earlier fricatives, contrast the rough labourers with the vision the poet sees. The patterning of the present participles, the internal rhyme—*labour/game*, and the alliterative sounds enhance this morning vision.

The poet has used enjambement to intensify the effect of this poem. It provides cohesion by mirroring the movement of the men and driving us forward to the final metaphor. He does not present us with a typical image of men at work, but transforms the mundanity and indignity of physical labour into something magical.

Example 9

"Is there anybody there?" said the Traveller,
Knocking on the moonlit door;
And his horse in the silence champed the grasses
Of the forest's ferny floor.
And a bird flew up out of the turret,
Above the traveller's head:
And he smote upon the door a second time;
"Is there anybody there?" he said.
But no one descended to the Traveller;
No head from the leaf-fringed sill
Leaned over and looked into his gray eyes,
Where he stood perplexed and still.
But only a host of phantom listeners
That dwelt in the lone house then
Stood listening in the quiet of the moonlight
To that voice from the world of men:

Stood thronging the faint moonbeams on the dark stair
That goes down to the empty hall,
Hearkening in an air stirred and shaken
By the lonely Traveller's call.
And he felt in his heart their strangeness,
Their stillness answering his cry,
While his horse moved, cropping the dark turf,
'Neath the starred and leafy sky;
For he suddenly smote the door, even
Louder, and lifted his head:--
"Tell them I came, and no one answered,
That I kept my word," he said.
Never the least stir made the listeners,
Though every word he spake
Fell echoing through the shadowiness of the still house
From the one man left awake:
Aye, they heard his foot upon the stirrup,
And the sound of iron on stone,
And how the silence surged softly backward,
When the plunging hoofs were gone.

(*The Listeners:* Walter de la Mare)

Substance: The poem builds up an eerie atmosphere by using suggestion, mystery and fear. It describes a lone traveller's visit to a solitary medieval castle. The castle is abandoned giving a weird look in the moonlight. There is no one present in the castle, except some strange ghosts who listen to the question asked by the visitor.There are two worlds: one alive, and the other dead.They are cast side by side presenting dramatic moment charged with suspense and fear. As the reader waits with suspended expectation for something strange to happen, the lone visitor leaves the place.With this, normalcy is restored in the forest. Peace and silence again prevail over the woodland, leaving the reader puzzled by the unsolved mystery of drama just witnessed by him. The poem is essentially about silence and loneliness. The only human voice in the poem is that of the Traveller's; the listeners, who say nothing, are phantoms. The listeners can hardly be separated from the silence surrounding them. Into the silence and solitude there rides a single man. The Traveller may be regarded as Any Man, the episode Any Time, and the location Any Place, as in a sense they are.

Critical Note: The poem is a masterpiece of suggestion and it shows the poet's mastery of the art in creating an uncanny atmosphere. The poem is based on the mystery and suspense that surround one's experience of visiting a deserted house. The poet describes how one night a traveller came riding to a lonely house in the forest, knocked on the moonlit door and shouted: "Is there anybody there?" Nobody responded to the traveller's call. The traveller thought that his cry was heard only by some phantom listeners. He at last shouted:

"Tell them I came, and no one answered,
That I kept my word."

Then the traveller rode away in silence. Thus the whole poem hinges on certain unsolved mysteries—the mystery surrounding the identity of the traveller, the mystery of the deserted castle, the mystery of the strange message left by the traveller, and mystery surrounding the phantom listeners. The real charm of the poem lies in the subtle manner in which the poet created an eerie atmosphere.

Suspense sustains the attention of the readers. It is built up by using various skills in narration. Without any introduction, the poem begins with a question against the background of the moonlit door. This whets the reader's curiosity to know many things about the visitor—his name, the purpose of his visit why he has chosen the particular time. The poem says nothing to satisfy the curiosity of the reader.

Besides building up suspense, the poet creates an atmosphere of mystery and fear. A bird flies up out of a turret above the traveller's head. When the visitor asked the question a second time, no one came down to open the door; neither any head leaned over from the leaf-fringed sill to look at him. It is only the phantom listeners who "stood listening in the quiet of the moon light". The atmosphere of mystery pervades the whole narration. Towards the end, the words of the visitor 'fell echoing through the shadowiness of the still house'. The silence prevailed in the gloomy background even after 'the plunging of hoofs were gone'.

The poem is a narrative poem. It has the element of a dramatic monologue. There is only one speaker who asks questions. His listeners are a host of phantoms, who show no reaction to what he says. The main purpose of the poem is to present a strange atmosphere.

To create an atmosphere compatible to the theme, various figures of speech and other literary devices have been used by the poet. For example, the poet has used alliteration to create the hissing sounds in the following lines:

Aye, they heard hi**s** foot upon the **s**tirrup,
And the **s**ound of iron on **s**tone,
And how the **s**ilence **s**urged **s**oftly backward,
When the plunging hoof**s** were gone.

Personification is used to re-create an atmosphere of silence in the following line:

'the silence surged softly backward'.

The tone and the mood of the poem is dreamlike, in that the scene is unlocalised, yet remarkably clear and precise too in the details, as dreams often are. The moonlight is the moonlight of all romantic poetry, a setting for experience heightened beyond the commonplace towards what might be insight, might even be hallucination. The horse, the bird, the forest, the turret, the leaf-fringed sill are fixed in a moment of intense expectation, against the moonlight and the unfolding silence. They help like the words of the traveller himself, to define the silence. His question 'Is there anybody there?' his last challenge 'Tell them I came, and no one answered' resonate against the silence, underlining its enigma and its finality.

The people are shadowy; we have no way of knowing anything about them, except that they are very old, very beautiful, very gay, very sad. When they turn into ghosts, as they sometimes do, they seem scarcely altered. The landscape alters round them; the silence steals gradually closer, as it does in the poem. They have no class, no period, no *Zeitgeist*, no personal history. We can push them indefinitely into the world of the dead. Despite pushing them into the past, they do not exist in any historical past.

Their isolation is that of the soul itself; their one major relationship, as the absence of particular relationship serves to underline, is with transience. If they live anywhere, it is in the world of the family album, and the strangely timeless reality and unreality of that. Their gaiety, beauty, sadness, just because they have no immediate context, directly confront the certainty of decay. The loneliness here is defined against nothing; it relates to the perennial human awareness of nothing. The loneliness of the soul in itself is somewhere between waking and sleeping, between midnight and dawn.

The time and place are unspecific; yet everything is so vivid. The poem haunts the mind with a resolute resistance to exorcism. This is so, partly because the very remotences of the Traveller and his situation from historical particulars sets them free as symbols. The whole poem is like a dream. The dream may be diversely and plausibly interpreted after we wake, but which has its own symbolic vividness beyond any or all of the meanings it can be shown to have. In the poem, the human protagonist is the Traveller, who had journeyed to the moonlit door to keep faith with whoever he expects to find there. We have no idea where he comes from or where he rides off to at the end. All that we are told about him is that he comes on a horse, that his eyes are grey, and that he is the one man left awake. We know of nothing of the purpose of his journey except that the other side does not seem to have kept faith. He appears to be a lone man lost in a world of illusions. His parting words have a finality, heroic yet forlorn, which resonates, against the other finality of the silence.

The poet dramatizes with exquisite precision the moment of challenge and doubt when the isolated soul questions the unanswering universe. At the same time, he dramatizes the silence and the enigma of the listeners; the meeting of a human with the great and strange silence, in a moment that is not without dignity.

It is to this silence that the poem always returns. It is so tangible, we can almost touch it. Nothingness itself comes near to incarnation. No one descends to the Traveller; no head leans over and looks: it is the nearest approach to meeting no one that we are likely to make. And the listeners themselves, who walk off with the title of the poem, make no stir, but *are* the silence they lurk in, just as the witches in Shakespeare's *Macbeth* are the air into which they vanish. At the end, the silence 'surges softly backwards', and remains when the plunging hoofs are gone.

Despite the shadowiness of time and place, the poem is all so vivid. The language of the poem is almost paradoxically concrete and clear. Throughout the poem, the poet makes frequent use of words like *love, empty, phantom, strangeness*; the numinous words belong to, rather than create, the atmosphere. The whole effect of the poem is paradoxical and unusual. In order create suspense, the poet resorts to alternately rhyming lines—*abcb*.

Example 10

I wonder by my troth, what thou, and I
Did, till we Iov'd ? were we not wean'd till then ?
But suck'd on countrey pleasures, childishly?
Or snorted we i'the seaven sleepers den?[1]
'Twas so; But this, all pleasures fancies bee.
If ever any beauty I did see,
Which I desir'd, and got, 'twas but a dreame of thee.

And now good morrow to our waking soules,
Which watch not one another out of feare;
For love, all love of other sights controules,
And makes one little roome, an every where.
Let sea-discoverers to new worlds have gone,
Let Maps to others, worlds on worlds have showne,
Let us possesse our world, each hath one and is one.

My face in thine eye, thine in mine appeares.
And true plaine hearts doe in the faces rest,
Where can we finde two better hemispheares
Without sharpe North, without declining West?
What ever dyes, was not mixt equally:
If our two loves be one, or thou and I
Love so alike, that none doe slacken, none can die.[2]

(*The Good Morrow*: John Donne)

1. The legend tells of seven young men of Ephesus who took refuge in a cave during the persecution of Diocletian and were entombed there. They were found alive after almost two centuries later.
2. Only the simple or uncompounded, and things compounded of elements between which is no contratiety are free from corruption and are immortal.

Substance: The lover bids good morning to his beloved, whom he has met for the first time after a rather prolonged slumber, as it were. He speaks of the time before their first meeting and falling in love. He wonders how they had lived, like weanlings separated from the mother's breast, in baby days, when they required sucking the mother's milk. They fed upon the various beauties of the countryside and these probably served as the source of nourishment to them, instead of the mother's milk. Or it may be that like the seven sleepers of Ephesus they slept a long sleep in some mountain cave. All these are the pleasurable fancies of the lover. But this much he is sure that he always dreamt of his beloved. Their souls are now aroused from slumber and they are united by love into one whole, without any rift between them. Love has enlarged their world, so that a small room in which they meet appears are large as the vast universe. In their universe there is no North Pole of ice and cold, no warm sunset in the west. It is even bright and sunny. Their souls have been refined into 'quintessence' by love and as such they are immortal.

Comment: To some extent this poem is highly conventional. It takes place at dawn, after a night of making love, and as such can be described as an *aubade*. The term *aubade* (applicable to poetry or music) is always associated with the drowsy bliss of a post-coital dawn. The poet does not make it clear that this is an aubade until the second verse:

And now good morrow to our waking souls.

Even then we are not quite sure whether these are souls or bodies waking. The image which begins the third verse, of his seeing his own reflection in his lover's eyes, provides the confirmation that the two lovers are physically close, so close that they can see each other's reflections clearly in their eyes.

There are a series of rhetorical questions (*erotema*) in the opening stanza. The poet begins by asking as to what they did before they fell in love. Then he asks whether they were such infants and whether they were not weaned till then. Continuing the breast-feeding image, the poet enforces the idea of their previous experiments as childish by calling them 'country pleasures' is so often alluded to with the use of the word 'country' in sixteenth and seventeenth-century writing, an indecent pun is intended. Apart from raising the possibility of an indecent pun on 'country' which would also heighten the quality of this new love, the word signifies unsophisticated.

The seven sleepers (of line 4) refers to the myth of seven Christian youths of Ephesus who escaped Roman persecution by sleeping in a cave for almost two centuries. (Christian legend tells us of seven young men who were walled up alive during religious persecution and slept for 187 years.) All these combine to create a sensation familiar to lovers: the notion that whatever has taken place before was in some fundamental way only fragmentary, nullified, substantially impoverished in some essentially human way we find difficult to quantify.

The poet opts for childishness as his central metaphor until the final three lines of the opening verse where a triple rhyme reinforces a new point. The poem explains:

> 'Twas so; But this, all pleasures fancies bee.

This love is the only reality, everything else is imagination. Beautiful women he had formerly desired, and enjoyed, now become mere dreams compared to the girl in his bed. It is, indeed, a potent compliment. The girl in the poet's bed becomes so superb that the realities of his experience of love with other beautiful women are turned into dreams of her. Hyperbole seems to be an instinctive gift in the poet.

The form of address adopted in the poem is that there is no dialogue, no direct speech. Despite this the girl's presence is not in question. The frequent use of personal pronouns—*I*, *thou*, *we*—and emphasis on joint experience make this clearly a love poem in its need to communicate.

The three stanzas correspond to three stages. In terms of time we have a progression from past to present to future. The opening of the poem is ordinarily felt as explosive. The first question is abrupt; it differs in tone from the three questions that then follow. They offer three strikingly individual images of physical activity, but they all serve the purpose of presenting possible answers to the first question:

> I wonder by my troth, what thou, and I
> Did, till we lov'd ?

The tone of an oath is difficult to judge. The first stanza, as first stage, brought the memory of the unconscious past of flesh toward a conscious relationship with the mind of the present. The second stanza makes declarations concerning that present; it prepares for the next stage but also looks back. Their activities are dismissed from the present, not because they are contemptible or a passionate threat, but because they are inconsequential.

In the third stanza the external world enters again, as another intellectual recollection of the past. In a way the reference is even further remote and abstract. The two hemispheres are those of a merely objective world, with which there can be no significant human relationship, except at the point of contact, the idea of time and change. The 'sharpe North' and the 'declining West' belong to the world of passion and death from which the lovers have awakened. That world, like their preconscious past, has not been annihilated by the poetic imagination; it has been transformed by the lovers' consciousness of purpose; if defines by its cold externality the warm centre of a living present. The line:

What ever dyes, was not mixt equally

introduces the idea of death, not imaginatively immediate or threatening, but not quite abstract either. It sums up all the images from the external world of change, sums them up as a gentle reminder that they have been defeated and that the triumph of the warm present has been won in spite of this. The end of the poem turns, as the end of each preceding stanza has turned, to a summing up that consolidates the stage attained and looks forward to the next. It is this fact that accounts for the strange tone at the end. The tone is not triumphant; it is not the tone of an enthusiastic voice proclaiming transcendence. Instead it is quiet, even modest. The argument does not undertake to prove the infallible safety of the lovers' final arrival. It points that wisdom toward the future, with the modest tentativeness of two possible propositions, both based upon an *if*:

If our two loves be one, or thou and I
Love so alike, that none doe slacken, none can die.

The world of love as it takes shape in the poem, defines pure centre both by exclusions and by inclusions:

For love, all love of other sights controules,
And makes one little roome, an every where.

It is a world of twoness united. The unity of love depends on their twoness being one. When we come to the line:

My face in thine eye, thine in mine appears

we get a proof of the lovers' identification: the objective recognition of self in another and the feeling of another in self. In that experience, the lover sees his own reflected face directly, while he sees directly the other face, but only feels its image reflected in his own eyes, there exists the most delicate point of contact between the subjective and the objective. The two lovers are one in the image.They are one, and they do love alike. They have been mixed equally, and present an ancient proof of human integration, the transparency of the heart in the countenance. There is rhetorical emphasis, the emphasis of feeling coincide almost exactly, in the line, where there is stress on '*thine... thine... mine*', with internal rhyme. This is reinforced by he single sound '*my... eye*'—these draw together in a singleness of effect.

The poem illustrates wonderfully the range and variety of imagery. From the homely activities of breast-feeding and heavy sleeping, we pass to the more exotic activities of the explorers, the geographers, and the philosophers. There is also a considerable range of language, from the 'unpoetic':

> Or snorted we i'the seaven sleepers den?

to the conventionally 'poetic':

> Let Maps to others, worlds on worlds have showne.

The rhythm of the poem reflects the comparative straight forwardness of its subject matter, as in the lines:

> If ever any beauty I did see,
> Which I desir'd, and got, 'twas but a dreame of thee.

Nowhere in the poem, except in the last two lines, where the thought becomes knotty, do we meet irregularities of rhythm. The limpid rhythm adds to the serene and affirmative note of the poem.

Example 11

> Stern Daughter of the Voice of God!
> O Duty! if that name thou love,
> Who art a light to guide, a rod
> To check the erring and reprove;
> Thou, who art victory and law
> When empty terrors overawe;
> From vain temptations dost set free;
> And calm'st the weary strife of frail humanity!
>
> There are who ask not if thine eye
> Be on them; who, in love and truth,
> Where no misgiving is, rely

Upon the genial sense of youth:
Glad hearts! without reproach or blot;
Who do thy work, and know it not:
O, if through confidence misplaced
They fail, thy saving arms, dread Power! around them cast.

Serene will be our days and bright,
And happy will our nature be,
When love is an unerring light,
And joy its own security.
And they a blissful course may hold
Even now, who, not unwisely bold,
Live in the spirit of this creed;
Yet seek thy firm support, according to their need.

(*Ode to Duty*: *the first three stanzas*: William Wordsworth)

Substance: The Ode begins with an invocation to Duty. Duty is the stern daughter of the Voice of God. The poet asks whether or not Duty likes its name. Duty is the light that guides human beings; it is a threat to prevent men from following the path of evil. It blames when they go astray. When hollow imaginary fears are built up. Duty becomes a law and leads us to victory by protecting us from such baseless fears. It sets us from the clutches of vain temptations and claims the minds of morally feeble human beings in their struggle between right and wrong.

There are some persons who instinctively follow the right path without being supervised by Duty. They do not require her guidance. They are led in love and truth by their own impulses which are dominant during their youth. They perform their duty happily without being conscious that their way of acting is in order. Some times, such people may go astray because of their over confidence in their instincts. Then Duty comes to their rescue by putting them on their right path.

Our days will be bright and we shall be happy when we are correctly guided by our instincts. Such a life gives us spontaneous joy and happiness. We may have a blissful life in this imperfect world. We should live by the basic principles of this good belief. Yet we should seek the help of Duty whenever we are in doubt.

Critical Note: In his younger days, William Wordsworth was a lover of individual freedom. He was impressed by the ideals of the French Revolution which advocated absolute freedom. However, after the Revolution, things changed. Unbridled freedom gave rise to dictatorship and bloodshed. The poet then changed his ideas of freedom. He maintained that absolute freedom has to be curtailed by the dictates of discipline. This poem is a milestone in the history of the poet's mind. He repudiates the unchartered freedom in favour of something greater—obedience to eternal law. So, the Ode may be said to have an autobiographical element.

Wordsworth was a didactic poet. He once wrote: "Every great poet is a teacher: I wish either to be considered as a teacher or as nothing." A careful study of the extract from the ode shows that he seeks to impart to his reader a set of moral lessons. According to him the secret of happiness is that one must perform his duty under all circumstances.

Serene will be our days and bright,
And happy will our nature be,
When love is an unerring light,
And joy its own security.

Mysticism is an atmosphere rather than a systematic philosophy of life. The basis of mysticism is the firm belief in a world of divine reality. To the mystic there is 'one undivided changeless life in all lives'. The poet believes that all things in the visible world are but forms and manifestations of the one divine life.

Wordsworth was a mystic in the true sense of the term. He was also a seer. He himself had caught a vision of life. He believed that every man could attain peace and happiness by following stern law and order.

Ode to Duty is a fine example of what is called 'reflective or meditative poetry', that is a type of poetry which chiefly conveys the thoughts of the poet, either in his own person or as an imaginary person.

In a didactic, moralistic poem, imagery is drawn from different areas. Imagery of terror and authority is used in the poem. Duty is a *stern Daughter, of the Voice of God.* It is said to be the light to guide, *a rod to check the erring, dread power.*

Example 12

Had we but World enough, and Time,
This coyness Lady were no crime.
We would sit down, and think which way
To walk, and pass our long Loves Day.
Thou by the *Indian Ganges* side
Should'st Rubies find: I by the Tide
Of *Humbcr* would complain. I would
Love you ten years before the Flood:
And you should if you please refuse
Till the Conversion of the *Jews.*
My vegetable Love should grow

Vaster than Empires, and more slow.
An hundred years should go to praise
Thine Eyes, and on thy Forehead Gaze,
Two hundred to adore each Breast:
But thirty thousand to the rest.
An Age at least to every part,
And the last Age should show your Heart.
For Lady you deserve this State;
Nor would I love at lower rate

But at my back I always hear
Times winged Charriot hurrying near:
And yonder all before us lye
Desarts of vast Eternity.
Thy Beauty shall no more be found;
Nor, in thy marble Vault, shall sound
My echoing Song: then Worms shall try
That long preserv'd Virginity:
And your quaint Honour turn to dust;
And into ashes all my Lust.
The Grave's a fine and private place.
But none I think do there embrace.

Now therefore, while the youthful hew
Sits on thy skin like morning dew,
And while thy willing Soul transpires
At every pore with instant Fires,
Now let us sport us while we may;
And now, like am'rous birds of prey,
Rather at once our Time devour,
Than languish in his slow-chapt pow'r.
Let us roll all our Strength, and all
Our sweetness, up into one Ball:
And tear our Pleasures with rough strife,
Thorough the Iron gates of Life.
Thus, though we cannot make our Sun
Stand still, yet we will make him run.

(*To His Coy Mistress*: Andrew Marvell)

Substance: The poem has a clearly defined syllogistic structure. It is in three sections, which contrast not only what they say, but also in their imagery, wit, and tone. In its structure, the poem presents an argument, a demonstration of a case. The first two sections give different points of view, and the third gives a conclusion. In the first section, the poet imagines how they would love if time and space did not restrict them. In the second, he gives the reality—that time passes and we die. In the third, he draws the conclusion that they should make the most of life while they can, and make love now.

Comment: The poem displays great variation in tone and pace. It falls into three sections. In the first section (comprising lines 1 to 20) the poet says that, if he and his beloved had illimitable time and space, it would be proper for her to be so modest and to repel his advances. She could find rubies beside the Ganges while he lamented by the Humber:

I would
Love you ten years before the Flood:
And you should if you please refuse
Till the Conversion of the *Jews.*

Their courtship could extend in time from before Noah's Flood until shortly before the Day of Judgment (when it was believed that the Jews would be converted to Christianity). And the lady, he says, deserves such protracted wooing.

The first section moves slowly and deliberately, and the tone is judicious and detached. The writing is witty, as in the striking *vegetable love* (in line 11), which refers to the traditional belief that the distinctive characteristic of the vegetable kingdom (as approved to the animal kingdom or minerals) is the power of growth; the word does not suggest the kitchen (a later development in its meaning), but the slow growth of something like on oak-tree.

In the second section of the poem (lines 21 to 32) there is a sudden increase in pace, and the mood becomes restless:

But at my back I always hear
Times winged Charriot hurrying near:
And yonder all before us lye
Desarts of vast Eternity.

The pace slows down again for the solemn contemplation of the marble vault where the lady will lie in death, and then modulates into a sardonic reflection on death and love, concluding:

The Grave's a fine and private place.
But none I think do there embrace.

The final section (comprising lines 33 to 46) is an ardent invitation to love is also an invitation to live, and to live energetically, to 'tear our Pleasures with rough strife,/Thorough the Iron gates of life', and to devour time rather than be devoured by Time's 'slow-chapt power'. So, if we cannot make time stop, we will at least use it to the full:

> Thus, though we cannot make our Sun
> Stand still, yet we will make him run.

The structure of the whole poem is one of logical argument: (1) *If* it were so... (2) *But* it is not so... (3) *Therefore* let us love: within this syllogistic framework the poet gives us a poem of enormous wit, clarity, poise and emotional range. Moreover, the poem is teeming with rhythmic energy and physical immediacy of experience is firmly rooted in idiomatic English. The phrase 'slow-chapt power' gives us the physical experience of people being inexorably ground down in Time's jaws.

In the different sections the poet uses different images, related to differences in tone. The imagery of the first section is extravagant and far-fetched, because he is indulging in pure fancy. In the second section, the imagery is gruesome as he presents grim reality. In the third, the imagery is full of vigorous activity and liveliness, as he asserts that they must live to the full.

In a similar way the tone changes. In the first section, he is lighthearted, using playful wit. He gives a precise portion of time for each part of her body. He gives the absurd detail '*ten years* before the flood', to be so precise about time in a timeless world is clearly absurd. He is politely considerate, 'if you please', as though this timelessness were more than a game. There is an element of irony in this thoughtfulness—it is a sarcastic consideration for her.

The tone of the second section is frank; he is stating the facts with concrete detail—*worms*, *marble vault* (on its literal level), *dust*, *ashes*, *Grave*. At the end of the section he uses grim irony:

> The Grave's a fine and private place.
> But none I think do there embrace.

The wit here is in marked contrast to the playing of the first section—after the ironic praise *fine* and the grim understatement *private*, the mock uncertainty of *I think*, emphasizes the stupidity of not being realistic and facing the facts. The poet's tone is becoming increasingly impatient (about the unreality of imagining that they have lots of time), and reaches its climax in the sarcasm of the final couplet.

In the final section, the poet writes much longer sentences, which build up the tension and create a sense of urgency. His assertive tone speaks quickly, with the excitement of what he is advocating. It culminates in the emphatic statement:

Let us roll all our Strength, and all
Our sweetness, up into one Ball:

His triumphant assurance that they can conquer time, produces a wit that is without any undercutting irony:

Thus, though we cannot make our Sun
Stand still, yet we will make him run.

In this couplet the wit lies in the switch from the literal, 'cannot make our sun/Stand still', to the figurative 'make him run', in the course of one sentence. The poet does this because in the human experience he is expressing, there is no distinction. In our consciousness time does not pass regularly, but quickly or slowly according to what we are doing.

Though in each section the poet uses different images, the imagery in all three sections is similar in being complex and consciously worked. In the first part, the conceits are firmly in a convention of love poetry in which the poet flatters his mistress with praise which is as hyperbolical as possible. In the second part, the factual basis of the conceits makes their wit a fanciful playing on the given facts, which serves to endorse their unavoidable reality. There is a great paradox of time in the poem.

Example 13

He clasps the crag with crooked hands;
Close to the sun in lonely lands,
Ring'd with the azure world, he stands.

The wrinkled sea beneath him crawls;
He watches from his mountain walls,
And like a thunderbolt he falls.

(*The Eagle*: Alfred Tennyson)

Substance: The poet is writing of a bird and its mastery of its environment, but also, perhaps, symbolically of a human ruler who conquers and reigns supreme in his kingdom. The opening simple clause 'He clasps the crag with crooked hands' creates an immediate and dramatic image. The ambiguity of reference to the pronoun *He* at the beginning of the poem underpins our feeling that the poem is doing more than literally describing a bird. There is a kind of semantic layering.

Comment: For the poet, the lexical choice is directly linked to a physical environment. The concrete nouns *crag* (in line 1), *lands* (in line 2), *sea* (in line 4), and *mountain* (in line 5) give the reader a sense of the terrain over which the bird flies. The modifiers are important because they develop our sense of perspective: both literally in terms of height, but also symbolically in terms of the bird's distance from others. The intensity of the blue sky surrounding the bird is indicated by the modifier *azure* (in line 3)—it symbolically represents the height of the bird's perch because he appears to be above the cloud, literally in a world of his own. This is reinforced by the verb modifier *wrinkled* (in line 1) and *lonely* (in line 2) create a different sort of perspective. The poet's bird is personified and this is reinforced by the choice of *hands* (in line 1) rather than *claws* and the reference to *walls* (in line 5) with its connotations of man-made constructs.

The poet uses the declarative mood throughout the poem, his manipulation of word order is an important means of guiding and influencing us. The delayed second main clause *he stands* (in line 3) draws attention to the fronted adverbials *close to the sun...* (in line 2) and *Ring'd with the azure world...* (in line 3) that begin to characterize the bird/ruler in terms of elevation, isolation and entrapment. A similar pattern is created in the final line of the poem in which the simile *like a thunderbolt* (in line 6) precedes the main clause *he falls*. The delay heightens our sense of the power in the bird's action as it drops down to strike its prey, or the ruler's meting out of punishment. The simile conjures up images of both the natural and god-like with its allusions to he Greek Zeus, all powerful father of the gods and ruler of the sky, and the Scandinavian thunder god Thor.

Form and meaning are also combined in the poet's use of the adverbial *beneath him* (in line 4) in the medial position. By delaying the main verb *crawls*, the poet reinforces the power of the bird/ruler—the connotations of the words; their order and the possible symbolic reading of the *sea* as the ruler's subjects suggest an unforgiving and potentially cruel tyrant alongside the literal description of the instinctive bird.

The poet uses two three-lined stanzas, or tercets, linked by rhyme to order his ideas, dealing first with the bird's location and then with his power. Internal rhyme—*close/lonely*, *sea/beneath*—the regular octosyllabic rhythm, and the importance of end-stopped lines where the final words are given extra weighting contribute to the overall effect of the poem. The tightness of the form emphasizes the poem of the bird/ruler and reinforces the sense of entrapment created by the verb *Ring'd* (in line 3).

Example 14

Move him into the sun—
Gently its touch awoke him once,
At home, whispering of fields unsown.
Always it woke him, even in France,
Until this morning and this snow.
If anything might rouse him now
The kind old sun will know.

Think how it wakes the seeds—
Woke, once, the clays of a cold star.
Are limbs so dear-achieved, are sides
Full-nerved,—still warm,—too hard to stir?
Was it for this the clay grew tall?
—O what made fatuous sunbeams toil
To break earth's sleep at all?

(*Futility:* Wilfred Owen)

Substance: The dead body of the soldier should be brought into the sun. He used to get light and heat from the sun so long as he was alive. These were the sources of his life. So, only the sun should know if it will be able to restore his life. The sun-beams help the seeds to germinate. Once they were instrumental in creating life on cold earth. Now the question is whether the sun will be able to restore the life of the dead soldier. The poet thinks that the sun will not succeed. So human life is futile and useless.

Critical Note: In this poem, the poet asks a fundamental question about the significance of human life.

A young soldier is dead. He has been killed on the battle-field while fighting against the enemy. For no fault of his own he has become a victim of war. Even the sun which is the source of energy and life on earth will not be able to rouse him from his eternal sleep. Then is it to be assumed that he was born only to die an early and tragic death? But as this is not a desirable thing, the poet does not find any reason for which man should live. If a man is to die in the prime of his life, why should he be born at all? Does war serve any purpose? These are the questions raised by the poet in his poem.

A note of protest is to be found throughout the poem. The horrors of the First World War (1914-'18) made him feel the intensity of the unfortunate victims. Some English poets glorified the World War as a national event of rejoicing. But Wilfred Owen thought it differently. Owen himself wrote: "I am not concerned with poetry. My subject is war and pity of war. The poetry is in the pity". The poem reflects the cruelty and viciousness of war. That the poet is a staunch hater of war is clear enough. At the same time his pity for the victims of war has also been properly emphasized. He feels for those who have no choice but to get killed in war.

The poem may be called a sonnet as it consists of fourteen lines. But instead of making the usual divisions that we find in a Petrarchan or Shakespearean sonnet, Owen divides the poem into two equal halves of seven lines each.

The poem is a memorial to an unknown soldier. It is a poetic equivalent, in its way, to the famous Tomb in Westminster Abbey. We have no idea who the dead man is; we do not know whether he was even known to the poet, except in his death. Like the unknown soldier he is nameless, but with an anonymity at the opposite pole to abstraction. Our most personal experiences of love and loss respond for him. He is every young man dead and squandered in war.

Comment: The economy of the poem is remarkable. It is short enough to be inscribed on a tomb; it has something of the same finality. The vocabulary is simple and homely. Nearly all the words are monosyllabic: they move with an even trend, until the second stanza, when this evenness is deliberately broken, to point the mounting emotional intensity. We may notice the very characteristic use of assonance and consonaince—*sun/ sown*; *once/ France*; *Snow/ now/ know*; *Seeds/ sides*; *star/ stir*; *tall/ toil/ all*. These half-rhymes and pararhymes leave a sense of incompleteness on the ear. Cheated of our natural expectation of rhyme, we are referred back from the poem itself as a formal triumph to the poem's theme: to the frustration of form, of pattern, in the ruthlessness of war.

The tone of the poem is governed by the imperatives and questions when there is nothing useful to be done, and to questions when there is nothing hopeful to be known. The words introducing these imperatives and questions are '*Move*' (in line 1), '*If*' (in line 6), '*Think*' (in line 8), '*Are*' (in line 10), '*Was it*' (in line 12), and '*O what*' (in line 13).

The word *move* is not a literal imperative, since the poet is not addressing anyone on the spot. The dead man is not really to be moved into the sun; it could no longer reach him if he were. The imperative is, therefore, profoundly ironic, though its main function is of another kind. The real directive is to the reader; we are mentally to move the dead body into contrast with the life-giving sun—a contrast which permeates the poem as a whole. The force of this is nearer to contemplation than to action, nearer to a question than to a normal imperative.

In the second line the word *gently* intensifies the ironic suggestiveness established in the opening line, of loving care in a situation where love and care are no longer of any use. Gentleness is linked with the sun, which takes on attributes first of parental love (the *kind old sun* waking a young man in the mornings of life), and then of godhead: 'Think how it woke the seeds,—/Woke, once, the clays of a cold star...'. The Sun is certainly a symbol of life, and may even in the chemistry of creation have been its cause, but all the suggestions surrounding it are ironic. The word *awoke* reminds us of our own summer wakings to a world of promise and hope, but the very reminder is through a desolating realization that for this man, in this place, waking and hoping already belong to the past. The word *always* in the fourth line is in fact an 'always until', though the word '*until*' is held back until the fifth line where it comes, after dominating line 4 by its unstated presence, with tremendous effect. The phrase 'fields unsown' simultaneously evokes the rich promises of youth, with all of life stretching out before, and the bitter certainty that these particular fields never will be sown: even in presenting itself, the promise is conjured from the future into the past. The agonizing *if* (in line 6) is all the more poignant, with which we ponder something that might once have been alterable, but is now fixed and terrible in the past. It directs our attention even more harrowingly to the Sun, in its enigmatic relationship with the dead man. We wonder why this life-giving warmth, which brought him gently and patiently to life, should be so utterly helpless at the very moment of death.

The second stanza opens with another imperative, even further removed from action than the first: '*Think how it wakes the seeds...*'. As the poet moves to a wider questioning of creation itself; the poet also deepens our sense of the personal. The soldier does not simply represent mystery, he is the mystery incarnate. The poem proceeds to its central questions, impassioned and resonant, which carry what has gone before to a new level of agonized clarity:

> Are limbs so dear-achieved, are sides
> Full-nerved—still warm—so hard to stir?

It seems to echo the forlorn cry of Job who asks why did all his suffering have to be. Behind the poem's very existence there is protest at the folly of men, who have turned creation into destruction, and effected this terrible despoiling of youth. Though the protest is certainly savage, it is never cynical. Though the poem's theme is war, it is also a poem about death. The poem moves through questions which are essentially religious, whether they are accompanied by religious belief or not.

Example 15

> My heart is like a singing bird
>   Whose nest is in a water'd shoot;
> My heart is like an apple-tree
>   Whose boughs are bent with thickset fruit;
> My heart is like a rainbow shell
>   That paddles in a halcyon sea;
> My heart is gladder than all these
>   Because my love is come to me.

Raise me a dais of silk and down;
        Hang it with vair* and purple dyes;
Carve it in doves and pomegranates,
        And peacocks with a hundred eyes;
Work it in gold and silver grapes,
        In leaves and silver fleurs-de-lys;
Because the birthday of my life
        Is come, my love is come to me.

Substance: The poet uses a certain rhetorical patterning to draw attention to the central idea of the poem. The poet emphasizes the excitement felt through a repeated pattern that builds to a climax at the end of each stanza. The poem is obviously patterned, using repeated words and clause structures to convey the poet's emotional state. In the first stanza, lines 1 to 6 repeat the noun phrase 'My heart' followed by 'is' and a simile made up of complex noun phrase; lines 7 to 8 replace the simile with a post-modified comparative adjective phrase—'gladder than all these'—and an adverbial clause of reason explaining the poet's state of mind. In the second stanza, in lines 9 to 14 consist of imperatives—*Raise, Hang it, Carve it, Work it*—concluding in lines 15 to 16 with a second adverbial clause of reason that provides the motivation for everything the poet wants done. The exuberance of the opening stanza is then replaced by the emphatic imperatives of the second stanza: *Raise, Carve, Work.*

Comment: The natural images of the 'bird', the 'apple-tree', and the 'shell' become bound up with the creation of a 'dais' raised in honour of the lover. The diction is ornate with references to opulent materials—'silk and down', 'vair', 'gold and silver', emblematic birds and flowers—'doves', 'peacocks', 'fleurs-de-lys', and rich colours—'purple dyes'. The visual image is sumptuous and the poet creates a fitting tribute to the poet's lover.

The climax is reached in the emphatic repetition of the final lines where the final line in the opening stanza:

Because my love is come to me

comes in a euphoric statement of justification. By using the verb phrase 'is come', the poet creates an interesting intensity—there is an emphasis on the realization of the poet's dream. From the usual structure of the English verb phrases, we would expect either 'is coming' (progressive) or 'has come' (perfective). By combining the two patterns, the poet has created a sense of immediacy that encompasses both the process of arriving and

**vair*—a kind of squirrel fur, bluish-grey and white in colour

its completion. The result is a present tense form that which emphasizes the moment of arrival and the poet's ecstatic state of being.

Example 16

Poet of Nature, thou hast wept to know
That things depart which never may return:
Childhood and youth, friendship and love's first glow,
Have fled like sweet dreams, leaving thee to mourn.
These common woes I feel. One loss is mine
Which thou too feel'st, yet I alone deplore.
Thou wert as a lone star, whose light did shine
On some frail bark in winter's midnight roar:
Thou hast like to a rock-built refuge stood
Above the blind and battling multitude:
In honoured poverty thy voice did weave
Songs consecrate to truth and liberty.—
Deserting these, thou leavest me to grieve,
Thus having been, that thou shouldst cease to be.

Substance: The poet in all probability, hails Wordsworth as the poet of nature in the sonnet. He alludes to the fact that Wordsworth has realized that things once departed never return. Childhood, youth, friendship, and love's first glow pass away like sweet dreams leaving the dreamer to mourn. The poet too feels these woes which are common to all mankind. He too like Wordsworth feels the loss, but he alone, stands to deplore the cause of his fall. The poet recollects Wordsworth's sunny days as a successful guide. Even in his dire poverty he wrote poetry of truth and liberty. Like a lonely star guiding a fair book on a tempestuous winter sea at midnight, and like a strong refuge built of a rock in the middle of a blind and battling mass of people, Wordsworth was inspiring to his contemporaries and younger poets of his time. Such a person of high inspiration and nobility deserted all this, simply for the sake of money. Wordsworth's decline disappoints the poet and he grieves over that fact.

Comment: Wordsworth, who was the champion of 'Liberty, Fraternity, and Equality', the three main props of the French Revolution, later renounced his faith in democracy and turned a Tory. It is, in fact, this transient nature of Wordsworth which is criticized and condemned by the poet. By this change in Wordsworth, the poet feels the loss of Wordsworth himself who was a creator of 'Songs consecrate to truth and liberty'.

The sonnet begins with an apostrophe to Wordsworth who is honoured as the *Poet of Nature*. The rhyming patern of the octave is Shakespearean—

ababcdcd. The rhyming of *return*: *mourn* is not to our fullest satisfaction. Further on, in the sestet, the Shakespearean rhyme scheme has been awfully disrupted with *eefgfg*, instead of *efefgg*. The couplet:

Thou hast like to a rock-built refuge stood
Above the blind and battling multitude:

is rather disturbing, as a couplet at the end of the sonnet (as in the Shakespearean sonnets) could be more effective. In the rhyming couplet too, the rhymes are not that satisfying. The liquid *l* sounds in words like fee*l*, fee*l*'st, a*l*one, dep*l*ore, *l*one, *l*ight adds a certain amount of fluidity to the lyric. The alliterations in phrases like '*r*ock-built *r*efuge' and '*b*lind and *b*attling' adds to the musicality of the lyric. The quibble in:

I alone deplore.
Thou wert as a love star...

attracts our notice. This quibbling makes the image of '*a lone star*' all the more conspicuous.

Example 17

Bards of Passion and of Mirth,
Ye have left your souls on earth!
Have ye souls in heaven too,
Doubled-lived in regions new?

Yes, and those of heaven commune
With the spheres of sun and moon;
With the noise of fountains wondrous,
And the parle of voices thund'rous;
With the whisper of heaven's trees
And one another, in soft ease
Seated on Elysian lawns
Browsed by none but Dian's fawns;
Underneath large blue-bells tented,
Where the daisies are rose-scented,
And the rose herself has got
Perfume which on earth is not;
Where the nightingale doth sing
Not a senseless, trancèd thing,
But divine melodious truth;
Philosophic numbers smooth;
Tales and golden histories
Of heaven and its mysteries.

(*Ode on the Poets* (Extract): John Keats)

Substance: The poem is addressed to all the dead poets who according to Keats, have a double life—they have lived on earth and now they are living on earth as well as in heaven. Poets, who die, leave their souls behind on earth in the form of their poetry. But their other souls live in heaven. The dead poets thus enjoy a two-fold immortality. On earth they live in their works; in heaven their souls enjoy all the heavenly pleasures.

Critical Note: In this extract of the poem Keats glorifies poets and poetry. He pays an eloquent tribute to all great poets who have ever lived on the earth. The idea of the poem is applicable to Keats himself as much as to other poets.

Keats's description of the heavenly life is fanciful and devoid of any realistic appeal. This description has an appeal to our imagination, not to our sense of reality. However, the opinion that the poetry of dead writers is a source of wisdom to us is true and convincing.

Keats is one of the major poets of nature. His nature poetry is based on his exact knowledge from his own observation of what he saw in nature. He is gifted with a keen insight of the beauty of the woods and fields. Keats is a poet of the senses of sight, hearing, smell, taste and touch. He loves flowers because of their appeal to the senses of delight and smell. He loves the streams because of their music.

The present poem is an ode that belongs to the category of subjective poetry. It deals with a dignified subject with personal feeling. In this extract, Keats expresses his feeling on the lasting contribution of poets during their life and after death.

The presentation of the pleasures of heavenly life has a sensuous charm. We are shown a new world where the daisies have the fragrance of roses and the roses have an unearthly perfume. Similarly, the songs of the nightingales in heaven have a philosophical significance and they present divine truths in a melodious voice. Only the fawns of Diana graze in the Elysian fields. Thus the description of the heaven, though brief, is an example of Keats's vivid and concrete imagery.

Various figures of speech enrich the expression and feelings, for example: "With the *whisper* of heavenly trees", "And the rose *herself* has got perfume which on earth is not": Personification; "And the rose *herself* has got perfume which on earth is not": Hyperbole.

Example 18

Downhill I came, hungry, and yet not starved,
Cold, yet had heat within me that was proof
Against the north wind; tired, yet so that rest
Had seemed the sweetest thing under a roof!

Then at the inn I had food, fire, and rest,
Knowing how hungry, cold, and tired was I.
All of the night was quite barred out except
An owl's cry, a most melancholy cry.

Shaken out long and clear upon the hill
No merry note, nor cause of merriment,
But one telling me plain what I escaped
And others could not, that night, as in I went.

And salted was my food, and my repose,
Salted and sobered too, by the bird's voice
Speaking for all who lay under the stars,
Soldiers and poor, unable to rejoice.

(*The Owl:* Edward Thomas)

Substance: It is winter. The poet, who has been walking all day, is cold, hungry and tired. But he knows that at nightfall he will find an inn to provide a fire for warmth, food to quench his hunger and a bed for rest. Then he hears the sad cry of an owl that reminds him of the poor and the soldiers at the front. They are just as exhausted, cold and hungry like him. But unlike him, they have no assurance of finding any shelter, fire or food. The poet finds little joy in his good fortune.

Critical Note: The poem reveals the poet's deep and sincere concern for those people who cannot enjoy the pleasures and comforts of life. Man is a social being and he cannot be truly happy unless he knows that his fellow beings also have their due share of happiness. It is one of the fundamental truths of human life that one's happiness is easily marred by other people's unhappiness.

In this poem Edward Thomas gives no details of the sufferings of the poor, and of the soldiers. He says simply that they sleep 'under the stars' and not, like him, in a warm and hospitable inn. Moreover, he is concerned, not to expand in sympathy towards the sufferings of others, but simply to record the feelings aroused in him by the melancholy cry of the owl. He does not exaggerate his distress; he says that his own comfort was 'salted and sobered', by the reflections started in his mind by the owl. His whole treatment of the experience is, in other words, restrained. He writes with a sober under-statement beneath which true feeling lies.

The Owl is a representative poem of Edward Thomas. It reveals his love of nature and his love of the countryside though in an indirect manner. His economy of expression is particularly noticeable in the poem. The gloom and melancholy that pervade the poem are the result of his deep concern for suffering humanity. This genuine concern for the sufferings of his fellow beings is the key-note of many of his poems.. In the first two stanzas , the poet makes a fine use of the poetic device—contrast—to drive home his point. In these two stanzas he has carefully created the proper atmosphere in which the owl's melancholy cry acquires a symbolic significance. There is a fine metaphor in 'salted was my food'. The style is simple and has the flavour of unpremeditated art.

There are four four-line verses written in iambic pentameters, the second and fourth in each verse rhyming. The verse form is simple and regular. The tone is quiet and conversational and the diction unaffected and almost bare. There is very little imagery; the owl's cry is the only thing in the poem which is described in detail.

Example 19

Success is counted sweetest
By those who ne'er succeed.
To comprehend a nectar
Requires sorest need.
Not one of all the purple Host
Who took the Flag today
Can tell the definition
So clear ofVictory.

As he defeated -- dying --
On whose forbidden ear
The distant strains of triumph
Burst agonized and clear!

(Emily Dickinson)

Word Notes: *nectar*—the drink of the Greek and Roman gods also any delicious drink. *comprehend*—understand; *sore*—causing pain or distress; severe; intense. *Purple*—purple robe emblematic especially of regal rank and authority.

Substance: The speaker says that those who never achieve success in life place the highest value on success. (They "count" it "sweetest".) To understand the value of nectar, the speaker says, one must feel "sorest need", must undergo a process of pain and suffering. The poet says that the members of the victorious army ("the purple Host/Who took the Flag today") are not able to define victory as well as the defeated, dying man who hears from a distance the music of the victors.

Critical Note: This is a poem written by Emily Dickinson. Many of Dickinson's most famous lyrics take the form of homilies, or short moral sayings, which appear quite simple but that actually describe complicated moral and psychological truths. The idea in this poem is that the person who lacks or does not have, understands whatever is lacking better than the person who possesses it. In this poem, the loser knows the meaning or "definition" of victory better than the winners. The implication is that he has "won" this knowledge by paying so high a price, with the anguish of defeat and with his death. "Success is counted sweetest" is such a poem; its first two lines express its homiletic point, that "Success is counted sweetest /By those who ne'er succeed" (or, more generally, that people tend to desire things more acutely when they do not have them). The subsequent lines then develop that axiomatic truth by offering a pair of images that exemplify it: the nectar--a symbol of triumph, luxury, "success"—can best be comprehended by someone who "needs" it; the defeated, dying man understands victory more clearly than the victorious army does. The poem exhibits Dickinson's keen awareness of the complicated truths of human desire (in a later poem on a similar theme, she wrote that "Hunger--was a way/Of Persons outside Windows—/The Entering—takes away—"), and it shows the beginnings of her terse, compacted style, whereby complicated meanings are compressed into extremely short phrases (e.g., "On whose forbidden ear").

The three stanzas of this poem take the form of iambic trimeter—with the exception of the first two lines of the second stanza, which add a fourth stress at the end of the line. (Virtually all of Dickinson's poems are written in an iambic meter that fluctuates fluidly between three and four stresses.) As in most of Dickinson's poems, the stanzas here rhyme according to an *abcb* scheme, so that the second and fourth lines in each stanza constitute the stanza's only rhyme.

Example 20

Milton ! thou shouldst be living at this hour:
England hath need of thee: she is a fen
Of stagnant waters: altar, sword, and pen,
Fireside, the heroic wealth of hall and bower,

Have forfeited their ancient English dower
Of inward happiness. We are selfish men:
Oh ! raise us up, return to us again;
And give us manners, virtue, freedom, power.

Thy soul was like a Star, and dwelt apart:
Thou hadst a voice whose sound was like the sea,
Pure as the naked heavens, majestic, free;

So didst thou travel on life's common way
In cheerful godliness; and yet thy heart
The lowliest duties on herself did lay.

(William Wordsworth)

Substance: The poet deals with Milton's presence by symbolically making him a star. The poet reduces Milton to a figure of speech (a simile) within the poem. The poem seems to alternate between two conflicting registers of language. The first register is hortatory and public (or even 'national'); the second, natural and private.

The poem opens in Miltonic tones: 'Milton ! thou shouldst be living at this hour:/England hath need of thee:'; shifting after the caesura in the second line to another level (? Wordsworthian): 'she is a fen/Of stagnant waters'. The next lines (that is, third line onwards) are Miltonic: 'altar, sword, and pen,/Fireside, the heroic wealth of hall and bower,/Have forfeited their ancient English dower.' However, all this is then renegotiated in Wordsworthian terms, fingering public experience in private language: '...their ancient dower/Of inward happiness.' This 'inward' rhetoric is itself in turn interrogated in the phrase: 'We are selfish men'. The poem returns to the Miltonic tone with a rousing appeal:

> Oh ! raise us up, return to us again;
> And give us manners, virtue, freedom, power.

After this comes the crux of the poem where the poet brings in a simile—'Thy soul was like a star'. Following this, the poem concludes in Wordsworthian fashion, with a series of natural images. By the closing line, the grand public rhetoric of the poem's opening lines ('England hath need of thee') has been both feminized (a feminization anticipated by the 'bower'/'dower' rhyme) and consequently domesticized: 'The lowliest duties on herself did lay'. Saviour, at the beginning of the poem, by its close, Milton is figured as a housewife. Thus, there is indeed a sense in which the poem enacts a poetic conflict between the poet and Milton.

Comment: The poet gives us an idealized portrait of John Milton. The poet laments the deterioration in English life and pays homage to Milton. English people, he says, have forgotten their high traditions and noble ideals and have fallen on evil days. Only a man like Milton with his moral calibre and spirit of service could uplift the English people. Thus the poem, besides being a tribute to Milton is a criticism of contemporary English conditions. The poem has, therefore, a social and didactic purpose.

The poet wishes that Milton should have been living in England in the poet's time when English life had become as unwholesome as the stagnant water in a low marshy place. All categories of people—the priests, the soldiers, the writers, and the aristocrats—have lost their spiritual happiness. They have become self-centred. So the poet wishes that Milton should return and make English people courteous, virtuous, freedom-loving, and powerful. Milton maintained a dignified aloofness from people who had unclean ways of life. His voice was as powerful as the roaring waves of the sea. His character was spotless like the cloudless sky. He had the cheerful life of a common man with abiding faith in God, and never shrank from doing the lowliest things circumstances so required.

This sonnet besides being a criticism of life, is a warm tribute to Milton. In it the poet's meditations are about the state of England's 'soul'. Compared with the heroic age of plain living and high thinking. England has turned out to be 'a fen of stagnant waters'. The poet's countrymen have forgotten their great traditions and high ideals, and have fallen upon evil days. Only a moralist like Milton could uplift them.

This sonnet is noteworthy for its neat structure and technical perfection. It is written in a very compact style. Here the poet is at once concise and dignified, and yet what he says brings out the particular emotion which was possessing him. The poem is shot through with beautiful images of stars, sea, and 'the naked heavens'.

Finally, it will be noticed that are a number of apt and expressive similes which serve to convey the poet's meaning effectively and forcibly. Milton's soul was 'like a star dwelling apart'. Milton's voice sounded 'like the sound of the sea'. At the end, Milton emerges 'pure as the naked heavens'.

Example 21

Yes! In the sea of life enisled,
With echoing straits between us thrown,
Dotting the shoreless watery wild,
We mortal millions live *alone.*
The islands feel the enclasping flow,
And then their endless bounds they know.
But when the moon their hollows lights,
And they are swept by balms of spring,
And in their glens, on starry nights,
The nightingales divinely sing;
And lovely notes, from shore to shore,
Across the sounds and channels pour;
Oh! then a longing like despair
Is to their farthest caverns sent;
For surely once, they feel, we were
Parts of single continent!
Now round us spreads the watery plain—
Oh might our marges meet again!
Who order'd, that their longing's fire
Should be, as soon as kindled. cooled?

Who renders vain their deep desire?-
A God, a God their severance ruled;
And bade betwixt their shores to be
The unplumbed, salt, estranging sea.

(Matthew Arnold)

Substance: The poet himself italicized the word *alone* (in line 4). Whether or not we like that particular device, it says clearly that the word needs to be pondered because its idea is startling and probably new. In any literal, obvious sense, what the poem says is false. If there are million, they are not alone.

Comment: The first word gives an almost unique emphasis to the fact that the poem is not an ordering of experience by some traditional understanding, but is about an experience newly arrived at and newly comprehended. One may ask as to what makes the poet dramatically burst out with *Yes*!—an exclamation of surprised conviction and discovery. It seems there has come to him just the very metaphor which expresses, all in one, both the nature of the unfamiliar experience and its universality. The word *enisled* hints at the predicament that the poem concerns itself with. It seems like a newly identified predicament.

In this poem the poet has nothing to say about a remedy for the predicament his poem defines: and the last stanza builds that lack of remedy deep into the scheme of things. It is 'a God' who 'ordered' it: made it part of the order of things. He did so when he *bade* the waters to cover the earth. The tragic divisiveness of life belongs to creation.

The poem is essentially a poem of the flagging and failing of the spirit. In one way or another, the poem links failure of the spirit and man's isolation from others. The poem decisively adds the idea of the newness and as yet uncomprehendedness of this condition of spiritual failure and flagging. It adds also, equally decisively, the thought that it is no personal and distinctive crisis, and that spiritual decline and collapse which go with isolation from one's fellows are part of the human lot. The link which this poem advances between despair and isolation is full of meaning.

Example 22

"Hope" is the thing with feathers—
That perches in the soul—
And sings the tune without the words—
And never stops—at all—

And sweetest—in the Gale—is heard—
And sore must be the storm—
That could abash the little Bird
That kept so many warm—

I've heard it in the chillest land—
And on the strangest Sea—
Yet, never, in Extremity,
It asked a crumb—of Me.

—*(Emily Dickinson)*

Word Notes: *perches*—alights. *abash*—embarrass, disconcert. *crumb*—a small fragment, a small particle.

Substance: The speaker describes hope as a bird ("the thing with feathers") that perches in the soul. There, it sings wordlessly and without pause. The song of hope sounds sweetest in the strongest of wind ("in the Gale,") and it would require a terrifying storm to ever "abash the little Bird/That kept so many warm." The speaker says that she has heard the bird of hope "in the chillest land—/And on the strangest Sea—", but never, no matter how extreme the conditions, did it ever ask for a single crumb from her.

Critical Note: This simple, metaphorical description of hope as a bird singing in the soul is an example of Dickinson's homiletic style, derived from Psalms and religious hymns. Dickinson introduces her metaphor in the first two lines ("'Hope' is the thing with feathers—/ That perches in the soul—"), then develops it throughout the poem by telling what the bird does (sing), how it reacts to hardship (it is unabashed in the storm), where it can be found (everywhere, from "chillest land" to "strangest Sea"), and what it asks for itself (nothing, not even a single crumb). Though written after "Success is counted sweetest," this is still an early poem for Dickinson, and neither her language nor her themes here are as complicated and explosive as they would become in her more mature work from the mid-1860s. Still, we find a few of the verbal shocks that so characterize Dickinson's mature style: the use of "abash," for instance, to describe the storm's potential effect on the bird, wrenches the reader back to the reality behind the pretty metaphor; while a singing bird cannot exactly be "abashed," the word describes the effect of the storm—or a more general hardship—upon the speaker's hopes.

Like almost all of Dickinson's poems, "'Hope' is the thing with feathers— ..." takes the form of an iambic trimeter that often expands to include a fourth stress at the end of the line (as in "And sings the tune without the words—"). Like almost all of her poems, it modifies and breaks up the rhythmic flow with long dashes indicating breaks and pauses ("And never stops--at all—").The stanzas, as in most of Dickinson's lyrics, rhyme loosely in an *abcb* scheme, though in this poem there are some incidental carry over rhymes: "words" in line three of the first stanza rhymes with "heard" and "Bird" in the second; "Extremity" rhymes with "Sea" and "Me" in the third stanza, thus, technically conforming to an *abbb* rhyme scheme.

Example 23

Sweet Echo, sweetest Nymph that liv'st unseen
Within thy airy shell
By slow Meander's margent green [green bank] ,
And in the violet-embroider'd vale
Where the love-lorn Nightingale
Nightly to thee her sad Song mourneth well.
Canst thou not tell me of a gentle Pair
That likest thy Narcissus are?'
O if thou have
Hid them in some flow'ry Cave
Tell me but where
Sweet Queen of Parley [speech], Daughter of the Sphere,
So mayst thou be translated to the skies.
And give resounding grace to all Heav'n's Harmonies.

Substance: This is sung by the Lady, who is lost in the forest and hopes that she may be heard by her two brothers (the *gentle Pair* of line 7). It is mythological in theme, being addressed to Echo, a Greek nymph who was punished by Hera (Queen of the Gods) for her chattering: she was made unable to speak, except that she could repeat the final syllable of anything said to her, and she would be washed away until only her voice remained (which is why she lives *unseen*). She is perhaps said to live in an *airy shell* (in line 2) because certain kinds of *conch*, when placed to the ear, produce a sound like that of the sea.The *Meander* (in line 3) was a winding river in Phrygia.The Lady asks Echo whether she has seen her brothers: if she will tell her where they are, the Lady wishes that the nymph may be carried up to Heaven without dying (*translated to the skies*), where she will add resonance to the celestial music. In these last two lines, the reference is Christian, for *translated* is used in a technical religious sense: the poem rises from the charming fancies of Greek mythology to the majesty of the Christian Heaven, and there is a corresponding change of style in the final line, with its greater length (an alexandrine) and its resonant effect.

Comment: The poem is delicately and exquisitely phrased. But it has neither the wit and ingenuity of Donne, nor the down-to-earth quality that lies beneath the elegance of Jonson, nor the stylish urbanity of the

Cavalier poets. The distinctive quality of the poem is perhaps its mellifluousness. This is not just a matter of smooth rhythms, but also of the actual sounds of the words, especially the vowel sounds, and the cunning ways in which they are arranged. This is evident in such a line as:

Nightly to thee her sad song mourneth well
(line 6)

—the sequence of vowel-sounds has no special relevance to the meaning, but is extremely pleasing aurally; it also gives a kind of physical pleasure to the reader/speaker when the line is read aloud. Pronunciation has of course changed since Milton's time, but the effect in present-day pronunciation is in fact very similar to that in seventeenth-century pronunciation; in the earlier pronunciation, the aural effects are if anything more marked; in particular, all the rhymes in the poem were exact ones. The absence of wit and the delight in sound effects make the poem decidedly different from the other seventeenth-century lyrics.

Example: 24

Two roads diverged in a yellow wood,
And sorry I could not travel both
And be one traveller, long I stood
And looked down one as far as I could
To where it bent in the undergrowth;
Then took the other, as just as fair,
And having perhaps the better claim,
Because it was grassy and wanted wear;
Though as for that the passing there
Had worn them really about the same.

And both that morning equally lay
In leaves no step had trodden black.
Oh, I kept the first for another day!
Yet knowing how way leads on to way,
I doubted if I should ever come back.
I shall be telling this with a sigh
Somewhere ages and ages hence:
Two roads diverged in a wood, and I—
I took the one less travelled by,
And that has made all the difference.

(*The Road Not Taken:* Robert Frost)

Substance: The speaker stands in the woods, considering a fork in the road. Both ways are equally worn and equally overlaid with un-trodden leaves. The speaker chooses one, telling himself that he will take the other another day. Yet he knows it is unlikely that he will have the opportunity to do so. And he admits that someday in the future he will recreate the scene with a slight twist: He will claim that he took the less-travelled road.

Critical Note: A careful reading of the poem brings us the following:

- This poem is set in a rural natural environment which encourages the speaker to look inward.
- The poem relies on a metaphor in which the journey through life is compared to the journey down the roads.
- The speaker of the poem must choose one path instead of the other.
- Although the paths look equally attractive, the speaker knows that his choice at this moment may have a significant influence on his future.
- He does make a decision, hoping that he may be able to visit this place again, yet realizing that such an opportunity is unlikely.
- He imagines himself in the future telling the story of his life and claiming that his decision to take the road "less travelled by," the road few other people have taken, "has made all the difference."
- The speaker is a lone traveller, speaking in first person, past tense.
- The speaker describes his observations and thoughts about his dilemma, and then he continues after he makes his decision.
- His audience is any listener or person who may find himself in a similar situation.

About the poem, Frost asserted, "You have to be careful of that one; it's a tricky poem—very tricky." And he is, of course, correct. The poem has been and continues to be used as an inspirational poem, one that to the undiscerning eye seems to be encouraging self-reliance, not following where others have led.

This is among the best-known, yet the most-often-misunderstood poems of Frost. But one can get to the true meaning of the poem—not alone with imagination, but simply with accuracy.

One of the attractions of the poem is its archetypal dilemma, one that we instantly recognize because each of us encounters it innumerable times, both literally and figuratively. Paths in the woods and forks in roads are ancient and deep-seated metaphors for the lifeline, its crises and decisions. Identical forks, in particular, symbolize for us the nexus of free will and fate: We are free to choose, but we do not really know beforehand what we are choosing between. Our route is, thus, determined by an accretion of choice and chance, and it is impossible to separate the two.

This poem does not advise. It does not say, "When you come to a fork in the road, study the footprints and take the road less travelled by". Frost's focus is more complicated. First, there is no less-travelled road in this poem; it isn't even an option. Next, the poem seems more concerned with the question of how the concrete present (yellow wood, grassy roads covered in fallen leaves) will look from a future vantage point.

"The Road Not Taken" consists of four stanzas of five lines. The rhyme scheme is *abaab*; the rhymes are strict and masculine, with the notable exception of the last line (we do not usually stress the *-ence* of *difference*). There are four stressed syllables per line, varying on an iambic tetrameter base.

Example 25

The world is charged with the grandeur of God.
It will flame out, like shining from shook foil;
It gathers to a greatness, like,the ooze of oil
Crushed. Why do men then now not reck his rod?
Generations have trod, have trod, have trod;
And all is seared with trade; beared, smeared with toil;
And wears man's smudge—and shares man's smell: the soil
Is bare now, nor can foot feel, being shod.

And for all this, nature is never spent;
There lives the dearest freshness deep down things;
And though the last lights off the black West went
Oh, morning, at the brown brink eastward, springs
Because the Holy Ghost over the bent
World broods with warm breast and with ah! bright wings.

(G. M. Hopkins)

Substance: The poem focuses on the distance between man, God and the natural world. This, for the poet, is the reason for man's machine-like existence in an industrial society. He is looking beneath the surface detail of nature to a visionary and ecstatic recognition of God's presence in the world and man's ignorance of it.

The poem has the structure of a Petrarchan sonnet, having the rhyme-scheme *abba abba cdcdcd*.

Comment: The end rhyme organizes the poet's ideas, allowing him to control and develop his theme through the tightness of the Italian or Petrarchan sonnet form. The four recurring end rhymes (*abbaabba cdcdcd*) provide cohesion: the octave describes man's description of nature and his disregard for God. The volta of the sonnet creates a turning point and the sestet then focuses on God's power. It concludes with an image of protection that celebrates the redemptive nature of God's love. The full rhymes create a strong cohesive sound and add to the hymn-like quality of the poem.

The rhythm created by the metrical pattern also contributes to the sound quality of the poem. The poet moves away from what may be called 'running rhythms'—the alternating weak/strong stress pattern of the traditional iambic meter, using instead less predictable rhythms in which a fixed number of stresses are accompanied by a varying number of weak syllables. Although the length of the lines is varied, the fixed number of stresses gives a sense of balance.

Metrical variations are used to emphasize key words and to challenge our complacency. In the opening line, for instance, the poet sets the lilting rhythm of the first two iambic feet against a weak pyrrhic-foot (two unstressed syllables) and an accented trochaic foot:

∪ / ∪ / ∪ ∪ / ∪ ∪ /
The world | is charged | with the | grandeur | of God

The substitution prepares us for a counterpoint—the unstressed foot leads us straight to the harder trochaic foot forcing us to recognize that this will not be a traditional Romantic poem in which the natural world is represented as a retreat from industrialization. A similar technique is used in the fifth line, where the trochaic opening is juxtaposed with the tedium of the repeated iambic foot:

/ ∪ / ∪ ∪ / ∪ / ∪ /
Gene | rations | have trod, | have trod, | have trod;

The metrical change here, as well as the monosyllabic words and recurring short vowel sounds, emphasizes the world-weariness of the people who have lost sight of their God.

The poet's use of the spondee also demonstrates how metrical pattern can underpin meaning. The consecutive stresses in 'bleared, smeared' (in line 6), 'man's smudge... man's smell' (in line 7) and 'brightnings' (in line 14) draw attention to key ideas. The first three instances emphasize man's distance from God while the final one is an emphatic recognition of the power of God despite man's abandonment of Him. By changing the metrical pattern, the poet is able to highlight important lexical items. When read aloud, the sounds of the stressed syllables guide us, helping us to feel our way through the complexity of the style.

Perhaps most important of all in creating the intensity of this poem is the density of sounds the poet creates. As auditors we are struck by the power of the music. The harshness of the octave is modified by the softness of the sestet as the poet moves towards the final lines. There are plenty of alliterations throughout the poem. Alliteration of the soft fricatives in 'shining shook' (in line 2) is juxtaposed with harsher sounds like the plosives in 'grandeur, God' (in line 1), 'gathers', 'greatness' (in line 3) and 'crushed' (in line 4). Similarly, long vowel sounds like 'foil'/'oil', 'ooze' and 'now' (in lines 2 to 4) can be contrasted with the harsher assonance created by the pure vowels in 'men then... reck' (in line 4). The contrast of these sounds reflects the two sides of God: His gentleness—represented by the protective image in the final lines; and his power—conveyed in the image of His 'rod' (in line 4).

For the poet, the sound is an integral part of the meaning: it enhances the poem's ideas and helps us to understand by working on our emotions. The internal rhyme in 's*eared*... bl*eared*... sm*eared*' (in line 6) and the alliteration of '*sm*eared... *sm*udge... *sm*ell' (in lines 6 and 7) mirror the repetitive nature of industrial life. The connotations of the words and our emotional response to the sounds affect the way in which we engage with the text.

In the sestet, however, the effects created are different. The soft alliteration of '*l*ast *l*ights' and *w*est *w*ent' (in line 11) creates a soothing tone that is quite different to the roughness of the octave. The poet marks the strength of nature to go on in spite of man's failures—it is the quiet moment before the dynamic return of morning, which is evidence of God's 'grandeur'. The assonance of 'H*o*ly Gh*o*st *o*ver' (in line 13) and the alliteration of '*b*roods... *br*easts... *br*ight' in the final line draw attention to the climax of the poem. The reassuring tone of the long vowels is heightened by the upbeat monosyllabic alliterative words: the positive connotations of the words and the sound patterning create an inclusive feel to the final lines.

Example 26

Break, break, break,
    On thy cold gray stones, O Sea!
And I would that my tongue could utter
    The thoughts that arise in me.

O, well for the fisherman's boy,
    That he shouts with his sister at play!
O, well for the sailor lad,
    That he sings in his boat on the bay!

And the stately ships go on
    To their haven under the hill;
But O for the touch of a vanisnh'd hand
    And the sound of a voice that is still.

Break, break, break,
At the foot of thy crags; O Sea!
But the tender grace of a day that is dead
Will never come back to me.

(Alfred Tennyson)

Substance: The poem is elegiac in tone even though the poet has not directly referred to the death of his friend. Instead, he portrays his state of mind and contrasts it with the world around him. The only references to death are symbolic, emphasizing the poet's sense of loss. The longing expressed by the interjection 'O' (of line 11) and the contrastive conjunction (*But*) that precedes it mark a turning point. The poet moves away from the physical world and attempts to express his feelings, 'the thoughts that arise in him.'

Comment: The poet becomes an outsider, detached from what is happening around him. The dynamic verbs *shouts* and *sings* (in lines 6 and 8 respectively) reflect a world that is going on, unaffected by death. Similarly, the ships can go to a 'haven under the hill' (in line 10), but there is no solace for the poet. His loss is conveyed by the complex turn of phrases—'the touch of a vanish'd hand' (in line 11), 'the sound of a voice that is still' (in line 12), and 'the tender grace of a day that is dead' (in line 15). The things he yearns for are not physical as the abstract nouns here—*touch, sound, grace*—indicate. The focus on abstract concepts is in direct contrast to the concrete lexis of the earlier stanzas. It reflects that the poet has moved beyond his physical location and his inability to communicate his feelings, to a point at which he can put his loss into words.

The repetition of the dynamic verbs in the opening line sets the tone. The strong plosives (*b*) suggest the poet's anger at the death of his friend, and this is reinforced by the hard consonants in line 2—'*c*old *g*ray s*t*ones'. The interjections of stanza 2 (in lines 5 and 7) moderate the poet's anger to bitterness and this is finally replaced by a tone of acceptance in the final stanza. The hypothetical *would* (in line 3) has become *will* (in line 16) with its connotations of certainty as the poet faces the reality of his friend's death.

The inevitability of the sea's cycle establishes the framework for the poem—we begin and end with the breaking waves. Within this framework, however, tone changes. The anger of the opening line and the negative modifiers *cold* and *gray* (in line 2) are replaced by the resignation of the final stanza. The harsh rhythm of 'cold gray stones' with its sequence of stressed syllables is replaced by the lilting 'the foot of thy crags'. The symbolism of the sea breaking on the shore is crucial to our understanding of the poem: as it breaks on the shore; it is a parallel to the poet's breaking heart; and yet its cyclical pattern of ebb-and-flow moves the poet towards an acceptance that life will go on.

The poem is more than a mere cry of despair. Five times the poet abandons the disguise of speech, then paints his sorrow in a vivid picture. The poet says that before them lies the sea, powerless to tell its sobbing trouble to the shore, as wave after wave the utterance dies broken on the cold gray stones. He points out that the children playing on the shore know little about death. He next speaks of the sailor-boy out on the bay who is singing on the happy activity of life. He then describes ships returning from a prosperous voyage, and sailing on majestically to the neighbouring port. In all these pictures the poet expresses more eloquently than in any words the sense of desolation made yet more desolate by contrast with joy it cannot share. The final picture is of the sea breaking hopelessly at the foot of the crags that seem to spurn its desire; so death stands inexorably between him and all that he loved. This is a pictorial rather, than an articulate representation of grief.

The rush of the sea on the old gray stones is used to prepare the mind for the feeling of helplessness with which the deep emotions break against the hard and rigid element of human speech.

The picture is then widened out till we see the children laughing on the seashore, and the sailor-boy singing and the stately ships passing on in the offing to their unseen haven, all with the view of helping us to feel the contrast between the satisfied and the unsatisfied yearnings of the human heart. The poem in the end returns again to the helpless breaking of the sea at the foot of the crags it cannot climb, not this time to express the inadequacy of human speech to express human yearning, but the defeat of those very yearnings themselves. The poet turns an ordinary seashore landscape into a means of finding a voice for the dumb spirit of human loss.

It should be noted that the eye moves from the breaking waves to the children on the shore, then from the young sailor in his boat on the bay to the ships farther out, then back to the sea again breaking on the stones. The movement is circular, and the poem ends with the despair and inability to understand with which it began.

The rhythm used in the poem is anapaestic. Anapaestic rhythm is usually with lightness and speed; but here the anapaestic rhythm is rather slow:

∪ ∪ / ∪ ∪ / ∪ ∪ /
That he shouts | with his sis | ter at play

Apart from the remorseless and hopeless breaking of the sea on the rocks, the poem seems content with observation in place of imagery. This is probably its essential meaning: the world is meaningless.

Example 27

Obscurest night involved the sky,
        The Atlantic billows roar'd,
When such a destined wretch as I,
        Wash'd headlong from on board,
Of friends, of hope, of all bereft,
His floating home for ever left.
No braver chief could Albion's coast
        Than he with whom he went,
Nor ever ship left Albion's coast
        With warmer wishes sent.
He loved them both, but both in vain,
Nor him beheld , nor her again.
Not long beneath the whelming brine,
        Expert to swim, he lay;
Nor soon he felt his strength decline
        Or courage die away;
But waged with a death a lasting strife,
Supported by despair of life.
He shouted: nor his friends had fail'd
        To check the vessel's course,
But so the furious blast prevail'd
        That, pitiless perforce
They left their outcast mate behind,
And scudded still before the wind.
Some succour yet they could afford;
        And such as storms allow,
The cask, the coop, the floated cord,
        Delay'd not to bestow.
But he (they knew) nor ship nor shore,
Whate'er they gave, should visit more.
Nor, cruel as it seem'd could he
        Their haste himself condemn,
Aware that flight, in such a sea,
        Alone could rescue them;
Yet bitter felt it still to die
Deserted and his friends so nigh.
He long survives, who lives an hour
        In ocean, self-upheld;

And so long he, with unspent power,
His destiny repell'd;
And ever, as the minutes flew,
Entreated help, or cried 'Adieu!'
At length, his transient respite past,
His comrades, who before
Had heard his voice in every blast,
Could catch the sound no more;
For them, by toil subdued, he drank
The stifling wave, and then he sank.
No poet wept him; but the page
Of narrative sincere,
That tells his name, his worth, his age.
Is wet with Anson's tear:
And tears by bards or heroes shed
Alike immortalize the dead.
I therefore purpose not, or dream,
Descanting, on his fate,
To give the melancholy theme
A more enduring date:
But misery still delights to trace
Its semblance in another's case.
No voice divine the storm allay'd
No light propitious shone,
When snatche'd from effectual aid,
We perish'd, each alone:
But I beneath a rougher sea,
And whelm'd in deeper gulfs than he.

Substance: The case of the poem is unique; it proves to be written into the very metaphor of the poem: if a man is castaway from a ship that speeds on, he is lost while the others are saved.The speaker's tragic isolation is an isolated tragedy, one peculiar word in the poem underlines this uniqueness. It is the word *snatch'd* in the lines: 'When *snatch'd* from all effectual aid, we perish'd, each alone'.These lines are themselves especially prominent. Only a single couplet from the end of the poem, they are what confirm the analogy between the literal castaway, and the poet. Since *effectual aid* is a synonym for the religious term 'effective grace', they indicate exactly how the two cases can be agonizingly alike,'snatch'd' is so expressive, because it almost self-evidently refers not to the working of the system of providence, but to a special and abnormal dispensation.

Comment: The poem is written to a pattern which is frequent in poetry. This pattern comprises the detailed description in literal terms of an incident or situation; and then the brief and dogmatic application of that to some wholly other incident or situation. The poet's application is apt and ingenious. In the first stanza, the line 'when *such* a destin'd wretch as I' (in line 3) affords us, at the beginning, hint that in due course there will be an application: though not necessarily that it will be an eschatological one it turns out to be.

In the last stanza, the detail of the application is terse and close. Sea, storm, darkness, light, and 'voice divine' which might speak over a stormy sea, all prove to be familiar ideas in either the vehicle-situation, or the tenor-situation—the literal, or the figurative. In spite of this, the standing conditions in which any 'application-poem' has to be read do not fail to have their effect. A poet who can express his conviction that he is eternally damned, through the elaborate description of an event in the life of an unknown mariner, has set that conviction at a distance. 'Application' entrails remoteness be foreseen in the poem.

One cannot say that this amounts to an orthodoxy in the strict sense, because Christianity has a certain place for it. Yet, it is a little as if the poet were trying to deal not with a traditional and long-standing but with some new spiritual ailment; something which he does not quite identify, which he lacks the terms to describe rightly, and which it is beyond him to deal with. If he really had a straightforward religious conviction that he was spiritually damned, he ought to feel more agonized than to write so near a poem. Perhaps, also, he ought to find more hope in the traditional reassurances which the religious cultural heritage could offer him.

Example 28

To Mercy Pity Peace and Love,
All pray in their distress:
And to these virtues of delight
Return their thankfulness.

For Mercy Pity Peace and Love,
Is God, our father dear:
And Mercy Pity Peace and Love,
Is Man his child and care.

For Mercy has a human heart
Pity, a human face:
And Love, the human form divine,
And Peace, the human dress.

Then every man of every clime,
That prays in his distress,
Prays to the human form divine
Love Mercy Pity Peace.

And all must love the human form,
In heathen, Turk or Jew.
Where Mercy, Love & Pity dwell,
There God is dwelling too.

(*The Divine Image*: William Blake)

Substance: The personified figures of Mercy, Pity, Peace, and Love are listed as the four "virtues of delight." The speaker states that all people pray to these in times of distress and thank them for blessings because they represent "God, our father dear." They are also, however, the characteristics of Man: Mercy is found in the human heart, Pity in the human face; Peace is a garment that envelops humans, and Love exists in the human "form" or body. Therefore, all prayers to Mercy, Pity, Peace, and Love are directed not just to God but to "the human form divine," which all people must love and respect regardless of their religion or culture.

Critical Note: This is one of Blake's more rhetorical *Songs*. The speaker praises both God and man while asserting an identity between the two. "The Divine Image" thus differs from most of the other *Songs of Innocence*, which deal with the emotional power of conventional Christian faith, and the innocent belief in a supreme, benevolent, and protective God, rather than with the parallels between these transcendent realms and the realm of man.

The poem uses personification to dramatize Christ's mediation between God and Man. Beginning with abstract qualities (the four virtues of Mercy, Pity, Peace, and Love), the poem makes these abstractions the object of human prayer and piety. The second stanza explains this somewhat strange notion by equating the virtues with God himself. But the idea is still slightly unorthodox, suggesting as it does that we pray to these abstract virtues because they are God, rather than praying to God because he has these sympathetic qualities. The poem seems to emphasize that Mercy, Pity, Peace, and Love are not God's characteristics but his substance--they are precisely what we mean when we speak of God.

The speaker now claims that Mercy, Pity, Peace, Love are also equivalent to Man: it is in humans that these qualities find a kind of embodiment, and they become recognizable because their features (heart, face, body, clothes) are basically human. Thus when we think of God, we are modelling him after these ideal human qualities. And when people pray, regardless of who or where they are, or to what God they think they are praying, they actually worship "the human form divine"--what is ideal, or most godly, in human beings. Blake's "Divine Image" is therefore a reversed one: the poem constructs God in the image of man rather (whereas, in the Bible, God creates man in his image). The implication that God is a mental creation reflects Blake's belief that "all deities reside in the human breast."

The poem does not explicitly mention Christ, but the four virtues that Blake assigns alternately to man and God are the ones conventionally associated with Jesus. Because Christ was both God and man, he becomes the vehicle for Blake's mediation between the two. But the fact that he is given an abstract rather than a human figuration underscores the elaborate intellectualization involved in Christian doctrine. Blake himself favors a more direct identification between what is human and what is divine. Thus the companion poem in *Songs of Experience*, "The Human Abstract," goes further toward exposing the elaborate institutions of religion as mental confabulations that obscure rather than honor the true identity of God and man.

The poem is comprised of five ballad stanzas--quatrains in which the lines have four and three beats, alternately, and rhyme *abcb*. This stanza form, in English poetry, conveys a sense of candour and naturalness, and it is common in songs, hymns, and nursery rhymes. The lilting rhythm and the frequent repetition of words and phrases combine with a spiritual subject-matter to create the poem's simple, hymn-like quality.

Example 29

Suddenly I saw the cold and rook-delighting heaven
That seemed as though ice burned and was but the more ice,
And thereupon imagination and heart were driven
So wild that every casual thought of that and this
Vanished, and left but memories, that should be out of season
With the hot blood of youth, of love crossed long ago;
And I took all the blame out of all sense and reason,
Until I cried and trembled and rocked to and fro,
Riddled with light. Ah! when the ghost begins to quicken.
Confusion of the death-bed over, is it sent
Out naked on the roads, as the books say, and stricken
By the injustice of the skies for punishment?

Substance: These twelve lines are an expression of an overwhelming experience which is at the same time staring at the sky filled with the flight of rooks, the poet sees it transformed into a sheet of burning ice.

This kindles his imagination. Standing beneath a cold winter sky the poet has suddenly had a vision. The experience is inexpressible; its intensity can only be suggested by saying that it 'seemed as though ice burned and was but the more ice.' The poet's anguished utterance is also that of all humanity. His whole being was in such tumult that imagination, feeling, thought no longer functioned; he was haunted by a memory alone, that of 'love crossed long ago'—his love of his beloved. All casual thought disappears from his mind and his whole being remembers only the frustrated love experienced in youth. Blaming himself irrationally and beyond the bounds of sense he had been overcome by a paroxysm of grief in which at the same time he was aware of light that seemed to be sifting over him. His old (and cold) heart is heated with a sense of regret in which he takes the whole blame of the failure upon himself, and shakes and rocks to and fro as his heart is *riddled* (shot through or confused) with the light of reality issuing from the past memories. The recalling of this moment beyond time, this glimpse of eternity leads him to end this poem with a question. He wonders if his tortured soul when released from the confession of death-bed, will be sent to wander, exposed to the burning ice of the sky, to be punished. He wonders, whether the soul after death journeying to its longed for heaven, experience only punishment to its guilt, in an eternity where there is no justice.

Comment: The complexity of the poem leads us to interpret the poem variously. On a trivial level, it could signify the poet recalling how much he loved his beloved. But on a rich symbolic level, the poem gives rise to speculations about an after-life. The poem is the crystallization of a moment of intense dream-like perception, where physical surroundings remained fixed in the mind, accumulating the years of thought and reality that passed in review.

Vague nostalgia hardens into a heart-breaking emotion. Many different sentiments—desire, desperation, and terror—are interwoven into a composite pattern of feeling. The atmosphere is strange and weird—the frozen snow burns as the sun-rays fall on it. This image is enough to explain the nature of the poet's agony. The burning ice ties two apparently opposed subjects in a felt unity—the burning passions of youth balance the freezing naked soul of a dead old man. And the soul, 'naked on the roads' is stricken by the coldly burning skies for punishment, the poem seems to offer two possibilities for the soul being punished. The naked soul is to be burned by the cold sky for his failure to bring his passion to fruition in love; or he is to be punished for his recklessly assuming the blame for the failure of love, in which case the cold skies will ultimately force an anguish on his soul the vision of which he has already seen—in being 'riddled with light' or shot through with light and insight. However, these two possibilities do not seem entirely right or entirely wrong in themselves. There is a hint of confusion—the poet seems 'riddled with light' in the sense of being puzzled and tormented by the shining light of reality. Thus the poem ends with a question.

The word *riddled*, usually found in a construction in a phrase like 'riddled with bullets', suggests perhaps stinging arrows of light (as well as the idea of light pouring over him as from a sieve or riddle) and at the same time the light, the whole vision, is enigmatic (like the Sphinx). This awareness of more than one approach is contained in the opening line:

> Suddenly I saw the cold and rook-delighting heaven

the sky, which is literally overhead but is also the image of the agonizing experience, is ice-cold (and therefore painful) for the poet but a source of delight for the rooks. It is significant to contrast the cold burning sky here to the heavens overlaid with 'embroidered cloths'.

The vast expanse of the sky tears away illusions and shatters emotional well being. The poet's mind regrets lost opportunities as he is tormented by the searing memories of 'love crossed long ago'. The cold burning sky has no shelter, or hope of escape from the responsibilities of self, and pierces the poet's innermost being with cruel light. As the memories of his past emotional life overwhelm the poet's mind, he speculates whether after death a ghost has also to undergo the memories of past life as a purgatorial experience inflicted by 'the injustice of the skies'.

A flash of memory of love frustrated comes to the poet's mind. He does not blame his beloved for his misery. He realizes that his love affair has been a miserable failure and that he had washed his life in a pursuit of something that did not exist. The feeling that his whole past has been meaningless leads him to the thought of death and he imagines what might happen to his ghost. The poet wonders whether the ghost would be sent out naked on the roads for punishment. The vision of the agony of the spirit in the burning frost inspires terror.

Suffering and controlled passion are felt in the powerful verbs, which, like the majority of the nouns, are unqualified:

> And I took all the blame out of all sense and reason,
> Until I cried and trembled and rocked to and fro,
> Riddled with light.

Although imagination is helpless in the face of the memory and the remarks, yet the poet recognizes that at the very moment of being overwhelmed he is aware of the cold light—with which the sentence both begins and ends. It is as though he recognizes the presence of something good, but such recognition is bound up with the crippling of the imagination and heart and the terrible sense of loss and remorse. This prompts the question about life after death. The poet presents an accepted idea of the soul's journey after the 'confusion of the death-bed'. 'As the books say', however, begins to cast doubt, and the question (as well as the poem) ends by suggesting an appalling alternative to the believer's conception of an afterlife.

Example 30

I'm nobody! Who are you?
Are you nobody, too?
Then there's a pair of us—don't tell!
They'd banish us, you know.
How dreary—to-be-somebody!
How public—like a frog—
To tell your name the livelong day
To an admiring bog!

(Emily Dickinson)

Substance: The poem's first stanza tells how the speaker meets a fellow "nobody"—a friend. Together, the two nobodies can enjoy each other's company and their shared anonymity.

The speaker exclaims that she is "Nobody," and asks, "Who are you? / Are you—nobody—too?" If so, she says, then they are a pair of nobodies, and she admonishes her addressee not to tell, for "they'd banish us—you know!" She says that it would be sad and gloomy to be "Somebody"—it would be "public" and require that, "like a frog," one tell one's name "the livelong day—/To an admiring bog!"

Critical Note: This poem is a playful defense of the kind of spiritual privacy the poet favoured, implying that to be a Nobody is a luxury incomprehensible to the dreary Somebodies--for they are too busy keeping their names in circulation, croaking like frogs in a swamp in the summertime. This poem is an outstanding example of jaunty approach to meter (the poet uses the dashes quite forcefully to interrupt lines and interfere with the flow of her poem, as in "How dreary—to be—Somebody!"). Further, the poem vividly illustrates the poet's surprising way with language. The juxtaposition in the line "How public—like a frog—" shocks the first-time reader, combining elements not typically considered together, and, thus, more powerfully conveying its meaning (frogs are "public" like public figures—or Somebodies—because they are constantly "telling their name"—croaking—to the swamp, reminding all the other frogs of their identities.

The two stanzas of "I'm Nobody!" are constituted of loose iambic trimeters occasionally including a fourth stress ("To tell your name—the livelong day—"). They follow an *abcb* rhyme scheme (though in the first stanza, "you" and "too" rhyme, and "know" is only a half-rhyme, so the scheme could appear to be *aabc*), and she frequently uses rhythmic dashes to interrupt the flow.

Example 31

I will arise and go now, and go to Innisfree,
And a small cabin build there, of clay and wattles made;
Nine bean rows will I have there, a hive for the honey bee,
And live alone in the bee-loud glade.

And I shall have some peace there, for peace comes dropping slow,
Dropping from the veils of the morning to where the cricket sings;
There midnight's all a glimmer, and noon a purple glow,
And evening full of the linnet's wings.

I will arise and go now, for always night and day
I hear lake water lapping with low sounds by the shore;
While I stand on the roadway, or on the pavements gray,
I hear it in the deep heart's core.

(*W.B. Yeats*)

Substance: Yeats expresses his desire to build a small cabin at Innisfree, out of natural materials, and live alone. He will find peace on the lake, where it drops from the morning, and the beautiful midnight. He determines to leave immediately, because even when he stands in a road or on a city pavement, he hears the lapping of the lake waters in his heart.

Critical Note: First published in the collection The *Rose* in 1893, "The Lake Isle of Innisfree" is an example of Yeats's earlier lyric poems. Throughout the three short quatrains the poem explores the speaker's longing for the peace and tranquility of his boyhood haunt, Innisfree.

"The Lake Isle of Innisfree" suggests that a life of simplicity in nature will bring peace to the troubled speaker. However, the poem is the speaker's recollection of Innisfree, and therefore the journey is an emotional and spiritual escape rather than an actual one. Innisfree may be a symbol for the speaker's passed youth, which the speaker is unable to return to in the "real," or physical, world. Emotionally, the speaker can return again and again to the tranquility of Innisfree. Innisfree, whose name means "heather island" in Gaelic, is an island off the coast of Ireland of intense natural beauty.

Yeats's poem is perhaps most interesting for what it does not say.

Although the speaker expresses the desire to arise and "go to Innisfree," he never explicitly states what it is that motivates this desire. This absence asks readers to infer what compels the speaker to be other than where he is. People often daydream when they are dissatisfied with their lives. They fantasize about how circumstances might be different and how new surroundings would make them more content, perhaps even how such a change would make them different persons. They see themselves in daydreams differently.

"The Lake Isle of Innisfree" is one of Yeats's earlier poems and also one of his best known. It is perhaps so widely known due to its universal subject matter, that of the conflict between youth and aging, and the longing for emotional escape. Author William York Tindall, in his book *W. B. Yeats*, terms "The Lake Isle of Innisfree" "a vision of escape." However, some find the poem overtly sentimental and prefer Yeats's later poems.

"The Lake Isle of Innisfree" is written with an *abab* rhyme scheme corresponding to each of the three quatrains in the poem, which are defined as a stanza composed of four lines which may or may not have a set line length. Also prevalent is the use of alliteration and assonance, both of which emphasize the musical tone and rhythm of the piece.

Example 32

My heart cries like a beaten child,
Ceaselessly, all night long;
And I must take my own heart cries
And thread them neatly into a song.

My heart cries like a beaten child,
And I must listen, stark and terse,
Dry-eyed and critical, to see,
What I can turn into a verse.

Thus was a sob at the hour of three,
And this when the first cock crew.
I wove them into a dainty song,
But no-one thought it true!

Substance: The poem is about writing; it is about turning painful experience into the subject matter of verse. The language therefore reflects both the detachment of the creative process and the intensity of an individual's emotional response to a particular event. It is the opposition created between these two attitudes that lies at the heart of the poem.

Comment: The concrete noun *heart* functions figuratively and its repetition is a haunting reminder of the feeling underpinning the poem.

Linked to the verb *cries* (in lines 1 and 5), and the plural noun *cries* (in line 3), and the emotive image of the *beaten child* (in line 5); it emphasizes the emotional tone. The repetition of the possessive determiner *my* and the use of the adjective *own* (in line 3) create an intensely personal field of reference in which both subject and object can be traced back to the poet. This enhances the mood of entrapment that pervades the poem, reinforced by the adverb *ceaselessly* (in line 2) and the phrase *all night long* (in line 2)—the poet can escape only when only the poet has contained the personal emotions within the pattern of verse.

While the immediacy of the present tense verbs—epitomizes an emotional state, the emphatic modal—*must*—represents the certainty of the winter. The foregrounded conjunctions *And*—reinforce this since they represent the poet's attempt to take control. Similarly, where the repeated image of the suffering child is emotive and disturbing, the adjectives—*stark, terse, Dry-eyed, critical*—suggest detachment. Developing this contrast between the instinctive emotion and conscious discipline, the verbs *thread* and *turn* and the adverb *neatly* (in lines 4 and 8) suggest something of the creative process as the poet curbs his/her feelings.

The structure of the poem's neat quatrains reflects the movement towards control. In the first stanza, there is a balance between the subjectivity of feeling and the objectivity of the writing process, with two lines focusing on the poet's emotional state and two representing her need for constraint. The second stanza restricts personal emotion to one line, leaving three lines to describe the detachment of the writer. The process is brought to its conclusion in the third stanza, where the change of tense suggests that the poet has achieved the goal: the poet is now in a position to be able to talk in a detached way about the emotions. The possessive determiner *my* has been replaced by the indefinite article *a* (in line 9). The heartfelt plural noun *cries* has been replaced by the less emotive singular noun *sob* (in line 9). The infinite reference to line (in line 2) is contained by specific references—*at the hour of three, when the first cock crew* (in lines 9 and 10).

Picking up the connotations of *thread* in the first stanza, the poet uses the past tense *wove* to describe the completed creative process that has taken a painful personal experience and transformed it into a *dainty* song (in line 11). The lexical link forces us to remember the emotional opening lines, and the juxtaposition of the adjective *dainty*, with its connotations of something delicate and neat, with the disturbing image of the beaten child reinforces this.

The poem reaches its climax in the final line:

> But no-one thought it true!

The dismissive use of the conjunction *But* and the exclamative tone draw attention to the distance that exists between the poet, the subject matter and the reader. The neatness of the poem's structure with its masculine rhymes throughout the poem is set against the reality of the experience that lies behind the poem.

Example 33

Forgetfulness is like a song
That, freed from beat and measure, wanders.
Forgetfulness is like a bird whose wings are reconciled,
Outspread and motionless,—
A bird that coasts the wind unwearyingly.

Forgetfulness is rain at night,
Or an old house in a forest,—or a child.
Forgetfulness is white,—white as a blasted tree,
And it may stun the sybil into prophecy,
Or bury the Gods.

I can remember much forgetfulness.

Substance: The poet uses rhetorical patterning to draw attention to the ideas. The poet repeats his key word, the abstract noun *Forgetfulness*. He draws attention to its qualities through similes (in Stanza 1) and metaphors (in Stanza 2). The poet takes an abstract quality and gives it a concrete presence through the comparisons he makes. The images represent forgetfulness as a stage of freedom and perfect balance in which we no longer need to be bound by the conventions and expectations of day-to-day life. An adjective phrase like *freed from beat and measure* (in line 2), verbs like *wanders* (in line 2), *reconciled* (in line 2), and *coasts* (in line 5), and the adverb *unwearyingly* (in line 5) suggest that the poet is approaching forgetfulness from an untraditional angle. For him, it seems to be representative of a life without stress or responsibility, where everything can be lost in the sound of rain, the isolation of the forest, or the innocence of a child who is not bound by the rules of the adult world. It is a stage of exultation, rather than an impairment.

Comment: The patterning of the stanzas is effective because it provides a sequence of images that counter the connotations of forgetfulness as a 'failure', or as 'neglectfulness'. The repetition of the key word *Forgetfulness* in the initial position (in lines 1, 3, 6, 8) followed by *is like* or *is.../or..., or* creates a balanced structure that draws into the poet's vision. The richness of the images appeals to our senses and develops a positive rather than negative context for the poet's theme. They build to a climax in the description of forgetfulness as *white* with its connotations of purity and blankness. This is not an obviously negative image—it seems to develop the positive associations of the metaphors in the previous lines. The post-modified adjective phrase 'white as a blasted tree' (in line 8), however, seems to alter the tone: as a symbol of lifelessness. The dead tree not only is a symbol of lifelessness but also offers perhaps another view of forgetfulness. It is an absence from life; it represents a detachment from the world of the living.

The final lines of the second stanza capture the paradox: while forgetfulness can 'stun the sybil into prophecy', unexpectedly revealing life's secrets; it can also 'bury the Gods', leaving the individual disconnected and remote. The poet's use of the modal verb *may* emphasizes the unpredictability of 'forgetfulness'.

The main body of the poem offers a detached view of 'forgetfulness', but the last line introduces a more personal element. The use of the first person pronoun *I* adds a subjective note. The bringing in of *I* makes the poem a statement about a particular individual's experience of life. It is left to stand alone, as a reflective overview. The juxtaposition of *remember* and *forgetfulness* is not illogical, but a recognition of a life that is notable for its periods of blankness. The tone is neither nostalgic, nor regretful—the speaker has experienced both the freedom and state of balance created by forgetfulness, and the sterile detachment from life.

In short, the entire poem is structured around the repetition of the key word *forgetfulness*, the patterning of the similes and metaphors, and the recognition of the paradoxical nature of his theme.

Example 34

On moonlit heath and lonesome bank
    The sheep beside me graze;
And yon the gallows used to clank
    Fast by the four crossways.

A careless shepherd once would keep
    The flocks by moonlit there,
And high amongst the glimmering sheep
    The dead man stood on air.

They hang us now in Shrewsbury jail;
    The whistles blow forlorn,
And trains all night groan on the rail
    To men that die at morn.

There sleeps in Shrewsbury jail to-night,
Or wakes, as may betide,
A better lad, if things went right,
Than most that sleep outside.

And naked to the hangman's noose
The morning clocks will ring
A neck God made for other use
Than strangling in a string.

And sharp the link of life will snap,
And dead on air will stand
Heels that held up as straight a chap
As treads upon the land.

So here I'll watch the night and wait
To see the morning shine,
When he will hear the stroke of eight
And not the stroke of nine;

And wish my friend as sound a sleep
As lads' I did not know,
That shepherded the moonlit sheep
A hundred years ago.

Substance: The basic contrast of the poem is brought out in the first two stanzas. We may consider the implications of *moonlit heath*, *sheep*, and *graze* as against *gallows* and *clank*; and of *careless* (carefree), *shepherd*, *flocks*, *moonlight*, and *glimmering sheep* as against *the dead man stood on air*. The language is very simple, but the clashing associations of those two groups of words give us a key to the very intense emotions that lie beneath the surface. The image of 'The dead man stood on air' suggests grotesqueness. With mention of Shrewsbury jail, the whistles blowing, and the trains groaning all night, a new note enters—another contrast, this time between the stillness of the old rural setting at the crossroads and the new conditions under which condemned criminals are executed, the speaker, certainly, does not approve of the new system.

Comment: In the fourth stanza the precise situation is made clear: the speaker, sheepherder, is thinking of someone in particular who is awaiting execution in Shrewsbury jail. In the fifth stanza there is a pun on the word *ring* (being used in two senses); it is rather unusual to find a pun in a poem about some about to be hanged. It is definitely not a humorous pun. The poet selected the word *string* in the last line of the stanza for a special reason: not merely because of the rhyme scheme. The difference in implication between *rope* and *string* is brought out prominently. In fact, the effect of *string* harmonizes with the tone of the poem as a whole.

The sixth stanza recalls to mind the earlier image of the criminal 'standing on air'. The earlier reference was to the gallows at the crossroads; here it bears reference to the modernized gallows in the jailyard. But the effect of hanging is the same under both conditions. And that is a point that the poet wishes to drive home. Suddenly, at the beginning of the seventh stanza, we are taken back to the original setting—the moonlit heath and lonesome bank, with the sheep peacefully grazing beside the speaker. The idea of death is now conceived of as the difference between hearing the stroke of eight o'clock and not hearing the stroke of nine. Of all the ways in which the poet might have epitomized the fact of death, he chose that one, perhaps, to convey the sense of suddenness of death.

Finally, the speaker alludes to the men who were hanged long years ago—'A hundred years ago'—and thus 'Kept sheep by moonlight.' And we realize with a shock—if we have not done so before—that he too is 'Keeping sheep by moonlight'. In other words, the ultimate effect of the poem is centred in the double meaning of the phrase. The phrase can be applied with equal accuracy to both the speaker and condemned man, as the speaker implies. This is an irony, or a bitter contrast, which underlies the whole poem—the association of sheep-watching by moonlight (the most peaceful and inoffensive of occupations and the most tranquil of settings) with the gruesome practice of hanging convicted criminals. It is the interplay of these two sets of completely diverse associations which gives the poem its dominant tone.

The rhythm of the poem is as incongruous to the subject as is the highly colloquial diction: instead of having a measured, grave tempo, it fairly skips along. The short line is aided by the simple rhyme scheme *abab*—alternately rhyming couplets. In fact, the poem is composed in a series of ballad stanzas. The stanzas sound almost like something children memorize in kindergarten.

To a superficial reader, the poem seems, perplexingly enough, to be more or less flippant treatment of a serious subject. There is some sort of humour in the image of the dead man standing on air, in the pun on *ring*, in the familiar *lad* and *chap* , in the offhand way in which death is imaged in the seventh stanza. But the careful reader will realize that the humour is of a peculiar and significant kind. It is humour with the faintest suggestion of a smile; on the contrary, it is grim, bitter humour. The lightness suggested by the colloquial diction and the lilting rhythm is just as deceptive.

The effect of the poem lies in the complete incongruity between what is said, for anyone to read, and what is left unsaid, for the attentive reader to discover. The flippancy, the offhand manner, point not to any callousness on the part of the speaker. On the contrary, they are simply a camouflage for very deep and bitter feelings. The truth about the speaker's emotions resides almost completely in the implications, rather than the external meaning of what he says. The half-humorous tone makes the actual subject of the poem—the impending execution—all the more terrible.

Example 35

I

Only a man harrowing clods
In a slow silent walk
With an old horse that stumbles and nods
Half asleep as they stalk.

II

Only a thin smoke without flame
From the heaps of couch-grass;
Yet this will go onward the same
Though Dynasties pass.

III

Yonder a maid and her wight
Come whispering by:
War's annals will fade into night
Ere their story die.

(*In Time of "The Breaking of Nations"* : Thomas Hardy)

Substance: A lonely farmer with a tired horse is working in the field. A thin line of smoke rises from a heap of dry grass. And, this line of smoke announces the victory of man's basic activities over the great social and political changes. A girl and her lover whisper lovingly to each other. This primal sentiment of the human heart will triumph over the ruins caused by a great war.

Critical Note: This is basically a poem about war, especially the First World War. But the poet does not depict the spectacular heroic aspects of war. He has rather emphasized those aspects of life which remain unaltered and unaffected by the changes that take place in the outer world.

The poem deals with the outer as well as the inner aspects of man's life. The first two stanzas deal with the outer aspects while the third and final stanza deals with the inner aspect.

We should particularly note the elegiac cast of the verse. It is a highly reflective poem. But the reflection does not inspire hope. It simply conveys a sense of the continuity of man's labour.

In this poem, the poet observes a strict artistic restraint. The scene of desolation and decay serves as a convenient background for the theme. One should also note the intensity and the economy of expression in the poem. The subject-matter is stated as briefly as possible. The poet shows his modernity by avoiding the melodious music of Tennyson and insisting on strong and harsh rhythms. But we should note that the poet here turns focus of his attention chiefly on the contents of his poem, and hardly bothers whether or not it attains formal grace.

Example 36

Tears, idle tears, I know not what they mean,
Tears from the depth of some divine despair
Rise in the heart, and gather in the eyes,
In looking on the happy autumn-fields,
And thinking of the days that are no more.
Fresh as the first beam glittering on a sail,
That brings our friends up from the underworld,
Sad as the last which reddens over one
That sinks with all we love below the verge;
So sad, so fresh, the days that are no more.

Ah, sad and strange as in dark summer dawns
The earliest pipe of half-awakened birds
To dying ears, when unto dying eyes
The casement slowly grows a glimmering square;
So sad, so strange, the days that are no more.

Dear as remembered kisses after death,
And sweet as those by hopeless fancy feigned
On lips that are for others; deep as love,
Deep as first love, and wild with all regret;
O Death in Life, the days that are no more!

(Alfred Tennyson)

Substance: The poem begins with a paradox. The poet considers the nature of the tears as 'idle' man's, but when we look deeper into the poem we realize that the tears are not 'idle', rather they are the most meaningful of tears. They are described as 'idle' because the tears are occasioned by no immediate grief. In fact, the tears spring from a deeper and more universal cause. The poem alludes to the fact that the origin of the tears swells up from 'the depth of some divine despair'. The tears 'rise in the heart'. It is for this that they have been declared as 'idle' at the very outset of the poem.

Comment: We may observe that the poet has chosen to open the poem with some dramatic boldness by asserting the fact that he does not know what 'idle tears' mean. The poet takes a bold step of equating 'idle' with 'from the depth of some divine depth of some divine despair', there is a bold and violent reversal of the speaker's initial characterization of his tears.

The tears 'rise in the heart' as the speaker looks upon a scene of beauty and tranquility by looking on the 'happy autumn-fields' the poet does not recall the days that are no more. The poet does not stand responsible for any closer linkage between these actions, though most of us will want to make a closer linkage here. The fields are described as 'happy autumn fields' allude to something which is over and finished, yet happy; it does not connect them with the past. Despite this it significantly suggests to the observer thoughts about the past.

The past is fresh as with freshness of a daw—as fresh as the first beam glittering on the sail of an upcoming ship. The ship is evidently expected: it brings friends, friends 'up from the underworld.' The comparison, on the surface, is innocent: the 'underworld' merely refers to the antipodes, the world which lies below the horizon—an underworld in the sense displayed in old-fashioned geographies with their sketches illustrating the effects of the curvature of the earth. The sails, which catch the light and glitter, will necessarily be the part first visible of any ship which is coming 'up' over the curve of the earth. At the same time the word *underworld* will also suggest the realm of the shades, the world above of the dead. The attempt to characterize the freshness of the days that are no more has, thus, developed, almost imperceptibly into a further characterization of the days themselves as belonging, not to our normal daylight world, but to an *underworld*. This suggestion is strengthened in the lines that follow in which the ship metaphor is reversed so as to give us a picture of sorrowfulness by referring to approaching evening when the last glint of sunset light falls on the sail of a ship:

> That sinks with all we love below the verge...

The conjunction of the qualities of sadness and freshness occur in the image of the light on the sails of a ship hull down. This image has been employed to suggest both qualities. This is all the more evident when we see the process carried one stage further: the two qualities (with the variant of 'strange' for 'fresh') are explicitly linked together:

Ah, sad and strange as in dark summer dawns...

In the third stanza the sadness and strangeness is suggested by one and the same figure. The figure is developed in some details, which involves a dawn scene. It is ironical, because the beginning of the new day is to be considered as the beginning of the long night for the dying man. The dying eyes have been for some time awake—long enough to have had time to watch:

The casement slowly grows a glimmering square;

The dying man soon goes to sleep the lasting sleep; he is more fully awake than the 'half-awaken'd birds' whose earliest pipings come to his dying ears. The pipings are sad. They are strange because to the person hearing a bird's song for the last time, it will seem that he has never before really heard one. Even the familiar sound will take on a quality of unreality—of strangeness.

The sense of desperation runs through the concluding lines of the poem. In fact, the lines are full of ironic contrast. The kisses feigned by 'hopeless fancy' are made the more precious because of the very hopelessness; but memory takes on the quality of fancy. It is equally hopeless—the kisses can as little be renewed as those 'feign'd/On lips that are for others' can be obtained. The realized past has become as fabulous as the unrealizable future. The days that are no more are as dear as the one, as sweet as the other. The days that are no more are not merely 'dear' and 'sweet' they are at the same time 'deep' and 'wild'. We are astounded as to how the days can be 'deep as love' or even 'wild with all regret'. The poem ends with an exclamation which sounds paradoxical, 'O Death in Life!' It sounds like tortured cry. The grammatical status of the phrase is perhaps that of a loose appositive which could mean 'the days that are no more are a kind of death in life'.

The poem shows the poet's delight in pure sound, and his tendency to give intense expression to a simple emotion. The deep nostalgia, the despair at the lost past is contemplated, not analyzed or judged. In structure, the poem is a series of comparisons, each introduced by the comparative word *as*.

Each of the unrhymed stanzas is built round a single image or idea, becoming progressively more intense and hopeless. In the first stanza, tears 'gather to the eyes' simply from contemplation of the present autumn scene (with its Keatsian hint of maturity and approaching winter) and memory of the past.

In the second, the sail on the horizon belongs to the ship of birth and then of death. It suggests the mysterious places from which we go, with which we have no communication except when we make the voyage ourselves. The word *underworld* could simply mean 'the Antipodes', but it was also used to mean the abode of the dead in classical mythology.

In the third stanza, a dying person hears early morning bird-song as the window slowly becomes visible in the dawn. It might be thought that death should be the climax of the poem, but the poem is about memories.

The final stanza gives us even greater intensity of the memory of the dead—'remembered kisses after death'. But the days that are no more are also *sweet* (in line 17), even if the sweetness is that of unfulfilled desire. The poet is enjoying the nostalgia as well as fringing for what is lost.

The speaker sings of the baseless and inexplicable tears that rise in his heart and pour forth from his eyes when he looks out on the fields in autumn and thinks of the past.

This past, ("the days that are no more") is described as fresh and strange. It is as fresh as the first beam of sunlight that sparkles on the sail of a boat bringing the dead back from the underworld, and it is sad as the last red beam of sunlight that shines on a boat that carries the dead down to this underworld.

The speaker then refers to the past as not "fresh," but "sad" and strange. As such, it resembles the song of the birds on early summer mornings as it sounds to a dead person, who lies watching the "glimmering square" of sunlight as it appears through a square window.

In the final stanza, the speaker declares the past to be dear, sweet, deep, and wild. It is as dear as the memory of the kisses of one who is now dead, and it is as sweet as those kisses that we imagine ourselves bestowing on lovers who actually have loyalties to others. So, too, is the past as deep as "first love" and as wild as the regret that usually follows this experience. The speaker concludes that the past is a "Death in Life."

"Tears, Idle Tears" is part of a larger poem called *The Princess*, published in 1847. Tennyson wrote *The Princess* to discuss the relationship between the sexes and to provide an argument for women's rights in higher education. However, the work as a whole does not present a single argument or tell a coherent story. Rather, like so much of Tennyson's poetry, it evokes complex emotions and moods through a mastery of language. "Tears, Idle Tears," a particularly evocative section, is one of several interludes of song in the midst of the poem.

In the opening stanza, the poet describes his tears as "idle," suggesting that they are caused by no immediate, identifiable grief. However, his tears are simultaneously the product of a "divine despair," suggesting that they do indeed have a source: they "rise in the heart" and stem from a profoundly deep and universal cause. This paradox is complicated by the difficulty of understanding the phrase "divine despair": Is it God who is despairing, or is the despair itself divine? And how can despair be divine if Christian doctrine considers it a sin?

The speaker states that he cries these tears while "looking on the happy autumn-fields." At first, it seems strange that looking at something happy would elicit tears, but the fact that these are fields of autumn suggests that they bear the memories of a spring and summer that have vanished, leaving the poet with nothing to look forward to except the dark and cold of winter.

"Tears, Idle Tears" is structured by a pattern of unusual adjectives used to describe the memory of the past. In the second stanza, these adjectives are a chiasmatic "fresh...sad...sad...fresh"; the memory of the birth of friendship is "fresh," whereas the loss of these friends is "sad"; thus when the "days that are no more" are described as both "sad" and "fresh," these words have been preemptively loaded with meaning and connotation: our sense of the "sad" and "fresh" past evokes these blossomed and withered friendships. This stanza's image of the boat sailing to and from the underworld recalls Virgil's image of the boatman Charon, who ferries the dead to Hades.

In the third stanza, the memory of the past is described as "sad...strange...sad...strange." The "sad" adjective is introduced in the image of a man on his deathbed who awakes for his very last morning. However, "strangeness" enters in, too, for it is strange to the dying man that as his life is ending, a new day is beginning. To a person hearing the birds' song and knowing he will never hear it again, the twittering will be imbued with an unprecedented significance—the dying man will hear certain melancholy tones for the first time, although, strangely and paradoxically, it is his last.

The final stanza contains a wave of adjectives that rush over us—now no longer confined within a neat chiasmatic structure—as the poem reaches its last, climactic lament: "dear...sweet...deep...deep...wild." The repetition of the word "deep" recalls the "depth of some divine despair," which is the source of the tears in the first stanza. However, the speaker is also "wild with all regret" in thinking of the irreclaimable days gone by. The image of a "Death in Life" recalls the dead friends of the second stanza who are like submerged memories that rise to the surface only to sink down once again. This "Death in Life" also recalls the experience of dying in the midst of the rebirth of life in the morning, described in the third stanza. The poet's climactic exclamation in the final line thus represents a culmination of the images developed in the previous stanzas.

This poem is written in blank verse, or unrhymed iambic pentameters. It consists of four five-line stanzas, each of which closes with the words "the days that are no more."

Example 37

Dawn edges its way through the crowd of huddled trees,
a mole scurries away behind a fallen log. Somewhere
the sound of a truck starting, like the question
one had sullenly fallen asleep with, resuming
in the brain. A flight of parakeets
circling for a while before their cries are lost
in the distance that holds the sunken river,
stoically silent. Cries that fill and empty the mind
at the same time , touching the decaying timber
by the shore, a train losing itself in life,
saying nothing. How do we know what we are alike, when we
can turn to the dreams we find, and build
the pose of distance to serve as a symbol?

(*An October Morning (extract)*: Jayanta Mahapatra)

Substance: It is the beginning of the dawn. It emerges pushing its way through the cluster of trees which were not visible in the dark. The mole runs in the darkness and hides behind a log. One hears the sound of a truck starting after the ignition. Its dithering sound resembles the vexing question in the mind of a man who had gone off to sleep. The question had been troubling him and it came back to him again.

The flight of parakeets symbolizes our natural ideas of the past. The parakeets circled overhead. Their cries get lost at some distance near the dry river. The cries of the birds fill and empty the mind. It all looks like the path of life that is lost, without a protest, while running after the modern materialist civilization.

We do not come to know what we are like—that is, to know our identity—when we keep a distance from our dreams. We build up an excuse for deserting our distant past while following our materialistic pattern of living. The distance of time has become a symbol for desertion.

Critical Note: Emergence of the dawn and morning are occasions for the poet to express his feelings. The dawn exposes its futility, pointless ambition and competition in the modern world. This is done against the background of our tradition, culture and values of the past. Through a rich imagery and symbolism, the poet makes the readers to reflect and find a new way to life.

The poet adopts an anti-conventional approach to treat the natural phenomenon of the dawn. There are poems written on the dawn as the creator of all that is new in life. The dawn is supposed to make us forget the past. It ushers in a fresh life by infusing new hopes. Mahapatra differs from the poets who give a positive picture of the dawn. He gives us a negative picture. In this way he adopts an anti-conventional approach.

The dawn in this poem is a deceptive entity. At its arrival, dawn is described as edging its way through the crowd of huddled trees. The mole has a negative connotation. The dawn brings in futility, inhumanity, and ugliness of the modern life, symbolized by the starting of the truck, a perennial question haunting people.

The whole poem represents human longing for traditional values.

A flight of parakeets
circling for a while before their cries are lost
in the distance that holds the sunken river,
stoically silent.

By using symbolism from our surroundings, the poet builds up his theme of finding shelter in our own Indian way of life. He does this by asking questions. The reader has to note the negative points of modern culture. The answers to the poet's queries or suggestions are not given. The reader has to change his conscience and decide what he has to do. An appropriate example is given below:

How do we know what we are alike, when we
can turn to the dreams we find, and build
the pose of distance to serve as a symbol?

The poet sets the poem against the background of several voices of the nature and of man. First of all, there is the sound of a truck. The truck is a symbol of modern civilization which creates tension and anxiety. The question haunts the man while he is awake and asleep.

Nature has its own voices, represented by the cries of the parakeets. These protests against the modern culture and they have no place in our society. There are cries that fill and empty the mind at the same time. Other voices are the lone cry.

An October Morning is a modern poem using symbolism and imagery in a complex way. It is a philosophical attempt to examine the relationship between the past and the present conditions. The present is represented by the sound of the truck, while the past is represented by the flight of the parakeets and their cries 'lost in the distance of that holds the sunken river, stoically silent'.

The poet uses rhetorical questions. Such questions are asked to get an answer which the poet wants.

How do we know what we are alike, when we
can turn to the dreams we find, and build
the pose of distance to serve as a symbol?

The poem abounds in symbolism. For example:

i) Dawn edging its way—the dawn is stealthily moving hiding its identity.
ii) The mole scurrying—symbolizes a spy or an informer who is hiding from the public.
iii) The flight of the parakeets—symbolizes the natural values lost in the modern times.

Example 38

It was a lover and his lass,
With a hey, and a ho, and hey nonino,
That o'er the green, cornfield did pass,
In spring time, the only pretty ring-time,
When birds do sing, hey ding a ding ding,
Sweet lovers love the spring.

Between the acres of the rye,
With a hey, and a ho, and hey nonino,
These pretty country folks would lie,
In spring time,
In spring time, the only pretty ring-time,
When birds do sing, hey ding a ding ding,
Sweet lovers love the spring.

This carol they began that hour,
With a hey, and a ho, and hey nonino,
How that a life was but a flower,
In spring time,
In spring time, the only pretty ring-time,
When birds do sing, hey ding a ding ding,
Sweet lovers love the spring.

And therefore take the present time,
With a hey, and a ho, and hey nonino,

For love is crowned with the prime,
In spring time,
In spring time, the only pretty ring-time,
When birds do sing, hey ding a ding ding,
Sweet lovers love the spring.

(William Shakespeare)

Substance: The subject-matter of the poem is simple. It begins as if it were going to be a narrative poem, but in fact there is no story. The poem simply evokes a mood of carefree gaiety: it is a celebration of youth and love and spring. The intellectual context is slight, a fact that is reinforced by the extensiveness of the refrain, with its repetitiousness and its nonsense phrases. The refrain does contribute, however, to the atmosphere of springtime joyousness. The poem is typical of sixteenth-century song-lyrics in its lack of complexity and its evocation of a simple mood or feeling. This feeling, however, may be extremely intense, as it is in some of Thomas Wyatt's lyrics like 'Forget not yet', 'And wilt thou leave me thus?', and 'My lute awake'.

Comment: Like most lyrics, this poem is stanzaic, and for obvious reasons: in songs, the music repeats and so demands a repeating pattern in the words. The rhythms of the poem are relatively simple and regular, for the same reason, with few departures from the iambic pattern. The number of syllables is identical in corresponding lines in each stanza. This is not, indeed, essential in a stanzaic song, since the music can be varied slightly from stanza to stanza; but it certainly makes it easier for the words to be fitted to the tune. This particular lyric also has a refrain: line 2 and lines 4 to 6 are repeated in each stanza, so that each stanza contains only two new lines while having three lines of refrain. Parts of the refrain are meaningless: 'with a hey, and a ho, and a hey nonino' simply expresses mood of carefree celebration while 'hey ding a ding ding' represents birdsong. Refrains are common in sixteenth-century lyrics. When the poems are read aloud, they often sound ridiculous, but when the poems are sung they become perfectly acceptable.

Simple lyrics of this kind are often regarded as the purest form of poetry, because they lack features which poetry can share with other types of literature (the novel, drama), such as plot, character, and dialogue. In such lyrics, consequently, form plays a large part and much of the reader's pleasure may come from the neatness and elegance of the poem.

The compound 'ring-time' may be taken to be a reference to the exchange of wedding rings and/or the chiming of wedding bells. It may also refer to ring dances. A carol was a song which accompanied a ring dance. This song may be comparable to Thomas Nashe's song played in about 1592 'Spring, the sweet spring...then maids dance in a ring' in *Summer's Last Will* (1600). The phrase 'Between the acres of the rye' refers to the unploughed balks in an open field. Again, the word 'prime' in the phrase 'For love is crowned with the prime' may allude to spring time or may signify youthfulness at its best.

Originally a lyric was a poem which was set to music for performance as a solo song. The word is now commonly used of poems with similar characteristics even if they have never been set to music. It is usually confined to short poems which have no narrative element (though they may present a situation). A lyric tends to be the expression of a mood or an emotion, and is often written in the first person.

In the sixteenth century, the link between lyric poetry and music was still strong: lyrics were the words of songs. Such lyrics occur in Shakespeare's plays, like the above poem from *As You like It* (*c.* 1599), which was set to music by Thomas Morley (1558-1603).

In the age of Shakespeare we see the divorce between lyric poetry and music; during the seventeenth century it becomes increasingly common for poets to write lyrics which are not intended for singing. Freed from the demands of song, lyrics can be less regular in rhythm, and can offer greater intellectual content. But some poets continue to write songs, so that there is a double tradition, and two poets in particular are influential: Ben Jonson (1572-1637) and John Donne (1573-1631). Most seventeenth-century poets are influenced by one or other of these, and many by both.

Example 39

In the garden

A bird came down the walk:
He did not know I saw;
He bit an angle-worm in halves
And ate the fellow, raw.
And then he drank a dew
From a convenient grass,
And then hopped sidewise to the wall
To let a beetle pass.
He glanced with rapid eyes
That hurried all abroad,—
They looked like frightened beads, I thought;
He stirred his velvet head
Like one in danger; cautious,
I offered him a crumb,
And he unrolled his feathers

And rowed him softer home
Than oars divide the ocean,
Too silver for a seam,
Or butterflies, off banks of noon,
Leap, splashless, as they swim.

Substance: The speaker describes once seeing a bird come down the walk, unaware that it was being watched. The bird ate an angleworm, then "drank a Dew / From a convenient grass--," then hopped sideways to let a beetle pass by. The bird's frightened, bead-like eyes glanced all around. Cautiously, the speaker offered him "a Crumb," but the bird "unrolled his feathers" and flew away--as though rowing in the water, but with a grace gentler than that with which "Oars divide the ocean" or butterflies leap "off banks of noon"; the bird appeared to swim without splashing.

Critical Note: In this poem, the simple experience of watching a bird hop down a path allows the poet to exhibit extraordinary poetic powers of observation and description.

The poet keenly depicts the bird as it eats a worm, pecks at the grass, hops by a beetle, and glances around fearfully. As a natural creature frightened by the speaker into flying away, the bird becomes an emblem for the quick, lively, ungraspable wild essence that distances nature from the human beings who desire to appropriate or tame it. But the most remarkable feature of this poem is the imagery of its final stanza, in which the poet provides one of the most breath-taking descriptions of flying in all of poetry. Simply by offering two quick comparisons of flight and by using aquatic motion (rowing and swimming), the poet evokes the delicacy and fluidity of moving through air. The image of butterflies leaping "off banks of noon," splashlessly swimming though the sky, is one of the most memorable features of the poem.

Structurally, this poem is in iambic trimeters with occasional four-syllable lines, following a loose *abcb* rhyme scheme, and rhythmically breaking up the meter with long dashes.

Example 40

I died for beauty—but was scarce
Adjusted in the tomb,
When one who died for truth was lain
In an adjoining room.

He questioned softly why I failed?
"For beauty," I replied.
"And I for truth,--the two are one;
We brethren are," he said.

And so, as kinsmen met a night,
We talked between the rooms,
Until the moss had reached our lips,
And covered up our names.

(Emily Dickinson)

Substance: The poem "I died for beauty—but was scarce", is about two dead people having a conversation about their previous lives. One of them died for truth, one of them died for beauty. They talk and at the end of the poem, moss comes and covers up the names on the tombs. "I died for beauty—but was scarce", by Emily Dickinson is a poem about death and man's insignificance over the course of time.

Critical Note: Dickinson associates beauty and truth in this poem. The speakers' deaths are described in parallel language; they are buried in "adjoining" rooms and are "brethren" and "kinsmen." These descriptions also make it clear that they are not identical; otherwise they would be buried in the same room and be twins.

This bizarre, allegorical death fantasy recalls Keats ("Beauty is Truth, Truth Beauty," from *Ode on a Grecian Urn*), but its manner of presentation belongs uniquely to Dickinson. In this short lyric, Dickinson manages to include a sense of the macabre physicality of death ("Until the Moss had reached our lips--"), the high idealism of martyrdom ("I died for Beauty. . . One who died for Truth"), a certain kind of romantic yearning combined with longing for Platonic companionship ("And so, as kinsmen, met a night--"), and an optimism about the afterlife with barely sublimated terror about the fact of death. As the poem progresses, the high idealism and yearning for companionship gradually give way to mute, cold death, as the moss creeps up the speaker's corpse and her headstone, obliterating both her capacity to speak (covering her lips) and her identity (covering her name).

The ultimate effect of this poem is to show that every aspect of human life—ideals, human feelings, identity itself--is erased by death. But by making the erasure gradual--something to be "adjusted" to in the tomb--and by portraying a speaker who is untroubled by her own grim state, Dickinson creates a scene that is, by turns, grotesque and compelling, frightening and comforting. It is one of her most singular statements about death, and like so many of Dickinson's poems, it has no parallels in the work of any other writer.

This poem follows many of Dickinson's typical formal patterns--the *abcb* rhyme scheme, the rhythmic use of the dash to interrupt the flow--but has a more regular meter, so that the first and third lines in each stanza are iambic tetrameters, while the second and fourth lines are iambic trimeters, creating a four-three-four-three stress pattern in each stanza.

Example 41

As virtuous men passe mildly away,
  And whisper to their soules, to goe,
Whilst some of their sad friends doe say,
  The breath goes now, and some say, no:

So let us melt, and make no noise,
  No teare-floods, nor sigh-tempests move,
'Twere prophanation of our joyes
  To tell the layetie our love.

Moving of th'earth brings harmes and feares,
  Men reckon what it did and meant,
But trepidation of the spheares,
  Though greater farre, is innocent.

Dull sublunary lovers' love
  (Whose soul is sense) cannot admit
Absence, because it doth remove
  Those things which elemented it.

But we, by a love so much refin'd
  That our selves know not what it is,
Inter-assured of the mind,
  Care less, eyes, lips, and hands to miss.

Our two souls therefore, which are one,
  Though I must go, endure not yet
A breach, but an expansion,
  Like gold to airy thinness beat.

If they be two, they are two so
  As stiff twin compasses are two:
Thy soul, the fix'd foot, makes no show
  To move, but doth, if the other do;

And though it in the centre sit,
  Yet when the other far doth roam,
It leans, and hearkens after it,
  And grows erect, as that comes home.

Such wilt thou be to me, who must,
Like the other foot, obliquely run:
Thy firmness makes my circle just,
And makes me end where I begun.

Substance: The poem is one of parting, and was perhaps addressed by the poet to his wife when he went abroad in 1611. The poet begins by telling his mistress that their parting should be a quiet one, not marked by violent demonstrations of emotion, their parting is to be like the peaceful death of a virtuous man, the soul leaving the body almost imperceptibly. This suggests that their parting is itself a kind of death, that they belong together like body and soul. There are to be no floods of tears or tempests of sighs (a reference to the extravagant expressions of much conventional poetry). Their love is a religion, of which they are the priests: and it would be profanation to disclose its mysteries to those who were not initiates (*the laity*). The third stanza compares earthly events with celestial ones. Earthquakes cause damage and frighten people, but the quaking of heavenly spheres, which is much greater, is harmless (*innocent*).

In traditional astronomy, which was still accepted by nearly all educated people during the poet's life-time, the earth was surrounded by a nest of concentric invisible spheres, which carried the 'planets' (the Moon, Mercury, Venus, the Sun, Mars, Jupiter, and Saturn) and the 'fixed stars'; the rotations of these spheres accounted for the movements of heavenly bodies. The 'trepidation of the spheres' was a movement of the ninth of these spheres which was used to explain the astronomical phenomenon now known as the procession of the equinoxes. The poet is saying that their love is a heavenly one; its disturbances are harmless and almost imperceptible to others, whereas the upsets of an earthly love are obvious and harmful.

The contrast between the earthly and heavenly love is continued in the next two stanzas. The word *sublunary* means 'below the sphere of the moon.' Of all the spheres, that carrying the moon was the one nearest to the earth. Beneath the sphere of the moon was the realm of mutability; everything there was composed of the four elements (earth, air, fire and water) and underwent continual change. But above the sphere of the moon were the heavens, which were composed of a fifth element (the quintessence, or ether), and which were perfect and unchanging. Such, the poet implies, is the love between himself and his mistress, whereas ordinary earthly (*sublunary*) lovers are imperfect and inconstant. Such earthly love whose essential animating force (*soul*) is the senses, cannot survive a parting of the lovers, because this removes the things of which it was composed (*elemented*). In contrast, the poet and his mistress are betrothed to one another (*Inter-assured*) spiritually, and are less concerned about bodily absence.

Comment: Their two souls are united, they are not really separated even when absent from one another:

Our two souls, therefore, which are one,
Though I must go, endure not yet
A breach, but an expansion,
Like gold to airy thinness beat [beaten].

This is one of the most celebrated metaphysical images of the poet, described by Dr Samuel Johnson as 'the most heterogeneous ideas... yoked by violence together'. The souls of the parted lovers are compared to a piece of gold beaten out into very fine leaf, which extends a long way but remains in one piece. The word *expansion* must be pronounced as four syllables, with stresses on the second and fourth. The image introduces associations of purity (because gold has to be pure to be beaten out in this way), and of richness, incorruptibility and nobility (traditional qualities of gold). It also suggests the spiritualization of the physical, the apparently solid gold becoming something of 'airy thinness' (like the soul).

The poem ends with perhaps the most famous of metaphysical images of the poet's:

If they be two, they are two so

As stiff twin compasses are two.... Unity-in-separation is conveyed by the comparison of the lovers' souls to a pair of compasses and the image is given immediacy by *stiff* (in line 26), which makes us feel the physical effort of adjusting them. The woman is the stationary foot in the centre, while the poet is the foot that moves out across the map. The word *fix'd* (in line 27) also refers to the woman's constancy, as does the word *firmness* (in line 35). The image suggests their union on a higher plane: the compass-legs are used for drawing on two-dimensional paper, but are joined in the third dimension above the paper. It also shows the sympathetic connexion between the lovers: neither leg can move without a corresponding movement in the other leg. Especially expressive is the phrase 'leans, and harkens after it' (in line 31), giving the reaching-out of the woman's soul towards her parted companion.

In the final stanza, the compasses are used for drawing a circle: the firmness of the central foot ensures that the outer foot draws it perfectly. The woman exercises moral and emotional control over her partner, so that his behaviour is *impeccable* (the circle was considered a 'perfect' figure). He will ultimately return to her, his journey ending where it began.

In this lyric we have moved a long way from the simple song. The rhythms are often speech-like, as in *admit/Absence* (in lines 14 and 15). There is an intricate argument, drawing on specialized knowledge (such as that about the procession of the equinoxes). There are surprising and ingenious images, sometimes (like that of the compasses) developed at length. But weight of intellectual contents and ingenuity of imagery do not preclude feeling: the poem is charged with emotion; it appears to be a 'passionate paradoxical reasoning.'

Example 42

Spring, the sweet Spring, is the year's pleasant king;
Then blooms each thing, then maids dance in a ring,
Cold doth not sting, the pretty birds do sing,
    Cuckoo, jug-jug, pu-we, to-witta-woo!

The palm and may make country houses gay,
Lambs frisk and play, the shepherds pipe all day.
And we hear aye birds tune this merry lay,
    Cuckoo, jug-jug, pu-we, to-witta-woo!

The fields breathe sweet, the daisies kiss our feet,
Young lovers meet, old wives a-sunning sit,
In every street these tunes our ear do greet,
    Cuckoo, jug-jug, pu-we, to-witta-woo!
Spring! the sweet Spring!

Substance: The poet is engaged in gathering happy instances like flowers, in the poem . The emotion is fuelled by more than repetition; images of delight are delightedly accumulated. In argument or passion, we may choose illustrations, or images which outstrip the original purpose. Hence the surprise of currents of feeling or thought, inside or outside poetry. In a poem, the metrical exigencies play an important part in generating new material, for they insist on certain arbitrary choices and patterns . The poet's scheme of internal rhyme probably produced the music that pervades nature in spring time:

Spring, the sweet *Spring*, is the year's pleasant *King*,
Then blooms each *thing*, then maids dance in a *ring*,
Cold doth not *sting*, the pretty birds do *sing*,

In the midst of all these internal rhymes the sudden arrival of the negative instance in the middle of the positives, 'Cold doth not sting' comes as a surprise. The onomatopœic refrain: 'Cuckoo, jug-jug, pu-we, to-witta-woo!' also introduces a stylized pressure. It reminds us that each verse must get round, or get back, to the bird-song. It also has a sub-verbal effect, like that of lover's or parents' brooding murmurs.

Comment: Even this simple poem shows a characteristic effort of growth. The first two verses do little more than create accurate images and the feeling alive in a perfectly valid and delightful exercise, but the last verse starts up and connect, the fields' sweet breath moving into the precise and metaphorical daisies which then move back again into the metaphor of the kiss. Young lovers are poised against old wives. By particularization and antithesis, the list becomes more shapely than a list. In the final verse the simple repetition of the refrain itself is not sufficient for a climax, but has to be capped by the salute, 'Spring! the sweet Spring!' The poem does more than return to the beginning and appeals finally in an extra line, exuberant in an exclamation which has gone a long way beyond the quiet indicative of the beginning.

Delight, even in such a simply presented poem, is mixed with the conscious brooding on delight. As it lists and shapes pleasures, the poem also reflects on them: 'Spring, the sweet Spring, is the year's pleasant king.' The adjectives *pretty*, *merry*, *sweet*, insist that the feeling of delight is a delightful possession. The poem contains its own motive and reveals its own mainspring.

Example 43

When the voices of children are heard on the green
And laughing is heard on the hill,
My heart is at rest within my breast
And every thing else is still

Then come home my children, the sun is gone down
And the dews of night arise
Come come leave off play, and let us away
Till the morning appears in the skies

No no let us play, for it is yet day
And we cannot go to sleep
Besides in the sky, the little birds fly
And the hills are all cover'd with sheep

Well well go & play till the light fades away
And then go home to bed
The little ones leaped & shouted & laugh'd
And all the hills echoed

("*The Nurse's Song*": William Blake)

Substance: The scene of the poem features a group of children playing outside in the hills, while their nurse listens to them in contentment. As twilight begins to fall, she gently urges them to "leave off play" and retire to the house for the night. They ask to play on till bedtime, for as long as the light lasts. The nurse yields to their pleas, and the children shout and laugh with joy while the hills echo their gladness.

Critical note: This is a poem of affinities and correspondences. There is no suggestion of alienation, either between children and adults or between man and nature, and even the dark certainty of nightfall is tempered by the promise of resuming play in the morning. The theme of the poem is the children's innocent and simple joy. Their happiness persists unabashed and uninhibited, and without shame the children plead for permission to continue in it. The sounds and games of the children harmonize with a busy world of sheep and birds. They think of themselves as part of nature, and cannot bear the thought of abandoning their play while birds and sheep still frolic in the sky and on the hills, for the children share the innocence and unselfconscious spontaneity of these natural creatures. They also approach the world with a cheerful optimism, focusing not on the impending nightfall but on the last drops of daylight that surely can be evoked out of the evening.

A similar innocence characterizes the pleasure the adult nurse takes in watching her charges play. Their happiness inspires in her a feeling of peace, and their desire to prolong their own delight is one she readily indulges. She is a kind of angelic, guardian presence who, while standing apart from the children, supports rather than overshadows their innocence. As an adult, she is identified with "everything else" in nature; but while her inner repose does contrast with the children's exuberant delight, the difference does not constitute an antagonism. Rather, her tranquility resonates with the evening's natural stillness, and both seem to envelop the carefree children in a tender protection.

The poem has four quatrains, rhymed *abcb* and containing an internal rhyme in the third line of each verse: *rest/ breast*; *play/ away*; *sky/fly*; *leaped/ laugh'd*.

Example 44

'Love seeketh not itself to please,
'Nor for itself hath any care,
'But for another gives its ease,
'And builds a Heaven in Hell's despair.'

So sung a little Clod of Clay
Trodden with the cattle's feet,
But a Pebble of the brook
Warbled out these metres meet:

'Love seeketh only Self to please,
'To bind another to its delight,
'Joys in another's loss of ease,
'And builds a Hell in Heaven's despite'.

(William Blake)

Substance: The structure of the poem consists of a pattern of contrast or of contemplation. The poet presents two contrasting views of the nature of love, but makes no comment or judgment on them (though he does leave us to ponder on the choice of the Clod and the Pebble as spokesmen for these views). One structure of the poem suggests that antithesis is part of the nature of things, that conflicting concepts of love are inherent in the universe. The wonderfully structured poem opposes two views of love: the first, regards love as a force whereby one gives oneself to and on behalf of the other; the second, speaks of a selfish, jealous love which is only really an excuse for the aggrandisement of the self. By putting them in this order, the poet clearly shows which is dominant in the world of experience.

Comment: We may be astounded at the fact as to why the poet puts the words into the mouths two unlikely protragonists—a clod of clay and a pebble. The poet has done this perhaps because the clod is above all things soft, it takes the imprint of the 'cattle's feet,' whereas the pebble is hard, resistant, unchanging, and is thus a fitting emblem for the soul which cannot change or adopt and cannot fully take on the reality of other people and other minds. The clod gives the selfless version of love, whereas a pebble gives the selfish version of love. The poem is a pellucid amplification of the Petrarchan and masochistic views of love. The clod stands in favour of selfless love, the love leads the lover to abnegate his own personal and private and in a sense, selfish appeasements. This very point of view is negated when the fragile clod is crushed under the feet of the cattle. The clod of clay pertains to love which is self-sacrificing. But this kind of love crumbles to pieces under the heavy feet of selfish love. On the contrary, the pebble's viewpoint is more plausible. After all, the pebble is cold and solid and it finds love tormenting, overpowering, and tyrannical, and even selfishly possessive.

From yet another perspective, the poem has a different bearing. The clod which is smooth, submissive, and pliant connotes the extreme of feminine nature. The pebble which has comparatively a solid, inflexible, massive structure hints at the extreme of masculine nature. These two aspects in nature are visibly apparent in any sexual relationship. The beautifully structured poem opposes the two views of love: the first regards love as a force whereby one gives oneself to and on behalf of the other;

the second speaks of a selfish, jealous love which is only really an excuse for the aggrandisement of the self.

Neither complete submission nor exclusively selfish tyranny yields the much sought after bliss of love because either extremes are futile and ineffective. Standing by the view of the clod we can see that its total subservience and resignedness and submit to the humiliation of tyranny but finally it becomes disgusting and provokes contempt in the mate. The clod that assumes the mild nature is soon lost in the sand for it is crumbled to pieces by the active and alert legs of experience. The clod's view, however, sounds impeccable when we see it in the light of human love or mercy or philanthropist. The other extreme is held by the pebble. In the eyes of the pebble love is ruthless and tyrannous. It has the tendency to overbear others and exploit them. One who is involved in such a love, the pebble contends, looks forward to enjoying the loved one's loss of comfort. As a matter of fact that sort of love is replacing the heavenly and natural rapture with a host of hellish suffering.

Two types of love are presented here—the selfless and the selfish—in the two stanzas, namely, the first and the third stanzas, each in a small sentence. They are symmetrically placed before and after the second stanza which indicates the speaking—the clod and the pebble respectively. The clod is humble and selfless, trodden by the cattle's fact.

The line, 'Warbled out these metres meet', is smooth and musical; it is ironically attributed to the sleek pebble. The phrases, 'Heaven in Hell's despair' and 'Hell in Heaven's despite' are well-balanced, as well as counter-balanced. There is beautiful consonance in the phrases and also zeugmatic. There are alliterations throughout the poem: *cl*od and *cl*ay, *B*ut a pe*bb*le of the *b*rook, Love *s*eeketh only *s*elf to plea*s*e.

Example 45

A sudden blow: the great wings beating still
Above the staggering girl, her thighs caressed
By the dark webs, her nape caught in his bill,
He holds her helpless breast upon his breast.
How can those terrified vague fingers push
The feathered glory from her loosening thighs?
And how can body, laid in that white rush,

But feel the strange heart beating where it lies?
A shudder in the loins engenders there
The broken wall, the burning roof and tower
And Agamemnon dead. Being so caught up,
So mastered by the brute blood of the air,

Did she put on his knowledge with his power
Before the indifferent beak could let her drop?

(*Leda and the Swan*: W.B.Yeats)

Substance: The speaker retells a story from Greek mythology, the rape of the girl Leda by the God Zeus, who had assumed the form of a swan. Leda felt a sudden blow, with the "great wings" of the swan still beating above her. Her thighs were caressed by "the dark webs," and the nape of her neck was caught in his bill; he held "her helpless breast upon his breast." How, the speaker asks, could Leda's "terrified vague fingers" push the feathered glory of the swan from between her thighs? And how could her body help but feel "the strange heart beating where it lies"? A shudder in the loins engenders "The broken wall, the burning roof and tower, and Agamemnon dead." The speaker wonders whether Leda, caught up by the swan and "mastered by the brute blood of the air," assumed his knowledge as well as his power "Before the indifferent beak could let her drop."

Critical Note: William ButlerYeats's daring sonnet describing the details of a story from Greek mythology—the rape of Leda by the God Zeus in the form of a swan—was written at the height of the poet's career, the same year he received the Nobel Prize for literature. "Leda and the Swan" is a violent, sexually explicit poem that has all of the lyricism and complexity ofYeats's later work, with its plain diction, rhythmic vigor, and allusions to mystical ideas about the universe, the relationship of human and divine, and the cycles of history. It can be seen as a poem about the way a single event is to be understood as part of a larger scheme; the result of the god's assault on Leda is the birth of Helen ofTroy, the subsequent destruction of early Greek civilization, and the beginning of the modern era.

"Leda and the Swan" has been considered one of the most technically masterful poems ever written in English. In the work,Yeats uses the fourteen lines of the traditional sonnet form in a radical, modernist style. He calls up a series of unforgettable, bizarre images of an immediate physical event using abstract descriptions in terse language, while at the same time offering a distanced view of that occurrence in the sweep of time. Yeats himself considered the poem one of his major accomplishments, and in addition to praising its economy of language and skillful use of rhythm, critics have seen it as a fine example of how ideas that were central to the poet's life found expression in his poetry.

The title of the poem is important, because it is the only indication of the characters who are the subject of the poem. In the poem,Yeats assumes that the reader is familiar with the myth referred to in the title.Throughout the fourteen lines, he never uses the names of either of the characters. Zeus's name in fact appears neither in the title nor in the text of the poem; the reader is expected to understand that the swan is an incarnation of the all-powerful god.

"Leda and the Swan" is a difficult poem to grasp fully on a casual reading because it assumes considerable background knowledge on the part of the reader of the event being described and its place in Greek mythology.The poem is also inspired by Yeats' strange and difficult theory of historical cycles. Even when one is acquainted with Yeats' sources and theories, the poem is a challenge for the student because of the complexity of the ideas to which it makes subtle reference. However, the lyrical quality and force of description in the poem can be appreciated.

"Leda and the Swan" is a sonnet, a traditional fourteen-line poem in iambic pentameter. The structure of this sonnet is an intermixture of Shakespearean and Petrarchan forms with a clear separation between the first eight lines (the "octave") and the final six (the "sestet"), the dividing line being the moment of ejaculation--the "shudder in the loins." The rhyme scheme of the sonnet is *abab cdcd efgefg*.

Example 46

That time of year thou may'st in me behold
When yellow leaves, or none, or few, do hang
Upon those boughs which shake against the cold,
Bare ruin'd choirs, where late the sweet birds sang.
In me thou see'st the twilight of such day
As after sunset fadeth in the west,
Which by and by black night doth take away,
Death's second self, that seals up all in rest.

In me thou see'st the glowing of such fire,
That on the ashes of his youth doth lie
As the deathbed whereon it must expire,
Consumed with that which it was nourish'd by.

This thou perceiv'st, which makes thy love more strong,
To love that well which thou must leave ere long.

(William Shakespeare)

Substance: The structure is that of a Shakespearean sonnet. Here, the three quatrains consist of a single sentence each; the second and third beginning with an echo of the phrase *in me*, from the first line. Both, this coincidence of syntax with metrical form and repetition, help to emphasize the metaphorical structure of the poem. Each of the one-sentence quatrains presents a single image for growing old: autumn, twilight, the dying embers, all suggesting loss of light and warmth. Only in the couplet however, used to give a striking turn, do we discover the point of the sonnet. It becomes at last a kind of love poem. Incidentally, the poet likes to use the couplet as concluding device in his work—it ends with a striking double rhyme. The couplet in the sonnet does more than provide a strong final note: it is likely to begin with words like 'yet' or 'but', words that introduce a dramatic reversal and therefore often a witty or surprising conclusion.

Comment: The main attraction of the sonnet is the patterned movement of discourse, not the imagery. There are the three paralleled metaphors: 'That time of year...the twilight of such day...the glowing of such fire'—there is a progression by extending metaphors. The metaphors are picked up, changed, mixed, dropped and lilts while the sonnet runs its strong course as an utterance. There is not only the interplay of imagery but also the interplay of sound in the line: 'Bare ruin's choirs, where late the sweet birds sang'. The chord of vowels and '*r*'s' is noticeable in the phrase 'bare ruin'd choirs', sounded in three successive long, slow syllables: the mystery of the line comes from this music as much as from the wonderful complex of metaphors it holds in solution.

The poet uses three successive metaphors, one to a quatrain, in order to portray his developing old age and imminent death. The sonnet is attractive in its metaphoric structure. The metaphoric process helps exact the ageing of the man it describes. Behind the narrowing down from year to day to glowing embers the sonnet does something more, to an extent contrary to, its metaphors. This something else is contained in the verbs of the sonnet. In the opening line *thou may'st in me behold* is not likely to be interpreted by us as anything other than a general statement—an interpretation supported by the breadth of the metaphor which follows. In other words, we feel as much addressed as the person to whom the poet addresses his poem. Thus we take the statement as the poet's actual opinion of himself. In the second and third quatrains the phrase *thou see'st* modifies our position only a little. The absence of the auxiliary 'may' locates the sonnet as more particularly an address to a friend, but it remains one which we can share, as we all share supposedly intimate poems which, all they address themselves to a lover, describe the poet's general state.

The sonnet is charged with melancholy which is generated by the poet's reflection to the mortality and mutability of human life. The poet sees himself as a decrepit person tossed by the storms of life and troubled by the thought that death will soon swoop on him and take him to the region of eternal sleep. The mood of depression informs the whole poem and lends it a poignant note. The poet compares himself in his old age to a bare ruined tree standing as a skeleton in hoary winter or the glimmering twilight turning into a black night. Embers of his youth's fire, self-consumed, still linger glowing before the final extinction.

In this poem, the speaker invokes a series of metaphors to characterize the nature of what he perceives to be his old age. In the first quatrain, he tells the beloved that his age is like a "time of year," late autumn, when the leaves have almost completely fallen from the trees, and the weather has grown cold, and the birds have left their branches. In the second quatrain, he then says that his age is like late twilight, "As after sunset fadeth in the west," and the remaining light is slowly extinguished in the darkness, which the speaker likens to "Death's second self." In the third quatrain, the speaker compares himself to the glowing remnants of a fire, which lies "on the ashes of his youth"—that is, on the ashes of the logs that once enabled it to burn—and which will soon be consumed "by that which it was nourished by"—that is, it will be extinguished as it sinks into the ashes, which its own burning created. In the couplet, the speaker tells the young man that he must perceive these things, and that his love must be strengthened by the knowledge that he will soon be parted from the speaker when the speaker, like the fire, is extinguished by time.

Sonnet 73 takes up one of the most pressing issues of the first 126 sonnets, the speaker's anxieties regarding what he perceives to be his advanced age, and develops the theme through a sequence of metaphors each implying something different. The first quatrain, which employs the metaphor of the winter day, emphasizes the harshness and emptiness of old age, with its boughs shaking against the cold and its "bare ruined choirs" bereft of bird song. In the second quatrain, the metaphor shifts to that of twilight, and emphasizes not the chill of old age, but rather the gradual fading of the light of youth, as "black night" takes away the light "by and by". But in each of these quatrains, with each of these metaphors, the speaker fails to confront the full scope of his problem: both the metaphor of winter and the metaphor of twilight imply cycles, and impose cyclical motions upon the objects of their metaphors, whereas old age is final. Winter follows spring, but spring will follow winter just as surely; and after the twilight fades, dawn will come again. In human life, however, the fading of warmth and light is not cyclical; youth will not come again for the speaker. In the third quatrain, he must resign himself to this fact. The image of the fire consumed by the ashes of its youth is significant both for its brilliant disposition of the past—the ashes of which eventually snuff out the fire, "consumed by that which it was nourished by"—and for the fact that when the fire is extinguished, it can never be lit again.

In this sense, Sonnet 73 is more complex than it is often considered supposed by critics and scholars. It is often argued that Sonnet 73 and sonnets like it are simply exercises in metaphor—that they propose a number of different metaphors for the same thing, and the metaphors essentially mean the same thing. But to make this argument is to miss the psychological narrative contained within the choice of metaphors themselves. Sonnet 73 is not simply a procession of interchangeable metaphors; it is the story of the speaker slowly coming to grips with the real finality of his age and his impermanence in time.

The couplet of this sonnet renews the speaker's plea for the young man's love, urging him to "love well" that which he must soon leave. It is important to note that the couplet could not have been spoken after the first two quatrains alone. No one loves twilight because it will soon be night; instead they look forward to morning. But after the third quatrain, in which the speaker makes clear the nature of his "leav[ing] ere long," the couplet is possible, and can be treated as a poignant and reasonable exhortation to the beloved.

Example 47

Sunset and evening star,
And one clear call for me!
And may there be no moaning of the bar,
When I put out to sea,

But such a tide as moving seems asleep,
Too full for sound and foam,
When that which drew from out the boundless deep
Turns again home.

Twilight and evening bell,
And after that the dark!
And may there be no sadness of farewell,
When I embark;

For tho' from out our bourne ofTime and Place
The flood may bear me far,
I hope to see my Pilot face to face
When I have crost the bar.

(*Crossing the Bar*: Alfred Tennyson)

Substance: The poet has reached the last stage of his life and is calmly awaiting his death. Sunset and evening star are the signals for his final departure. He thinks of death as a great voyage into the unknown. He expects the sea to be quiet at the time of his departure. He also expects that the sea will be free from sound and foam, so that his passage over the sea may be smooth and easy. The poet will put out to sea in the evening and cross the bar. Then a deep darkness, that is, death will follow. He is confident that death will release his soul from bondage of flesh and carry it to God, the Divine Pilot. So his mind is free from all fear and trouble. He welcomes death and hopes that there will be none to mourn his final journey towards the greater mysterious unknown.

Critical Note: The poem describes Tennyson's placid and accepting attitude toward death. He uses the metaphor of a sand bar to describe the barrier between life and death. A sand bar is a ridge of sand built up by currents along a shore. In order to reach the shore, the waves must crash against the sand bar, creating a sound that Tennyson describes as the "moaning of the bar." The other important image in the poem is one of "crossing," suggesting Christian connotations: "crossing" refers both to "crossing over" into the next world, and to the act of "crossing" oneself in the classic Catholic gesture of religious faith and devotion.

This poem is a fine allegory of death. The poet looks upon death from a point of view which is uncommon and unconventional. For him death, the natural end of our life on earth, is something to be eagerly welcomed. In this poem Tennyson gives a new meaning to death. For him, death is the gateway through which we escape from the bonds of flesh to unite with our Divine Pilot, the Creator. Thus death, according to him is something to be wished for and heartily welcomed. For, it is the bridge that links us up with our Divine Father.

This poem consists of four quatrains rhyming *abab*. The first and third lines of each stanza are always a couple of beats longer than the second and fourth lines, although the line lengths vary among the stanzas.

Example 48

Gather ye rosebuds while ye may,
Old Time is still a-flying:
And this same flower that smiles to-day
To-morrow will be dying.

The glorious lamp of heaven, the sun,
The higher he's a-getting,
The sooner will his race be run,
And nearer he's to setting.

That age is best which is the first,
When youth and blood are warmer;
But being spent, the worse, and worst
Times still succeed the former.

Then be not coy, but use your time,
And while ye may, go marry:
For having lost but once your prime,
Ye may for ever tarry.

Substance: These lines may appear simple enough. The imagery of rosebuds and the lamp of heaven along with the theme of *carpe diem*,'seize the day', are perfectly conventional. And yet in using these images and this theme, the poet displays art and produces something more than a repetition of an old idea. The metrical scheme of the poem is extremely light and lyrical, with the movement of song or dance. The normally iambic tetrameter and iambic trimeter lines succeed each other, the short lines providing further variety by the addition of a final unaccented syllable that results in a feminine ending. And with this easy and gay-sounding rhythm goes the light and almost flippant diction: 'Old Time' describes the conventional personification of time, but it also has a hearty and familiar sound, as when one speaks of 'old-so-and-so'. Terms like *a-flying* and *a-getting* sound less than perfectly formal (whereas the poet could have written, 'Old Time is ever flying' and 'The higher he is getting'). This is a lively poem, then, about the subject of dying, and almost gaily spoken sermon in lyric form on the profoundly serious subjects of youth and age, love and death. In other words, the manner contrasts with the matter, that these lines have a half-mocking, half-serious effect.

Comment: In small details, too, the poet's complicating art is evident: 'The worse, and worst/Times' seems to repeat but actually varies a sound, to contrast the present with the future. The following of *today* at the end of one line by *to-morrow* at the beginning of the next (in lines 3 and 4) is another artful device for emphasis. Not only the tone and these details, furthermore, but also the logical and grammatical structures of the lyric give evidence of complication within an order. The first and last stanzas are primarily in the imperative voice—*gather ye rosebuds, be not coy, use your time, go marry*—while the sentences that compose the two central stanzas are statements illustrating the point of these comments. The first illustration, however, is that of the ephemeral flower, in the first stanza, and the others are variations on a theme: the sun rises only to sink, creatures grow not only to lose their youth and warmth, and all is *dying* and *setting*.

We might even argue that all these artful devices and complexities find their culmination and that tone is at last summed up, in a paradoxical ending. The moral of the poem appears until the end to be simply that no one stays young or lives forever; but the speaker's conclusion is that if you fail to enjoy youth, you may tarry, wait, 'forever'. Here the meaning is not that you may wait literally forever, all your life, but without fulfillment.

The fact that man can seize life only as he gradually dies is the lesson which the virgins have to learn from roses and sun: the fact that they can use, can enjoy their time instead of wasting life out passively. Like the bud that smiles, the sun that runs his race and the warmth that spends itself, they should act, smile, run and spend their lives, not waste them: they should marry. To be living, then is to be dying—this is the paradox—but it is better to die in a lively way than to languish and neither live nor die without much intensity.

Despite all these complexities, the contrast between subject and manner, the variety of poetic devices and the complicated even paradoxical ending, we notice the coherence of this poem, with its unified tone, at once deftly light and serious. Virtually every detail in these lines, of both imagery and diction, is directly relevant to the subject of passing time that robs life of spent and unspent beauty and vigour: the rosebud and the sun are thus related; and nouns and adverbs that refer to time recur insistently. All the emphatic rhyming words in the short lines of the first two stanzas are in progressive form that embodies knowledge of temporal forces—*flying, dying, getting, setting*. Even within stanzas there are special echoic arrangements of words. In the second stanza each of the series of comparative comes as the second word and the third and the fourth syllable in a series of three lines: *higher, sooner, nearer*. In the third stanza these are replaced by superlatives: the *best* is *first*, then the earlier series is recalled in the comparatives *warmer* and *worse*, with the climax coming in the word *worst*. Finally, the last word of the poem, *tarry* bears a negative importance (do not tarry, the speaker says, but spend your life or it will be spent): it is related to all other words, the verbs of movement and change, the adverbs of temporal qualification and the comparative adjectives, that carry the theme of time.

The lyric embodies complexity and coherence. In its brisk rapid movement it embodies an unmistakable economy in words, phrases and images. Not that it is a perfect poem; if its imagery were more vivid and particular it might be a richer lyric still. *Old Time* is fate personified; and the poet resorts to conventional poetic counters—*sun, rosebuds, Old Time*.

Example 49

O Rose thou art sick.
The invisible worm,
That flies in the night
In the howling storm:

Has found out thy bed
Of crimson joy:
And his dark secret love
Does thy life destroy.

(William Blake)

Subatance: The speaker, addressing a rose, informs it that it is sick. An "invisible" worm has stolen into its bed in a "howling storm" and under the cover of night. The "dark secret love" of this worm is destroying the rose's life.

Critical Note: While the rose exists as a beautiful natural object that has become infected by a worm, it also exists as a literary rose, the conventional symbol of love. The image of the worm resonates with the Biblical serpent. Worms are quintessentially earthbound, and symbolize death and decay. The "bed" into which the worm creeps denotes both the natural flowerbed and also the lovers' bed. The rose is sick, and the poem implies that love is sick as well. Yet the rose is unaware of its sickness. Of course, an actual rose could not know anything about its own condition, and so the emphasis falls on the allegorical suggestion that it is love that does not recognize its own ailing state. This results partly from the insidious secrecy with which the "worm" performs its work of corruption—not only is it invisible, it enters the bed at night. This secrecy indeed constitutes part of the infection itself. The "crimson joy" of the rose connotes both sexual pleasure and shame, thus joining the two concepts in a way that Blake thought was perverted and unhealthy. The rose's joyful attitude toward love is tainted by the aura of shame and secrecy that our culture attaches to love.

The two quatrains of this poem rhyme *abcb*. The ominous rhythm of these short, two-beat lines contributes to the poem's sense of foreboding or dread and complements the unflinching directness with which the speaker tells the rose she is dying.

Example 50

My luve is like a red, red rose
    That's newly sprung in June:
My luve is like the melodie
    That's sweetly play'd in tune.

So fair art thou, my bonnie lass,
    So deep in luve as I:
And I will luve thee still, my dear,
    Till a' [all] the seas gang [go] dry.

Till a' the seas gang dry, my dear,
And the rocks melt wi' the sun:
And I will love thee still, my dear,
While the sands o' life shall run.

And fare thee weel [well], my only luve,
And fare thee well awhile!
And I will come again, my luve,
Were ten thousand miles.

(Robert Burns)

Substance: The poet uses *luve* (meaning 'love') in various senses. In everyday usage, love (or 'luve') is used as a verb ('I love you') and as a noun (which can refer either to the emotion of love 'I am in love') or to the person loved. In the second stanza of the poem, it appears both as emotional stake ('So deep in luve am I') and as verb ('I will luve thee'). In the final stanza, however, the speaker refers to his beloved as *luve: fare thee weel, my only luve.* These different uses are all clearly distinguished from each other. But in the first stanza it is not clear whether *luve* refers to the speaker's emotional state or to his beloved: 'O my luve's like a red, red rose'. That the poet uses *luve* in both senses in subsequent stanzas which does not help us to resolve this. Nor does the fact that stanzas two to four are addressed to his beloved, since it does not follow that the first stanza which is also addressed to her. Thus the double meaning of *luve* in the first stanza remains unresolved and perhaps unresolvable. Yet the two distinct meanings of *luve* are not in conflict with one another and they add up to a coherent poetic statement. In fact, the second stanza seems to suggest that there is a direct ratio between extent of her beauty and the depth of his love:

So fair art thou, my bonnie lass,
So deep in luve am I.

The poet's usage of *luve* is ambiguous. It may be concluded that the meanings in question do not have to be contradictory or even incompatible to create ambiguity: the difference between senses which are distinct and disparate is a sufficient condition for ambiguity to occur.

Comment: Here we are back to song lyric, with relatively slight intellectual content, expressing strong and simple emotion. The poem is straightforward declaration of affection, relying a good deal for its effect on hyperbole (the seas going dry and the rocks melting) and on repetition, which is almost hypnotic in its effect, there are explicit affirmations (as in lines 7 and 11), together with the evocative comparisons of the girl to a rose (in lines 1 to 2):

My love is like a red, red rose
That's newly sprung in June

and a melody (in lines 3 to 4):

My love is like the melodie
That's sweetly play'd in tune.

These get their effect, not by any special or detailed ways in which she is like these things, but simply from the general loneliness of the rose and the melody. The final stanza introduces a poignant note of parting, which is itself made into a reaffirmation of the poet's commitment, again by means of hyperbole ('ten thousand miles'). These hyperbolic expressions in the poem get their effect from the simple way in which they are said, extravagant ideas being expressed in homely language. The overall effect of the poem is of a flow of pure feeling, but feeling under control.

In its personal declaration of emotional attachment the poem is unlike most eighteenth-century poetry: we do not find such declarations in the poetry of Pope, or Gray , or Johnson. This contrast stems from differences in tradition and audience. The southern poets were writing for a polite metropolitan audience, for whom poetry was public statement rather than private feeling; while the writer of this poem was not only a regional poet, but also a popular one, writing about and for ordinary country people of Scotland. While the English poets were part of a political and cultural elite; the poet of this poem was a rebel against the conventional pieties of his time, and his poetry makes more than one tilt at the Scottish Establishment. It is true that he was lionised for a time by polite Edinburgh society, but his poetry is not metropolitan, and draws its strength from everyday Scottish speech. The strength of the poem lies in its rootedness in Scottish rural life and in colloquial Scots speech.

The poet seems to be trying to reconcile two traditions, that of the native folk-song and that of the polite taste. The sprinkling of Scotch in it gives it an air of rustic naivete. The poet is successful in achieving a perfect consonance of words and music. The poem is a triumph of assimilation. The poet artistically raises folksong to perfection. It is unsurpassed as a simple, moving, and intense statement of undying love.

The repetition in the first line is inspired:

O, my love's like a red, red rose.

The simile is itself a commonplace but the poet transforms it by the repetition of 'red', so intensifying the effect and requiring us to look again at a rose and savour the depth of feeling which the image renders. The poem derives its effect from comparisons of telling simplicity, for instance the rose and the sweetly played melody.

In the imagery of the third stanza, the elemental terms movingly convey the original and eternal nature of the love:

Till a' the seas gang dry, my dear,
And the rocks melt wi' the sun!
O I will luve thee still, my dear,
While the sands o' life shall run.

The line of connotation—'*seas... rocks... sands o' life*', with the last of these evoking the sands of time in the hourglass—is brilliantly managed, conveying the notion that his love stands comparison with original elements but is doubly intense because he is mortal and timebound. This is mortal man's statement of eternal love.

In the final stanza he takes leave of his beloved, but he reaffirms the undying nature of his love, this time in terms of distance as well as duration—spatial and temporal dimensions; we may detect in this poem that swagger and tender protectiveness so characteristic of the male in love. It is so because it is recognizably an individual's response—deep and genuine—that it has such universal significance.

As a poem it is riotously metaphorical:

O my love is like a red, red rose
That's newly sprung in June:
My love is like the melodie
That's sweetly play'd in tune.

To the modern reader such ecstatic language is unsurprising, but it is certainly ludicrous and absurd. Untamed emotion is registered from the first line, with the repetition of *red*, a seeming tautology of a kind that would not be found in literary song anywhere else. The comparison of human emotion to vegetable and even abstract, inanimate (a tune) is also an exuberance (of 'pathetic fallacy'). From the notion of harmony with nature and song, the poem moves, in a sense, to a disharmony where nature is superseded by the potency of the speaker's love, which he pledges:

Till a' the seas gang dry, my dear,
And the rocks melt wi' the sun.

The rather elaborate musical tone tend, arguably, to tidy up the jangling, somewhat overwrought emotion of the poem.

Example 51

Some say the world will end in fire,
Some say in ice.
From what I've tasted of desire
I hold with those who favor fire.

But if it had to perish twice,
I think I know enough of hate
To say that for destruction ice
Is also great
And would suffice.

(Fire and Ice: Robert Frost)

Substance: The speaker considers the age-old question of whether the world will end in fire or in ice. This is similar to another age-old question: whether it would be preferable to freeze to death or burn to death. The speaker determines that either option would achieve its purpose sufficiently well.

Critical Note: An extremely compact little lyric, "Fire and Ice" combines humour, fury, detachment and forthrightness. Not a syllable is wasted. The aim is aphorism. But for Frost the truth remains ambiguous and the question goes unanswered; to settle for aphorism would be to over-simplify.

The poem is characterized by the contrast between the simple, clipped precision of its vocabulary and the vague gravity of its subject.

The language is simple, but the devastating, soaring anti-climax of the final two lines is lost.

It is one thing to pull off an offhand remark about the end of days; it is another to make it poetry. Frost masterfully accomplishes both in a single composition.

"Fire and Ice" follows an invented form, irregularly interweaving three rhymes and two line lengths into a poem of nine lines. Each line ends either with an *-ire*, *-ice*, or *-ate* rhyme. Each line contains either four or eight syllables. Each line can be read naturally as iambic, although this is not strictly necessary for several lines. Frost employs strong enjoinment in line 7 to great effect.

Example 52

The Brain—is wider than the Sky—
For—put them side by side—
The one the other will contain
With ease—and You—beside—

The Brain is deeper than the sea—
For—hold them—Blue to Blue—
The one the other will absorb—
As Sponges—Buckets—do—

The Brain is just the weight of God—
For—Heft them—Pound for Pound—
And they will differ—if they do—
As Syllable from Sound—

(Emily Dickinson)

Substance: The speaker declares that the brain is wider than the sky, for if they are held side by side, the brain will absorb the sky "With ease—and You—beside." She says that the brain is deeper than the sea, for if they are held "Blue to Blue," the brain will absorb the sea as sponges and buckets absorb water. The brain, the speaker insists, is the "weight of God"—for if they are hefted "Pound for Pound," the brain's weight will differ from the weight of God only in the way that syllable differs from sound.

Critical Note: One of Dickinson's famous poems, "The Brain—is wider than the Sky—" is in many ways also one of her easiest to understand. The poem's theme is the complicated relationship between the mind and the outer world. Using the homiletic mode that characterizes much of her early poetry—"the brain is wider than the sky" is as homiletic a statement as "success is counted sweetest by those who ne'er succeed"—Dickinson testifies to the mind's capacity to absorb, interpret, and subsume perception and experience. The brain is wider than the sky despite the sky's awesome size because the brain is able to incorporate the universe into itself, and thereby even to absorb the ocean. The source of this capacity, in this poem, is God. In an astonishing comparison Dickinson likens the mind's capabilities to "the weight of God", differing from that weight only as syllable differs from sound.

This final stanza reads quite easily, but is actually rather complex—it is difficult to know precisely what Dickinson means. The brain differs from God, or from the weight of God, as syllable differs from sound; the difference between syllable and sound is that syllable is given human structure as part of a word, while sound is raw, unformed. Thus Dickinson seems to conceive of God here as an essence that takes its form from that of the human mind.

This poem employs all of Dickinson's familiar formal patterns: it consists of three four-line stanzas metered iambically, with tetrameter used for the first and third lines of each stanza and trimeter used for the second and fourth lines; it follows *abcb* rhyme schemes in each stanza; and uses the long dash as a rhythmic device designed to break up the flow of the meter and indicate short pauses.

Example 53

When I have fears that I may cease to be
Before my pen has glean'd my teeming brain,
Before high-piled books, in charact'ry
Hold like rich garners the full-ripen'd grain;

When I behold, upon the night's starr'd face,
Huge cloudy symbols of a .high romance,
And think that I may never live to trace
Their shadows, with the magic hand of chance;

And when I feel, fair Creature of an hour !
That I shall never look upon thee more,
Never have relish in the faery power
Of unreflecting love—then on the shore

Of the wide world I stand alone, and think
Till Love and Fame to nothingness do sink.

Substance: The poet is haunted by the overshadowing thought of premature death. When he fears he may die before writing his thoughts in books, or feels he may not see his beloved or enjoy the joys of carefree love, the poet experiences such acute loneliness that love and fame become absolutely meaningless to him.

Comment: The poet effectively uses the formal divisions inherent in the Shakespearean form—three alternately rhyming quatrains, concluding with a clinching couplet. Thus the rhyme scheme resorted to here is *abab cdcd efef gg*. This structure greatly helps the poet for developing his thought gradually. The first quatrain expresses the poet's fears that he may die before he has written all the poems he wants to. This fear is further expanded upon in the second quatrain with a more specific reference to the possibility he may never trace all the 'high romance' he sees symbolized in the heavens. In the third quatrain he addresses a woman whom he met in a brief encounter to consider that he may also be prevented from ever experiencing love. Finally, in the concluding couplet, the poet presents an image of himself standing alone on the shore of the wide world with all personal ambitions and concerns erased from his mind by the immensity of what he contemplates.

The poem clearly demonstrates Shakespeare's influence upon the poet. The poet follows the basic requirements of the form quite closely. The ideas developed accord with the divisions offered by the three quatrains. In fact, the repetition of the opening words of the three quatrains as *When* or *And when* both link and simultaneously emphasize the divisions of the quatrains. The manner in which the sense of the couplet spills back to the last quatrain effectively undermines the epigrammatic tendency of the regular Shakespearean sonnet form which is greatly challenged by the poet, perhaps considering it to have a potentially trivializing effect. In addition, the Shakespearean influence is felt in the subject matter. Shakespearean sonnets have as their theme the destructiveness of Time. On reading this sonnet, we are reminded of 'when I have seen by Time's fell hand defaced' and 'like as the waves make towards the pebbled shore'.

The poet uses numerous natural images to describe the process of composition. He compares his fertile *teeming* (in line 2) brain to a field of corn: the act of writing is reaping of harvest, something he fears he may not live to complete; his books are the barns in which the grain is stored. Abstract ideas are repeatedly transformed into concrete and highly pictorial images.

It has been suggested that this sonnet is actually more concerned with self-doubt, with the threat of failure as a poet, rather than with the threat of early death which the poet so prophetically describes. While the poet may create a sense of fulfilment through the natural imagery described earlier, he also creates a sense of disappointment, a sense of individual insignificance. The lightness suggested by the lines describing the *fair Creature of an hour* (in line 9) is succeeded by a sense of heaviness.

The apprehensive tone of the poem is counterbalanced by the image of a barn full of ripened grain (to which a volume of poems is compared) in:

Hold like rich garners the full ripened grain.

This picture of perfection of rich autumnal harvest, suspends even if temporarily, the creeping fear of premature winter. The second quatrain shifts the perspective from the earth to the star-lit sky, to the resplendent expanse of infinite space, the imaginative parallel giving a new dimension to his poetic ambition. The vast idea of poetry—evident in the poet's use of the word *Huge* rolling before him suggests the nature of his enterprise. In the context of the poem, the word *romance* seems to have a general rather than a specific referent.

The third quatrain continues the idea of evanescence, the phrase *fair creature of an hour* adding a touch of tenderness to the poignant memory. The thought he will never again have relish in the *faery power of unreflecting love* indicates an awareness of a new direction in the poet's life. The sharp longing for the unalloyed beauty of the magic world (indicated by the use of the word *faery*) is tempered with the realization that he has virtually outgrown it. The farewell to *unreflecting love* implies a recognition (if not acceptance) of thought-ridden and time-ridden existence.

The concluding lines:

then on the shore
Of the wide world I stand alone, and think
Till love and fame to nothingness do sink

extend the area of meaning. Hitherto he had been reflecting on mutability in his own immediate, personal context. The thought of the transcience of his own existence leads to the discovery of the nature of reality itself, to the realization that flux and inexorable laws. The implied metaphor of the wide ocean—'on the shore/Of the wide world'—vididly conveys this phenomenon of flux, and this vision reduces to insignificance the longings and motives (particularized in Love and Fame) of individual human beings.

Example: 54

Does the road wind uphill all the way?
Yes, to the very end.
Will the day's journey take the whole long day?
From morn to night, my friend.

But is there for the night a resting place?
A roof for when the slow, dark hours begin.
May not the darkness hide it from my face?
You cannot miss the inn.

Shall I meet other wayfarers at night?
Those who have gone before.
Then must I knock, or call when just in sight?
They will not keep you standing at the door.
Shall I find comfort, travel-sore and weak?
Of labour you shall find the sum.
Will there be beds for me and all who seek?

(*Uphill*: Christiana Georgina Rossetti)

Substance: This allegorical poem is written in the form of questions and answers. A pilgrim is asking questions about the journey he is making and the destination he expects to reach. As for the answers, we may suppose that these come from a divine source. But it would be better and more natural to suppose that they spring from the very depth of the pilgrim's soul.

Here the pilgrim is the representative of all mankind. The journey referred to in the poem is man's long and toilsome journey through life. The inn which the pilgrim will reach at night is the abode where the tired pilgrim will finally find rest after life's long and toilsome journey.

The traveller as he journeys along, asks eight questions in all about the way and the resting place at night. And, he receives satisfactory answers to all these questions from the depth of his soul.

Critical Note: This poem is a frank and delicate meditation on death which takes the form of a series of questions and answers by unnamed speakers. Life is presented as a long, tiring uphill journey towards the *dark hours* of death, at the end of which one reaches an inn where one may rest, and where there are *beds for all who seek*. A story with an inner meaning is sometimes called an allegory and in this poem the presentation of life as an uphill journey may be said to be allegorical. The *inn* at the end of the journey, or the state after death is found to be equally restful for *all who seek*.

In spite of its strongly religious note, the poem remains a fine lyric. This has been possible because there was really no contradiction between the poet's religious convictions and her artistic sensibilities. This little poem reads like a fine devotional song.

Simplicity and directness appear to be the chief merit of this little poem. The inner and outer meanings have been simply and naturally woven into one another. Every important word used in the poem automatically assumes a double meaning.

The poem consists of four stanzas, and each stanza contains four lines. The first line in each stanza rhymes with the third, while the second line rhymes with the fourth. In each stanza two questions are asked and answered. The entire poem comprises anthypophora.

Example 55:

Bright Star ! would I were steadfast as thou art—
Not in lone splendour hung aloft the night,
And watching, with eternal lids apart,
Like Nature's patient sleepless Eremite,

The moving waters at their priestlike task
Of pure ablution round earth's human shores,
Or gazing on the new soft fallen mask
Of snow upon the mountains and the moors:—

No—yet still steadfast, still unchangeable,
Pillow'd upon my fair Love's ripening breast
To feel for ever its soft fall and swell.
Awake for ever in a sweet unrest;

Still, still to hear her tender-taken breath,
And so live ever,—or else swoon to death.

(John Keats)

Substance: The poet addresses a star; there is an apostrophe at the very outset of the poem, '*Bright Star*!'. The poet expresses his longing to be as steadfast, but not on the same terms. The star is alone, it is sleepless and watches constantly and dispassionately the ebb and flow of the tides and the various seasons of the year. Instead, the poet wishes to be as steadfast and unchangeable while upon his love's breast.

Comment: The sonnet is constructed in Shakespearean form. It is constructed around the contrast of cold isolation and warm communion. The *fair Love* of the sestet may be assumed to be the beloved of the poet. The octave centres on the image of the bright star, which is traditionally considered to be an image of permanence. The poet develops the star as a symbol of perfection, of the steadfastness for which he longs. The bright star is fixed, remote, and passionless, far above the mortal world of flux.

The example of the star is reflected at the turn or volta with the word *No*. The poet instead turns to the warmer erotic image of himself pillowed on his fair love's breast. The poet moves to seek immortality within the human condition to find an enduring perfection rooted in the world of constant change. The phrase *sweet unrest* (in line12) alludes to the contradiction and uneasiness. It is possible that the poet recognizes what he longs for is an impossibility, and that leads him to the alternative: *or else swoon to death* (in line14) at the end of the sonnet. Death here may suggest sexual climax, but the more literal meaning remains and this perhaps suggests the only way in which permanence can be achieved within the mortal world.

The adequacy of the symbol of the 'Bright Star' is to be questioned, and it seems to be almost repudiated in the sestet. This results in such a fundamental opposition that we find it difficult to reconcile the sestet with the octave—the two are unrelated. We may regard the sestet as a lapse from the majestic serenity of the preceding lines. The star is a symbol associated with an external order beyond flux. This pure, cold, passionless, yet externally wakeful consciousness is contrasted with the ardent warm sensuousness of the mortal lover who wishes, almost pathetically, to perpetuate his sensation. But the sonnet does not merely present this irreconcilable contrast; it also encloses within its structure attitudes and experiences that both clash and coalesce. Although the attempt at integration does not fully succeed—the failure also adds to the complexity of the poem's texture the parallelism and the opposition give a certain unity and coherence to the apparently disjointed pattern.

The apostrophe in the opening line:

Bright Star! would I were steadfast as thou art

conveys the urgency of the poet's desire to attain to the stability and repose symbolized by the North Star. The word *steadfast* suggests, besides changelessness, and unwavering purposiveness. The associations carried by and attributed to the symbol are enriched and elaborated in the succeeding lines of the octave that also mark a partial modification of the poet's initial aspiration. The almost instantaneous retreat—'Not in lone splendour hung aloft the night'—shows that the symbol because of its inherent character, cannot project the desired state. But the attitude, despite the withdrawal, is one of the veneration (blended with wistfulness). The star stands above the process and combines stillness with animation, wakefulness with disinterestedness. The transcendental remoteness of the star is equally stressed, but it has a very different function. It watches perpetually, in a state of contemplative vigilance (suggesting both aloofness and concern), the state of flux and the cyclic movement, involving death and change, is given a positive, purificatory function. The emphasis is on the need for continual vitalization and cleansing of the earth's body (and the human world), and the removal of all that is dead and putrid is part of the vitalizing process. The purgational act is presented in the form of a necessary ritual carrying religious sanction; in this connection we may note the word *ablution* (in line 6).

The meditative repose of the star contrasts with the dynamism of the sea—*moving waters*, but the sea (representing Time) serves, as it were, as the earthly agent of the unmoved mover who is eternally awake to see that the purifying of the earth is ceaselessly, unfalteringly performed. Rejuvenation presupposes and includes destruction.

The idea of death is suggested by the word *ablution* and is also implicit in the evocation of a shroud in the phrase 'the soft fallen mask/Of snow'. The epithet *soft fallen* underlines the silent, gentle, mysterious workings of nature, and the immaculate whiteness of snow indicates the purity of what is essentially a religious ceremony. Time that continually destroys life also causes a renewal of life, and the motionless and yet *open-lidded* star witnessess steadfastly this eternal ritual. The poet no longer seeks complete identification with the star, but he presents vividly the lovely splendour of the sleepless eremite and the magnificence of nature's operation.

In the sestet, the focus is shifted from the grand impersonal setting to the poignant personal context. Unlike the remote, disinterested star, the poet seeks an active, ardent, sensuous participation in physical beauty, but he also longs for a poised, changeless state. The implied connexions and contrasts become gradually clearer, sharpening (and reflecting) the dilemma of the mortal lover. The earth is imagined as the human body—macrocosm for the microcosm. The mountains and moons delicately correspond to the *breast* of the poet's love. The epithet *ripening* suggests process; the poet, like the North Star, watches the world of process; but he is more involved, and his participation is intenser. The pressure of his involvement also directs the course of his desire and sways him, at least partly, from the role of a steadfast observer. The sense of continuity is implicit in *ripening*; but a physical object, after attaining its fullness, inevitably decays, and this paradox of growth and regeneration is inherent in process. The descent from the climatic moment is also marked in human response, and the intensity of ardour cannot be permanently retained. The poet's problem as a mortal lover is to prevent the progressive erosion of physical beauty and emotional ardour, to rescue and preserve the climactic moment and achieve a condition in which the stability of the star can be reconciled with the pulsating rhythm of desire. This is the overt meaning of the sestet, but there are correspondences with the octave at a deeper level, bringing in a tonal complexity.

The poet, absorbed in physical passion and pillowed upon his fair love's breast, also experiences death—the process of becoming that nourishes objects and assures their fullness of growth also leads inevitably to decay—but he does not share the detachment of the star that watches the mutable scene with equanimity. The moment of highest exhilaration is thus also a moment of uncertainty and despair. This complex sensibility explains the sudden transition in thought in the closing line:

> And so live ever—or else swoon to death.

His desire to remain simultaneously at two levels and experience the sensation both as an observer and as an ardent participant seems unattainable, and he seeks release from process by plunging into the void of unawareness. It is true that *or* indicates the possibility of an alternative choice, the poet regards death as an alternative. But there is also the attendant feeling or realization that in the temporal order here is no escape from mutability, that the state of intense passion cannot be made permanent. Death is sought both as a consummation and as an escape. The yearning expressed in the closing line shows an almost despairing withdrawal from the ideal postulated in the opening apostrophe. At the same time the concluding line contains a fond, assuring thought that through the dissolution of consciousness he may achieve a reconcilement of contraries—repose and ardour, detachment and earnest involvement, changelessness and the intensity of human passion.

Example 56

Down the close, darkening lanes they sang their way
To the siding-shed,
And lined the train with faces grimly gay.
Their breasts were stuck all white with wreath and spray
As men's are, dead.

Dull porters watched them, and a casual tramp
Stood staring hard,
Sorry to miss them from the upland camp.
Then, unmoved, signals nodded, and a lamp
Winked to the guard.
So secretly, like wrongs hushed-up, they went.
They were not ours:
We never heard to which front these were sent.
Nor there if they yet mock what women meant
Who gave them flowers.

Shall they return to beatings of great bells
In wild train loads?
A few, a few, too few for drums and yells,
May creep back, silent, to village wells
Up half-known roads.

(*The Send Off*: Wilfred Owen)

Substance: The poet describes the departure of a band of soldiers to the front. The soldiers came to the station from some upland camp. They reached the siding-shed of the station and took their seats in the carriage. Their faces looked grave with anxiety, but they tried to look cheerful. No one was present there to bid them farewell.Only a few porters and a vagabond stood there watching the scene.The signal was given and the train left the station.The silent departure of the soldiers closely resembled a crime that must be hushed up. Nobody knows to which front the soldiers were sent. Nobody knows if they are still alive.Very few of the soldiers will ever return from the war.The trains will not bring back a great number of happy and healthy men wild with joy. Only a few sad and weary men, broken in body and soul will return silently to their village homes. No public welcome will be given to these few wretched men.

Critical Note: Owen had no faith in the much-trumpeted 'glory' of war. And, in this poem, he mercilessly exposes the inhuman cruelty and indifference with which millions of people are slaughtered.

Through a few and suggestive expressions, Owen vividly portrays the helpless state of the soldiers who are being sent to the front as cannon fodder. The *dull porters* and the *unmoved* signals symbolize the cruel indifference with which men are sent to the front to be slaughtered like flocks of cattle. The words like *wrongs hushed-up* mercilessly expose the hypocrisy of those who sing the *glory* of war. The soldiers' breasts, *stuck all white* with flowers, inevitably suggest the picture of dead bodies covered with wreaths and flowers. The last few lines reveal the great tragedy of war which kill millions of people and renders thousand others crippled in body and mind.

Example 57

Tyger! Tyger! burning bright
In the forests of the night,
What immortal hand or eye,
Could frame thy fearful symmetry?

In what distant deeps or skies
Burnt the fire of thine eyes?
On what wings dare he aspire?
What the hand dare seize the fire?

And what shoulder, and what art,
Could twist the sinews of thy heart?
And when thy heart began to beat,
What dread hand? and what dread feet?

What the hammer? What the chain?
In what furnace was thy brain?
What the anvil? What dread grasp
Dare its deadly terrors clasp?

When the stars threw down their spears,
And water'd heaven with their tears?
Did he smile his work to see?
Did he who made the Lamb make thee?

Tyger! Tyger! burning bright
In the forests of the night,
What immortal hand or eye,
Dare frame thy fearful symmetry?

(*The Tyger*: William Blake)

Substance: The tiger in the poem represents natural power and God is seen as the maker of such agents of destruction who have, as the expression of their perfection or symmetry, a tremendous completeness of nature; the poem consists entirely of unanswered questions, but its central image sees God as the divine blacksmith, creating from the forge of primitive energy.

Comment: There is a martial cadence in the poem. The words advance like a people's army, directly and spontaneously. The words used here are common; they are far removed from specialized, arcane diction. We consider them as a challenge—they begin by shouting:

Tyger! Tyger! burning bright
In the forests of the night...

Throughout the poem all the verbs are active, and all the actions are of *seizing, clasping, twisting, grasping, burning*. The poet wants us to imagine not only the tiger's appearance but his substance and volume. To give him depth and weight, the poet talks about his heart, which burns in the tiger's inwards just as brightly as the tiger himself burns in the forests of the night. Throughout the poem, the poet mentions only certain parts of the tiger, in order to emphasize the fact that we only partially see it. First, the poet gives us a medium close-up; the tiger is in a forest. Then, suddenly, we are inside the tiger, in the heart, sinews, and brain.

The trochaic rhythm and the end-stopped lines have a hypnotic effect on us. The rhythm somewhat resembles a heart beat, but it also resembles a measured hammering. The spelling of *tyger* makes us realize that we are in the presence of an unusual and striking creature. Furthermore, the slant of the *y* emphasizes the question that rises in our mind as to *why* (pun on *y*) has God created such a ferocious creature as the tiger. In fact, every sentence in the poem exists as a question. The wonderful thing about the poem is that through the form of questions, the tiger is both revealed and not revealed. He shines forth, and yet his mystery is preserved. This is because it is the mystery itself that shines forth, the unnameability that is named.

The tiger is mysterious, but this mystery has weight and substance, at the heart of the uncertainty and awe, the questions contain a residue of materiality; out of this residue, the tiger constructs a body. The questions help to create the tiger's body. The questions, in fact, are the substance of the poem.

The six stanzas of four lines each are in rhyming couplets, with fine *i* sounds and an insistent rhythmic beat, the kind of pounding rhythm which the poet sees as the 'framing' accompanying the tiger; it also conveys the movement of the tiger.

The symbol of strength, of beauty and of destruction is enclosed in a symmetry of form, with the opening stanza having the word *Could*—the ability of the divine creator to fashion such a beast—which in the closing stanza becomes *Dare*—a mixture of wonder and terror at the achievement of such power which touches on religious awe. The abbreviated, staccato phrases of the third and fourth stanzas seem to reflect the savage movements of what is savage, but the accompanying descriptions are vivid in both their sound and sense effects. In the repetition of the opening stanza at the end the poem is perhaps refusing to package, nail down, or conclude. It is because of this that the creature remains a never-ending mystery.

The poem is ruled by symmetry: symmetry between stanzas, between lines, and even within lines. Despite this, there is lack of symmetry between the opening and closing stanzas, where a single word—*Could* (in the opening stanza) is changed to *Dare* (in the closing stanza). The tiger, like all other beasts and like man himself, has been *framed*—in the sense of made—by God, even though the poem refuses to name the answer to the question. The tiger has been perfectly formed—*symmetry*. The fires with which the tiger burns is forever hidden in the 'forests of the night'—its stripes blending perfectly with its jungle backdrop. At the same time the fires of the creative soul, burning with the desire to *frame*—create—an image. This image, the poem appears to tell us, cannot in the end fully he made. Paradoxically at the same time, the very act of naming the impossibility of capturing the tiger actually captures it; so that in the poem we do indeed, despite everything, 'see' the tiger. We hear it too. The dull threatening stamp of the lines, the repetition of *dread*, are precisely incarnations of the tiger's walk out from the jungle to meet us.

The crux of the poem occurs in the fifth stanza:

> When the stars threw down their spears
> And water'd heaven with their tears

We wonder as to whether they are 'throwing down their spears' in the sense of attempting to ambush their mighty earth-bound opponent, or are they 'throwing down their spears' in the sense we might use today of 'throwing in the towel', abandoning all hope of divine, angelic supremacy in the face of a power which is nonetheless far more mighty than they. We set to wondering as to who really is in charge here—the stars or the tiger.

We might finally ask whether the tiger is a natural or an unnatural beast. He is natural, for tigers are real, they do exist. But here the tiger is unreal too, as he is a *made* beast. He is made in a quite specific way, made with hammer, chain and anvil, with the help of furnace. In other words, the tiger is made with all the apparatus of human making. We may thus be led to see in the tiger a figure for a monster—a monster constructed from bits and pieces, an emblem for the industrial revolution.

In the poem the strength and the terrifying beauty of the animal are gradually transferred to the description of its creation. Despite this we never for a single moment lose awareness of the animal. In the course of the poem there is a shift in perspective away from the animal and towards the mystery of its creator.

Example 58

Little Lamb, who made thee?
Dost thou know who made thee?
Gave thee life, and bid thee feed,
By the stream and O'er the mead;
Game thee clothing of delight,
Softest clothing, woolly, bright;
Gave thee such a tender voice,
Making all the vales rejoice?

Little Lamb, who made thee?
Dost thou know who made thee?

Little Lamb, I'll tell thee,
Little Lamb, I'll tell thee:

He is called by the name,
For He calls Himself a Lamb,
He is meek, and He is mild;
He became a little child.
I a child, and thou a Lamb,
We are called by His name.

Little Lamb, God bless thee!
Little Lamb, God bless thee!

(*The Lamb*: William Blake)

Substance: The child who is supposed to be speaking to the lamb gives a brief description of the little creature as he sees it. The lamb has been blessed with life and with the capacity to feed by the stream and over the meadow. It has been endowed with bright and soft wool which serves as its clothing. It has a tender voice which fills the valley with joy. Later, there is an identification of the lamb, Christ, and the child: the three entities seem to merge. Christ has another name, that is, Lamb, because Christ is meek and mild like a lamb. Christ was also a child, when he first appeared on this earth as the Son of God. The child in the poem speaks to the lamb, as if the lamb were another child and could respond to what is being said. The child shows his deep joy in the company of the lamb who is just like him, meek and mild. The poem conveys the very spirit of childhood—the purity, the innocence, the tenderness of childhood, and the affection that a child feels for little creatures. A religious note is introduced in the poem because of the image of Christ as a child.

Comment: The poet invites us to dwell upon the image of the lamb. It would appear that this is not the final purpose of the poem, which is rather to invite us to use this image of asking questions to about the whole of creation. The insistent question is, 'who made thee?' Though this might well seem a question most appropriately asked of young children, we should be in no doubt that the poet intends it also as a question he means to address to all the people, and especially as a reminder to those sunk in the travails of war or industrial labour that there remains a more innocent world. A child talking with the lamb obviously symbolizes love; it projects the kinship of man and nature in a state of innocence. The poem is written as the questioning song of a child, but clearly derives from the perpetual questions we human beings ask ourselves about our origins, from whence creation and all living things come. The lamb is to be equated with Jesus.

The first stanza is completely rural in emphasis, the second strongly spiritual, with the linking of the lamb in nature and in God. The use of the refrain makes the poem even more of a song. The vowel sounds have the softness and repetition both of bleating of the lamb and of the child lisping the song.

The opening stanza is in the form of a question and the closing stanza is in the shape of an answer which reveals the child's certainty in his faith and his innocent acceptance of all his teachings. The repetition of fact and description, and the hymn-like quality is finely sustained all through the poem. The fact that the child answers for the lamb, which exists in its own inarticulate completeness, gives the poem a moving, tremulous quality.

We may note how the repetition within the lines contributes to the music of the verse—*Clothing... Clothing...called...calls*. It is part of the running alliteration—*voice... vales* and *meek ... mild* (The two words most associated with Jesus and the Virgin Mary, as well the lamb and the child).

The first stanza contains a number of natural pictures so as to build up the lamb's habitat; but the emphasis is on the characteristics and qualities of the innocent creature. The second stanza states that the maker of the lamb is himself called a lamb. This bears reference to Christ, who because of his qualities of gentleness and meekness, is called the Lamb. Gentleness, meekness, and mildness are the basic qualities of a child. The lamb, the child, and Christ are identified in the poem. Christ is known as the lamb. Christ loved children for their innocence—'of such is the kingdom of God'. Christ was an incarnation of love and tenderness. Christ had the qualities of meekness and mildness which both a lamb and a child possess.

The poem is written as the questioning song of a child. The child who is supposed to be speaking to the lamb gives a brief description of the little lamb as he sees it. The lamb has been blessed with life and with the capacity to feed by the stream and over meadow. The little creature has been endowed with bright and soft wool which serves as its clothing. It has a tender voice which fills the valley with joy. There is an identification of the lamb, Christ, and the child. Christ has another name, that is, Lamb, because Christ is meek and mild like a lamb. Christ was also a child when he first appeared on this earth as the Son of God.

The structure of each stanza consists of a theme (in the first two lines), its exposition (in the six lines following), and finally a coda (in the concluding two lines). Technically it is a triumph of form. The first verse is completely rural in emphasis, the second strongly spiritual, with the linking of the lamb in nature and in God.

In the poem the poet appears to write of an orthodox Christian God, who as creator made the lamb, is also Jesus, who as Lamb of God was sacrificed to save mankind from sin. It is because of this creator 'calls himself a lamb.'

At the outset, the poem seems childish. In the first stanza questions are posed and the second stanza contains the answers to the questions. The use of refrain creates a song-like effect. The vowel sounds have the softness and repetition both of the lamb and of the child lisping the song. The opening verse is in the form of a question and the closing is in the shape of an answer which reveals the child's certainty in his faith and his innocent acceptance of all its teachings. The repetition of fact and description reflects the simplicity of the conception, and the hymn-like quality is finely sustained. The fact that the child answers for the lamb, which exists in its own inarticulate completeness, gives the poem a moving, tremulous quality.

Major part of the poem is made up of monosyllabic words. The images used to describe the clothing of the lamb—*softest clothing, ...woolly, bright*—is sensuous. *Softest* is a tactile image as much as *woolly* which is followed by a visual image—*bright*. Reference to the bleating of the lamb as *a tender voice* shifts to an auditory image.

The opening stanza contains a number of natural pictures—*stream* and *mead*—to build up the habitat of the lamb. It also refers to the source of sustainance, water of the stream and grass of the meadow—food and water. There is a faint echo of Psalm 23:

> The Lord is my shepherd, I shall not want. He maketh me to lie down in green *pastures*: he leadeth beside still *waters*.

The repetition (and alliteration) '*clothing*' ... *clothing...called...calls*' contributes to the music of the verse. It forms a part of the running alliteration '*voice* ... *vales*; This alliterative usage is continued in the line:

He is meek, and He is mild—

the two words are most associated with Jesus Christ, as well as the Virgin Mary—*meek...mild,*Along with this there is a conspicuous feature evident in the poem, where the conjunction *and* connect two items, as in the following lines:

Gave thee life, *and* bid thee feed
By the stream *and* o'er the mead
... ...
He is meek, *and* He is mild
... ...
I a child, *and* thou a lamb.

Another noticeable feature in the poem is the abundunt use *l* sound all through the poem which is present in words like: Litt*l*e *L*amb... *l*ife...c*l*othing...de*l*ihgt...woo*lly*... a*ll*...va*l*es...I'*ll*...ca*ll*s...ca*ll*ed...chi*l*d...b*l*ess'. The repetition of liquid *l* sound conveys the flowing of the stream.

The narrator of the poem asks us to relate the lamb's image as the most innocent of God's creatures to the image of his maker, the 'Lamb of God'. Although the poet invites us to dwell upon the image of the lamb, it would appear that this is not the final purpose of the poem, which is rather to invite us to 'use' this image as a means of asking questions about the whole of creation. This intention is what leads the poet to pose the insistent question:

'who made thee?'

The child-like qualities of this poem lie particularly in the little boy's unselfconscious and serious address to the lamb as to another child and in his delight in repetition.

In the line:

He is meek, and He is mild

—the child is echoing his early Christian instruction. In this case it echoes Charles Wesley's hymn:

'Gentle Jesus, meek and mild'.

Again the line:

We are called by His name

is reminiscient of *Jeremiah* (xiv. I):

Thou, O Lord, art in the midst of us, and we are
called by thy name; leave us not.

The poem begins with the question, "Little Lamb, who made thee?" The speaker, a child, asks the lamb about its origins: how it came into being, how it acquired its particular manner of feeding, its "clothing" of wool, its "tender voice." In the next stanza, the speaker attempts a riddling answer to his own question: the lamb was made by one who "calls himself a Lamb," one who resembles in his gentleness both the child and the lamb. The poem ends with the child bestowing a blessing on the lamb.

The poem is a child's song, in the form of a question and answer. The first stanza is rural and descriptive, while the second focuses on abstract spiritual matters and contains explanation and analogy. The child's question is both naive and profound. The question ("who made thee?") is a simple one, and yet the child is also tapping into the deep and timeless questions that all human beings have, about their own origins and the nature of creation. The poem's apostrophic form contributes to the effect of naiveté, since the situation of a child talking to an animal is a believable one, and not simply a literary contrivance. Yet by answering his own question, the child converts it into a rhetorical one, thus counteracting the initial spontaneous sense of the poem. The answer is presented as a puzzle or riddle, and even though it is an easy one—child's play—this also contributes to an underlying sense of ironic knowingness or artifice in the poem. The child's answer, however, reveals his confidence in his simple Christian faith and his innocent acceptance of its teachings.

The lamb, of course, symbolizes Jesus. The traditional image of Jesus as a lamb underscores the Christian values of gentleness, meekness, and peace. The image of the child is also associated with Jesus: in the Gospel, Jesus displays a special solicitude for children, and the Bible's depiction of Jesus in his childhood shows him as guileless and vulnerable. These are also the characteristics from which the child-speaker approaches the ideas of nature and of God. This poem, like many of the *Songs of Innocence*, accepts what Blake saw as the more positive aspects of conventional Christian belief. But it does not provide a completely adequate doctrine, because it fails to account for the presence of suffering and evil in the world. The pendant (or companion) poem to this one, found in the *Songs of Experience*, is "The Tyger"; taken together, the two poems give a perspective on religion that includes the good and clear as well as the terrible and inscrutable. These poems complement each other to produce a fuller account than either offers independently. They offer a good instance of how Blake himself stands somewhere outside the perspectives of innocence and experience he projects.

"The Lamb" has two stanzas, each containing five rhymed couplets. Repetition in the first and last couplet of each stanza makes these lines into a refrain, and helps to give the poem its song-like quality. The flowing *l*'s and soft vowel sounds contribute to this effect, and also suggest the bleating of a lamb or the lisping character of a child's chant.

Example 59

When I do count the clock that tells the time,
And see the brave day sunk in hideous night;
When I behold the violet past prime,
And sable curls all silver'd o'er with white;
When lofty trees I see barren of leaves
Which erst from heat did canopy the herd,
And summer's green all girded up in sheaves
Borne on the bier with white and bristly beard,
Then of thy beauty do I question make,
That thou among the wastes of time must go,
Since sweets and beauties do themselves forsake
And die as fast as they see others grow;
And nothing 'gainst Time's scythe can make defence
Save breed, to brave him when he takes thee hence.

(William Shakespeare)

Substance: The sonnet speaks of the sterility of bachelorhood and recommends marriage and children as a means of immortality. Additionally, the sonnet gathers the idea of using procreation to defeat time. The sonnet establishes a parallel way of measuring the passage of time, the passage of nature, and the passage of youth through life-decay. The poet then indicates the progression of the seasons, from *summer's green* to *the bier with white and bristly beard*, which is an image of snow and winter. The poet hopes that the young man will finally realize that time stops for no one; the only way the young man will ensure the survival of his beauty is through offspring. This final point, that having children is the single means of gaining immortality, is most strongly stated in the sonnet's concluding couplet. In these lines, *Time's scythe*, a traditional image of death, is unstoppable *Save breed*, meaning except by having children. The fast pace of time, or the loss of it, remains a major theme of the sonnet.

Critical Note: This sonnet is notable for its musical quality, largely to the effective use of alliteration and attractive vowel runs, which are of unusual merit. This sonnet, is notable for its musical quality. We note the striking concluding lines and how they convey the sense of sorrow and poignancy at the thought that youth and beauty must be cut down by time's scythe. The contrast of *brave day* with *hideous night* is particularly good. This is a Shakespearean sonnet and, as one critic has pointed out, the sonnets beginning with "*When*" are especially noteworthy because the structure of such sonnets is periodic (consisting of a series of repeated stages), making for tightness of organization, logical progression, and avoidance of a tacked-on couplet, while admirably evoking seasonal change.

Example 60

I leant upon a coppice gate
When frost was spectre-gray,
And winter's dregs made desolate
The weakening eye of day.
The tangled bine-stems scored the sky
Like strings of broken lyres,
And all mankind that haunted nigh
Had sought their household fires.

The land's sharp features seemed to be
The Century's corpse outleant,
His crypt the cloudy canopy,
The wind his death-lament.
The ancient pulse of germ and birth
Was shrunken hard and dry,
And every spirit upon earth
Seemed fervourless as I.

At once a voice arose among
The black twigs overhead
In a full-hearted evensong
Of joy illimited;
An aged thrush, frail, gaunt, and small,
In a blast-beruffled plume,
Had chosen thus to fling his soul
Upon the growing gloom.

So little cause for carolings
Of such ecstatic sound
Was written on terrestrial things
Afar or nigh around
That I could think there trembled through
His happy good-night air
Some blessed Hope whereof he knew
And I was unaware.

(*The Darkling Thrush*: Thomas Hardy)

Substance: On a certain day of winter when evening was approaching the poet saw all his neighbours had already returned to their respective homes to enjoy the comfort of their homefires. The poem describes the poet's feelings on viewing the landscape in winter, and his chance hearing of the courageous song of a thrush. The scene around was depressing and desolate; nature appeared to have stopped germinating. Yet a lone thrush burst into such joyful songs amidst such a desolate surrounding. The poet thought the little thrush had come to know of some hopeful future of which the poet was ignorant. This leads the poet to speculate in general terms whether there may be some 'Hope' of which he was 'unaware'.

Comment: The poet describes a cold and dreary afternoon of winter with whose grim features his own gloomy mood is in complete agreement.

The opening stanza begins by showing the poet alone in a desolate landscape:

> I leant upon a coppice gate.

The state of the mind of the poet is shown indirectly by the way in which the landscape is described. A variety of images combine to produce an idea of intense desolation and disintegration—*spectre-gray* frost, the sun as *the weakening eye of day*, the dead foliage as *winter dregs* and the powerful image of the bine-stems as *broken lyres*. The word *broken* itself emphasizes the sense of things petering out and disintegrating. The dimming of the sun and the sense of utter loneliness projects the poet's experience. He notices his neighbours' desire to sit by the cosy fireside at home. *All mankind*, excluding the poet, is missing from the scene. *Spectre-gray* and *haunted* might seem to suggest, additionally, some eerie quality to the landscape.

The grim landscape in the second stanza develops the idea of death and emptiness. The gaunt landscape is seen as a symbol of the dead century—'The Century's corpse outleant'. The alliteration of the lines:

> The Century's *c*orpse outleant,
> His *c*rypt the *c*loudy *c*anopy

emphasizes the starkness and harshness of the scene by the sound rhythm produced. The next comparison:

> The wind his death lament

develops still further the metaphors of bleakness and emptiness. The bleak landscape reminds the poet of the death of the century lying under a cloudy covering with the wind mourning the passing of an age. It seems that the principle of life is numbed which affects the poet's mind with intense apathy. The series of images reaches its culmination in the highly vivid and powerful lines:

The ancient pulse of germ and birth
Was shrunken hard and dry

which suggests the sterility of all life, with its ancient beginnings. The verse falls away into flat statement:

Seemed fervourless as I

which evokes the idea of complete despair.

At this point, the beginning of the third stanza introduces the voice of the thrush and thus the preceding stanzas depicting emptiness and despair are balanced by the following stanzas, which consider the possibility of Hope. The poet is startled on hearing a frail and small thrush bursting into an extremely joyous song.

This leads the poet to conclude in the final stanza that the bird is aware of a hopeful future not a trace he could find in the enveloping gloom. The final stanza shows the poet in a state of doubt. He is unable to see any cause for the apparent hope suggested by the bird's song:

So little cause for carolings
Of such ecstatic sound
Was written on terrestrial things.

The poet wonders if, perhaps, the bird possesses knowledge of some 'blessed Hope' of which he himself is unaware. His conclusion is hesitant and tentative in the extreme—'I *could* think there *trembled* through'—but at least admist the possibility of such hope.

The poem is in four regular, carefully structured stanzas of eight lines, where iambic tetrameters and iambic trimeters occur alternately. The poem is carefully balanced between reason and emotion. There is no overstatement of the case and the simplicity of the diction and rhythm help to emphasize the truth and intensity of the experience for the poet.

The poem is capable of touching on a universal subject though it contains a personal experience; it has been so enlarged by the poet's vision. The vision is fired with his passion, and shaped with his artistry, so as to have relevance and significance for mankind in general. Despite the poem being centred round an absolutely personal experience of the poet the poem is successful in universalizing the situation.

Gravity of tone pervades the entire poem. The intention behind writing this poem is to convey to other feeling hearts a mood of sadness that the poet personally experienced at the passing away of a century.

The poem consists of four eight-lined stanzas with alternately rhyming couplets, having the rhyme-scheme *ababcdcd*. Though the lines are in iambic tetrameters alternating with iambic trimeters, there are ample variations in the metrical pattern. In line 19 there occurs a delightful modulation of the basic rhythm:

In a full-hearted even song

This variation in the rhythm gives the reader a relief from the mechanical rhythmic pattern.

Further on, the immaculate description of the thrush by three perfectly chosen epithets is brought home by a shift in the usual accentuation:

An aged thrush, frail, gaunt and small

The steady beat of the rhythm is capable of communicating a gloomy mood, associated not only with the passing of an age but also the passing of a century.

The diction is remarkable in the sense that it is both fresh and apt. This is particularly evident in such words and expressions as: *spectre-gray, desolate, outleant, ancient pulse of germ and birth, fervourless, bleak, full-hearted, evensong, illimited, frail, gaunt, blast-beruffled, to fling his soul, growing gloom, terrestrial, trembled*, and *good-night air*. The most striking feature of the poem is its use of nouns, adjectives, and verbs in the entire poem.

The imagery resorted to is descriptive: *coppice gate, the weakening* eye of day, tangled *bine-stems, land's sharp features.* The descriptions are essentially of a sensuous nature—visual as in *cloudy canopy*; auditory as in *death-lament*, tactile as in *shrunken hard and dry*; thermal as in *household fires*; colour as in *spectre-gray*; kinesthetic as in *trembled*. The language used in the poem is basically figurative—simile is used in the expression *like strings of lyres*; alliterative as in *crypt the cloudy canopy.* The images appeal both to our emotion and intellect. Certain images are worth concentrating on: the dim sun in winter is likened to the 'weakening eye of day'; the tangled bine-stems are like the 'strings of broken lyres', the ancient principle of germination and birth seems to have 'shrunken hard and dry', the thrush is 'frail, gaunt, and small'; and its plume is 'blast-beruffled', the century is likened to a 'corpse' lying in a prone position underneath the 'cloudy canopy', while the wind sings a 'death-lament'. All these gloomy images far out-weigh the images of the bird's song expressive of 'joy illimited' or its 'good-night air' expressive of some 'blessed hope'.

There is assonance of long vowels in-b*i*ne, sk*y*, and l*y*res; and consonance in phrases like—*c*loudy *c*anopy, *b*last-*b*eruffled, *g*rowing *g*loom, occurrence of semi-vowels in the phrase— '*w*eakening e*y*e of da*y*', and use of liquid consonants in the lines:

Had chose*n* thus to fling his sou*l*
Upo*n* the growing gloo*m*.

Such effects aptly create a sense of musicality in the poem.

The poem expresses a relentless realism, and conveys a 'growing gloom' against the background of which the optimistic message brought in by the song of the thrush carries poor comfort and consolation. In a nutshell, the poem is successful in conveying a melancholy mood and sad reflections which arise in the minds of many at the end of a year, particularly at the silent and almost oblivious passage of an entire century.

Example 61

My mistress' eyes are nothing like the sun,
Coral is far more red than her lips' red;
If snow be white, why then her breasts are dun,
If hairs be wires, black wires grow on her head,
I have seen roses daimask'd, red and white,
But no such roses see I in her cheeks;
And in some perfumes is there more delight
Than in the breath that from my mistress reeks.
I love to hear her speak, yet well I know
That music hath a far more pleasing sound;
I grant I never saw a goddess go:
My mistress, when she walks, treads on the ground.
    And yet, by heaven, I think my love as rare
    As any she belied by false compare.

(William Shakespeare)

Substance: The poet debunks the beauty of his beloved by comparing her with certain excellent objects around us. Beloved of the poet looks less beautiful than those objects. Sunlight, coral, snow, rose, fragrance and music are more pleasing and attractive than her eyes, lips, breasts, cheeks, breath, and voice. Despite this, the beloved seems equal to any woman of rare beauty praised extravagantly with false comparisons.

Comment: This sonnet is a description of his mistress in the conventional style of Elizabethan idealism. Such passages of highly-wrought descriptions are to be found in Elizabethans like Spenser, Sidney, and Lodge. The sonnet is essentially a skit on the unreal comparisons, the unconvincing deifications of their mistress regular with the poets of the sonnet sequences. The poet attempts freshness through denying the usual images. Sonnets generally eulogize the features of the beloved, but strangely enough this sonnet denies the attractive features in the beloved.

If we look at the sonnet intently we will notice that this sonnet is not a denigration of the poet's mistress, or even an admission that she had not the conventional beauties and graces. It appears to be a satirical repudiation of false comparisons current in the poetry of the times—'complements of proud (but false) compare'. The poet is affirming by implication the physical qualities of the woman.

In the first quatrain the poet is seemingly critical of his beloved's beauty—sunshine, coral, and snow appear far more attractive. The poet is not saying that his mistress' breasts are 'dun', but denying that the colour of snow would be appropriate to her breasts, and, perhaps, by implication, to those of any desirable woman. The poet says that his mistress' eyes are not as bright as the sun, and her lips are less red than coral. The hair that grow on her head are like black wires, and not like golden wires that are generally held in admiration.

In the second quatrain the poet shows that the cheeks of his beloved are not conventionally red and white ('demask'd), so that they may be compared with red and white roses that the poet has seen. A variegation of hue in a woman's complexion was highly esteemed in Elizabethan court circles, where an even complexion would have been considered dull. In consonance with the whole drift of the sonnet the poet is saying, in effect, that he will not praise his mistress as bearing conventional colouring. The poet further adds that the scent of the breath of the woman that is being exhaled ('reek') from her mouth, is also not as pleasing ('delight') as the scent of some essences ('perfumes').

In the third quatrain the poet says that he loves to hear her speak though her speech is not as pleasing as the sound of music. The poet also admits ('grant') that whenever he has seen the lady walking, it had never come to his mind that he had been seeing a goddess—the lady could not be compared with a goddess, as the poet wished to. In other words, the poet felt that the lady fell short of being compared with a goddess. Rather, when she walks, the poet thinks that she is walking like any other woman who walks on the ground—and not in the heaven or over the ground like a goddess ('treads on the ground'). In short, the beloved's lacking in all these conventional feminine attractions has never come in the way of the poet's loving her.

In the conclusive couplet the poet asserts that his beloved is equal to any rare beauty whom other poets have praised highly by making exaggerated comparisons. The poet swears by heaven and thinks that his love for his beloved ('my love') is as rare and precious as any other true love ('As any'), and that she does not admit ('belied') of any comparison with any other lady, because such comparison will be false ('false compare'), or if she be compared with any other lady then that lady will be said to have false beauty:

> And yet, by heaven, I think my love as rare
> As any she belied with false compare.

The poet serves a two-fold purpose in writing this poem. On the one hand, he criticizes those who praise their beloveds so extravangantly as to make them unreal, and, on the other hand, teases his own beloved by stressing on her weak points, though at the end he wants to retrieve his position by equating her with a rare beauty.

The tone of the poem is satiric—it is apparent when directed to the poet's own mistress, and actual when directed to other contemporary poets who thought nothing of their beloveds to the skies.

The prevalent meter used in the sonnet is iambic pentameter with variations such as:

Coral is far more red than her lips' red

within the single line there are subtle variations with trochaic, pyrrhic, spondee feet. The variation appears to make the poet's point more emphatic. The steady beat of the iambic helps in heightening the point on a progressive basis. The rhyme scheme—*ababa cdcd efef gg*—three quatrains of alternately rhyming couplets and concluding with a couplet. The rhyme scheme conforms to the Shakespearean sonnet. All through the sonnet masculine rhyme has been used; it imbues the sonnet with a virility. The volta (or turn) towards the end of the sonnet is striking.

The style of the poem is lucid and forthright. The words used in the poem add a sharpness to the meaning. This is noticeable particularly in words such as: *dun*, *reeks*, *damask'd*, *belied*, and *treads.* The directness of expression gives a certain piquancy to the sense in such instances as: 'her breasts are dun', 'black wires grow on her head', 'My mistress, when she walks, treads on the ground', Ample references to colour—*red, white, dun, black*—is remarkable.

Imagery used in the poem is sufficiently rich. There are plenty of descriptive images—*mistress, coral, snow, roses, goddess*. Various kinds of sensuous images occur in the poem. Visual images found here are—*breasts, lips, eyes, hairs, cheeks.* There are a couple of auditory images—*speak, music, sound*; olfactory images—*roses, perfumes, breath, reeks.* There are also tactile images—*snow, lips, cheeks, hairs, wires*. Along with this the poet uses kinesthetic images like *go, walks, treads.* Finally, we find figurative images, such as similes in expressions like: 'My mistress' eyes are nothing like the sun', 'my love as rare as any she', and metaphor in 'but no roses see I in her cheeks'. These figures of speech heighten the aesthetic quality of the poem.

There is a great deal of musicality infused into the poem by means of consonance in words like spea*k*: musi*c*, hair*s*: wire*s*; assonance in words like *see*: ch*ee*ks; m*y*: *ey*es: *li*ke; alliteration in phrases like '*My mi*stress' eyes', '*w*hite, *w*hy'; 'a *g*oddess *g*o', mellifluousness is added by the use of long vowels—'That m*u*sic h*a*th a f*a*r m*o*re pl*ea*sing s*ou*nd' and 'As a*ny* *she* beli*e*d with false compare'. The repetition of the phrase 'My mistress' (in lines 1, 8 and 12) not only adds music to the poem but also emphasis; similar effect is created by the phrase 'coral is far more red than her lips' red'.

On the whole the poem is rich in its descriptive power. The satiric tone is evidently directed to contemporary sonneteers who exaggerated the beauty of their beloveds highly. There is a remarkable turn of thought at the end of the sonnet where, despite apparent slighting, the beloved is shown equal to 'any she' (meaning, any other beautiful woman).

This sonnet compares the speaker's lover to a number of other beauties—and never in the lover's favour. Her eyes are "nothing like the sun," her lips are less red than coral; compared to white snow, her breasts are dun-coloured, and her hairs are like black wires on her head. In the second quatrain, the speaker says he has seen roses separated by colour ("damasked") into red and white, but he sees no such roses in his mistress cheeks; and he says the breath that "reeks" from his mistress is less delightful than perfume. In the third quatrain, he admits that, though he loves her voice, music "hath a far more pleasing sound," and that, though he has never seen a goddess, his mistress—unlike goddesses—walks on the ground. In the couplet, however, the speaker declares that, "by heav'n," he thinks his love as rare and valuable "As any she belied with false compare"—that is, any love in which false comparisons were invoked to describe the loved one's beauty.

Critical Note: This sonnet, one of Shakespeare's most famous, plays an elaborate joke on the conventions of love poetry common to Shakespeare's day, and it is so well-conceived that the joke remains funny today. Most sonnet sequences in Elizabethan England were modeled after that of Petrarch. Petrarch's famous sonnet sequence was written as a series of love poems to an idealized and idolized mistress named Laura. In the sonnets, Petrarch praises her beauty, her worth, and her perfection using an extraordinary variety of metaphors based largely on natural beauties. In Shakespeare's day, these metaphors had already become cliche (as, indeed, they still are today), but they were still the accepted technique for writing love poetry. The result was that poems tended to make highly idealizing comparisons between nature and the poets' lover that were, if taken literally, completely ridiculous. My mistress' eyes are like the sun; her lips are red as coral; her cheeks are like roses, her breasts are white as snow, her voice is like music, she is a goddess. In many ways, Shakespeare's sonnets subvert and reverse the conventions of the Petrarchan love sequence: the idealizing love poems, for instance, are written not to a perfect woman but to an admittedly imperfect man, and the love poems to the dark lady are anything but idealizing ("My love is as a fever, longing still / For that which longer nurseth the disease" is hardly a Petrarchan conceit.) Sonnet 130 mocks the typical Petrarchan metaphors by presenting a speaker who seems to take them at face value, and somewhat bemusedly, decides to tell the truth. Your mistress' eyes are like the sun? That's strange—my mistress' eyes aren't at all like the sun. Your mistress' breath smells like perfume? My mistress' breath reeks compared to perfume. In the couplet, then, the speaker shows his full intent, which is to insist that love does not need these conceits in order to be real; and women do not need to look like flowers or the sun in order to be beautiful.

The rhetorical structure of Sonnet 130 is important to its effect. In the first quatrain, the speaker spends one line on each comparison between his mistress and something else (the sun, coral, snow, and wires)—the one positive thing in the whole poem—some part of his mistress is like. In the second and third quatrains, he expands the descriptions to occupy two lines each, so that roses/cheeks, perfume/breath, music/voice, and goddess/ mistress each receive a pair of unrhymed lines. This creates the effect of an expanding and developing argument, and neatly prevents the poem--which does, after all, rely on a single kind of joke for its first twelve lines--from becoming stagnant.

Example 62

To one who has been long in city pent,
'Tis very sweet to look into the fair
And open face of heaven ,—to breathe a prayer
Full in the smile of the blue firmament.
Who is more happy, when, with heart's content
Fatigued he sinks into some pleasant lair
Of wavy grass, and reads a debonair
And gentle tale of love and languishment?

Returning home at evening, with an ear
Catching the notes of Philomel,—an eye
Watching the sailing cloudlet's bright career
He mourns that the day soon has glided by:
E'en like the passage of an angel's tear
That falls through the clear ether silently.

(John Keats)

Substance: For a city-dweller, who has not been out in the countryside for a long time, it is an extremely pleasant experience to roam about the fields and meadows under a clear, bright sky. Having roamed the countryside for a long time he would feel tired. Then he may choose some pleasant nook and rest there for a while. He then could read some pleasant tale of love and languishment. Then towards evening when he returns home, he thinks of the pleasant memories of the day. And he laments that such a glorious day has come to its end so quickly.

Critical Note: This is one of the earliest poems of Keats. Yet one must say that it is a fine poem though not one of the best poems he wrote. Keats is essentially a poet of beauty—of sensuous beauty, beauty of form and colour, music and fragrance. He loves nature for her own sake. And this attitude towards nature is discernible even in this short poem of his early youth.

Here we see how the sights and sounds of Nature, the open countryside fill the London-bred poet with sensuous delights. 'The fair and open face of heaven' fills his heart with great joy. The simile of '*the blue firmament*' stirs up in him a longing *to breathe a prayer*. The *bed of wavy grass* and *gentle tale of love and languishment* make him perfectly happy. His ears are filled with *the sweet notes of Philomel*. His eyes feast upon the glorious beauty of *sailing cloudlets*, crimsoned with the rays of the setting sun. In this poem, as in many other poems of Keats, there is no attempt at philosophizing Nature. It only reveals a sweet sensuous experience, as the poet comes in contact with the sights and sounds of nature.

This poem is a Petrarchan sonnet divided into an octave and a sestet. The opening octave describes the poet's joy during a visit to the countryside. The concluding sestet conveys his emotions while returning to the city, a sadness mingled with the desire to continue to savour the beauties of nature and the tranquility it offers.

Example 63

I met a traveller from an antique land
Who said: Two vast and trunkless legs of stone
Stand in the desert... Near them, on the sand,
Half sunk, a shattered visage lies, whose frown,
And wrinkled lip, and sneer of cold command,
Tell that its sculptor well those passions read
Which yet survive, stamped on these lifeless things,
The hand that mocked them, and the heart that fed:
And on the pedestal these words appear:
'My name is Ozymandias, king of kings:
Look on my words, ye Mighty, and despair!'
Nothing beside remains. Round the decay
Of that colossal wreck, boundless and bare
The lone and level sands stretch far away.

(P. B. Shelley)

Substance: Technically the poem conforms to the sonnet form, but in its rhyme scheme—*ababacdcedefef*. The rhyme scheme conforms neither to a Shakespearean nor to a Miltonic sonnet. The poem, though beautiful, is so divergent from all accepted norms that it can hardly be styled a sonnet. No poet could ever dare to resort to rhymes such as *stone: frown* and *appear: despair*; they may at best be reckoned as near rhymes. In a nutshell, the poet has failed to churn out a successful sonnet. Despite its technical drawbacks, the theme of the sonnet is well established, that of the ravages of time, the favourite with Shakespeare in his sonnets. In the presentation of the theme of the ravages caused by the cruelty of time with detachment and poetic skill the poet has indeed come very near the great master. Had the poet not managed to wriggle out of the fetters of the sonnet form, he would never have been able to attain such magnificence for this poem. To make what he wants to say all the more convincing he maintains the detached tone throughout the poem.

Comment: Except the first ten words where the poet seems to imply that he will merely report and interpret, the entire poem is fashioned after a traveller's tale. The poet has deliberately employed this device because he fully knows that morals preached indirectly and through narration of events by supposed eyes. Witnesses can be much quicker to get home than plain and direct sermons; it sounds more convincing. The clear images at the beginning of the tale are meant to suggest the traveller's reliability and quick observation of relevant details. By supplanting the word *antique* in the opening line in place of *ancient* adds greater authenticity to the narration.

The abundance of sibilants in the narrator's utterance, especially in words like *sunk, shattered, visage, lies, whose, stone, sneer, its, sculptor, those, passions, survive, stamped, these, lifeless, things, pedestal, these, words, Ozymandias, kings, works, despair, beside, remains, colossal, boundless, sands* and *stretch* convey the utter desolation in the vast desert. The sibilants occurring in various positions—initially, medially, or terminally—does not in any way cause monotony. There are several instances of alliteration which not only add musicality to the poem but also seems to convey an echoing effect in the *vast desert, trunkless legs, cold command, boundless and bare, lone and level, sands stretch*.

In the poem the traveller relates how, in a vast and boundless desert he had seen the statue of King Ozymandias. Only its legs stand and its broken trunk lies half-buried in the sand. The inscription on the pedestal shows that Ozymandias thought himself mightier than God. The crux of the poem is in the inscription on the pedestal. It seems convincing because it seems to come from a reliable impartial traveller. In fact, the concluding quatrain puts forth two ideas which form a powerful and emphatic contrast to the idea expressed in the octave. The boastful lines of the inscription claims greatness and glory for Ozymandias. The boastful words are poignantly contrasted with the actual condition in which we find the statue at present. Juxtaposed against the broken statue of the great King Ozymandias is the vastness of the boundless desert which surrounds the ruins of the statue. This is further contrasted with the smallness of the "colossal" statue; the statue can stand no comparison with the vast desert. The sestet completes the poem through powerful contrasts as it presents the ideas of the vanity of human pomp and greatness, the boastfulness of man is nothing—his littleness is contrasted with the vastness of nature.

The most significant key to appreciating the poem resides in the verb 'to mock'. *To mock* most frequently means to treat an object, person, or idea with contempt or ridicule. It also means to imitate that object, usually for derision, or to produce an insincere or counterfeit version of the original object. Interstingly, a rather obscure meaning of the word *mock*, the origin of which is unknown, identifies the word with a stump or root of a tree, or refers to a large stick of wood, especially that turned at Christmas. Thus, the poet's play on the word *mock* makes the poem a pun-making room for a multiplicity of meaning. In fact, the poem utilizes puns to explore a variety of issues concerning the ravages of time and effacement of memory.

Ancient Egyptian culture was a civilization obsessed with death and personal survival, an obsession indicated by its foremost occupation—the construction of inscribed funerary monuments—pyramids, obelisks, stelae, and sarcophagi. It was a culture obsessed with time, and its fascination with the afterlife influenced all its earthly work and effort. These themes are prominent in the poem. It is simultaneously a poem concerned with poetic effort and the anxiety of whether that effort will be remembered.

Beginning with the first line, the narrating voice creates doubt as to the chronological time in which the poem is set, stating:

> I met a traveller from an antique land.

The word *antique* creates the first ambiguity in the poem. We are in doubt as to whether the traveller is a tourist living in the nineteenth century who merely refers to Egypt as the ancient world or is there some time warp in which the narrator meets with an actual inhabitant of antiquity. We are left a bit disconcerted as to the temporal location of the poem.

In the next two lines, we see the poet's adept and very oblique application of a mock as a stump of tree, when the strange visitor reports:

> Two vast and trunkless legs of stone
> Stand in the desert.

At the same time, the poet also introduces us to the multifaceted symbols and images he will employ to convey the erosive effects of time. First, time has 'amputated' this monument so that its representational value, a sculpture of a former ruler of this very same country, is seriously curtailed. Second, this sculpture is to be found in the desert, an arid and lifeless terrain, and as it is made of stone, it is also very much of the desert as well, its story composition reminding us that its physicality is inextricably linked to the same disintegrative processes that cause rocks to turn into silt. And finally, we are given additional details of this 'amputation' in a series of disturbing images:

> Near them on the sand,
> Half sunk a shattered visage lies, whose frown
> And wrinkled lip, and sneer of cold command.

Indeed, time has now grown violent, determined to annihilate any physical evidence that this person ever lived.

Most intersting is the poet's use of the word *visage* in reference to Ozymandias' face, a word derived from the Latin *visus*, meaning sight or appearance, and in English defined not only as the front part of the face, but an aspect of the person's true character and emotions. Through the multiple meanings of this word, the poet introduces the theme of a former leader whose monument has fallen into ruin and disgrace, one who was arrogant, mean-spirited, and tyrannical.

Finally, the poet uses one further meaning of the word *visage*, referring to something done merely for outward show, a falsehood of sorts. This indicates two important points—first, as the traveller tells us, the ancient sculptor did a brilliant job reading the ruler:

> Its sculptor well those passions read
> Which yet survive, stamped on these lifeless things,
> The hand that mocked them, and the heart that fed.

Thus, art remains the repository of truth; depite Ozymandias' obsessions with public works to celebrate his achievements, the artist captured his real character. Second, though the statue is in a state of ruin, the truth nevertheless remains with a tenacity that it is as irrepressible as the one it represents, and this truth will indeed withstand all attempts to obliterate it:

> And on the pedestal these words appear:
> 'My name is Ozymandias, king of kings:
> Look on my words, ye Mighty, and despair!'
> Nothing beside remains.

So Ozymandias' decaying statue, exposed to the elements and to human scrutiny, is left—

boundless and bare
The lone and level sands stretch far away.

This very same sand, commonly used to measure time has curiously lost that ability in a poem that is ultimately timeless.

Example 64

We are as clouds that veil the midnight moon;
How restlessly they speed, and gleam, and quiver,
Streaking the darkness radiantly—yet soon
Night closes round, and they are lost for ever:

Or like forgotten lyres, whose dissonant strings
Give various response to each varying blast,
To whose frail frame no second motion brings
One mood or modulation like the last.

We rest.—A dream has power to poison sleep;
We rise.—One wandering thought pollutes the day,
We feel, conceive or reason, laugh or weep;
Embrace fond woe, or cast our cares away:

It is the same.—For, be it joy or sorrow,
The path of its departure still is free:
Man's yesterday may ne'er be like his morrow;
Nought may endure but Mutability.

Substance: The poet compares the life of human beings to the clouds that veil the midnight moon. The clouds restlessly move fast in the brightness of the moon. But at the moment when the radiance of the moon is lost they once again become dark and are not seen. So also are human beings' lives—short and mortal. Following this, the poet distinguishes each man from the other and each action and experience from the other. Human life is compared to forgotten lyres. Just as each blast of wind produces its own note, so also is each human being different from the other. No two notes are similar; so also no two human beings are alike. Each and every man reacts differently to different situations and his experiences too are never alike. The poet then goes on to generalize human life which is transient and temporary. We go to sleep; but one bad dream is sufficient enough to poison our sleep. We rise; but one sad thought is cause enough to pollute the happy day. Our feelings, ideas, emotions, enjoyments, and sorrows—all are transient and different. With all these thoughts, the poet comes to a conclusion that whether yesterday or tomorrow—past or future—even if they are different from each other, they all are alike—being transient. The basic truth of life is that that nothing endures, except 'Mutability'.

Comment: In order to draw our attention to this basic truth of life, the poet has capitalized the keyword of the poem—'Mutability'. The prevalent meter of the short lyric is iambic pentameter (with some elisions here and there)—heroic meter. The poet faces the cruel fact of life heroically; thus the meter chosen for the poem is befitting. The entire poem has masculine (monosyllabic) rhymes, which again adds to the vigour and force of the poem.

The poem begins with a simile: 'We [human beings] are as clouds' and this comparison is maintained throughout the poem. Later the poet brings in another simile in the second stanza which is only half-formed 'or like forgotten lyres'. Throughout the poem there are alliterations—'*m*idnight *m*oon', '*fr*ail *fr*ame', '*m*ood or *m*odulation', '*po*wer to *po*ison', '*pa*th of its de*pa*rture'—in phrases, which add to the musical quality of the poem. There are also plenty of assonances in the poem:...sp*eed*, and gl*ea*m, and qu*i*cker str*ea*king the darkness rad*i*ant*ly* and again in:

> W*e* f*ee*l, conc*eiv*e, or r*ea*son, laugh or sl*ee*p...

That the poet is suffering from indecisiveness is evident from his abundant use of the conjunction *or* all through the poem in phrases like:

> ...conceive *or* reason, laugh *or* weep;
> Embrace fond woe, *or* cast our cares

Further on, there is:

> ...joy *or* sorrow.

The poem consists of four quatrains which are in alternately rhyming couplets—*abab cdcd*...

Example 65

> The art of losing isn't hard to master,
> so many things seem filled with the intent
> to be lost that their loss is no disaster.
>
> Lose something every day. Accept the fluster
> of lost keys, the hour badly spent.
> The art of losing isn't hard to master.
>
> Then practice losing farther, losing faster:
> places, and names, and where at was you meant
> to travel. None of these will bring disaster.

I lost my mother's watch. And look! my last, or
next to last, of three loved houses went.
The art of losing isn't hard to master.

I lost two cities, lovely ones. And, vaster
some realms I owned, two rivers, a continent,
I miss them, but it wasn't a disaster.

—Even losing you (the joking voice, a gesture
I love) I shan't have lied. It's evident.
the art of losing's not too hard to master
though it may look like (*write* it!) like disaster.

Substance: The poet has used the structure of the villanelle (a poetic form in which there are five tercets and a final quatrain, where the first and third lines of the first tercet recur alternately in the following stanzas as a refrain and form a final couplet) to develop an argument. The poem upholds the idea of an 'art'—something that can be learnt and practised with guiding principles. The opening noun phrase of the first stanza qualifies this art. Each tercet then relates the '*art of losing*' to a particular object or concept, growing in significance until we have moved beyond the personal to *cities*, *realms*, *two rivers*, and *a continent* (in lines 12 to 13). Having reacted to what would seem to be the pinnacle of the argument, the final quatrain changes direction, revealing a loss that seems to be harder to *master*. This time, we are not quite convinced by the poet's argument. The delay in the completion of the simile—'like...like disaster'—mirrors the poet's hesitation, suggesting that in this instance the loss is a disaster. This is an exceptionally disastrous loss and the poet is emphatic about it as he italicizes the fact that it should be written—well documented.

Comment: The poem conforms to the division of stanzas into five tercets and a final quatrain. In addition, there are only two rhymes and a repetition of the key words *master* and *disaster*. The poet does not, however, follow the repeating pattern of lines.

While line 1, the phrase 'the art of losing isn't hard to master', recurs exactly in lines 6 and 12, it becomes slightly less emphatic in line 18—'the art of losing's not too hard to master'. The addition of the adverb of degree *too* underlines the confident tone of the other stanzas in which the poet is able to *master* everyday losses of *door keys* (in lines 4 to 5), *places, and names* (in lines 8 to 9). Then the poet's *mother's watch* (in line 10) and so on. The loss in the final quatrain is different—it is emotional rather than physical; the poet therefore feels it more intensely. The tone of bravado or assumed confidence is an attempt to conceal her actual response.

The third line establishes the central idea that loss is not a *disaster*.

Although the poet does not repeat this line exactly as is traditional of the form (as in a refrain), the sentiments are echoed in lines 9, 15, and 19, and each ends with the abstract noun *disaster.* Again, the variation in the quatrain is more noticeable. The dash, marking the start of the final stanza, makes it appear like an afterthought, and yet the focus here is crucial to our understanding of the poem as a whole.

The tentative modal verb *may* (in line 19) suggests that the poet is not convinced by argument in this final instance of loss. Our sense of this is reinforced by the parenthesis and the repetition of the preposition '*like*'. The poet appears to be struggling to complete the line—as though the poet is trying to be convinced that losing the poet's lover is just as unimportant as losing the other things that has been listed. The change in grammatical mood from declarative mood to imperative mood and the use of italics in the parenthesis in the final stanza draw our attention to the underlying dilemma.

The villanelle is a complex form. It consists of 19 lines of any length divided into six stanzas with only two rhymes throughout. The five tercets rhyme of *aba* and the concluding quatrain rhymes *abaa*. In addition, line 1 is repeated in lines 6, 12 and 18; and line 3 is repeated in lines 9, 15 and 19.

The form was originally used for pastoral subjects, but in the twentieth century, it has been used in a variety of ways. Dylan Thomas' villanelle 'Do not go gentle into that good night' uses the repeated lines and recurring rhymes to create a haunting plea to his father in the face of death. William Earnest Henley adopts a lighter tone in his poem 'Villanelle' as he addresses the possibilities of the form itself.

—o—

CHAPTER V

Calcutta University Questions

1. In English writing we seldom speak of tradition, though we occasionally apply its name in deploring its absence. We cannot refer to "the tradition" or to "a tradition"; at most, we employ the adjective in saying that the poetry of so-and-so is "traditional" or even "too traditional." Seldom, perhaps, does the word appear except in a phrase of censure. If otherwise, it is vaguely approbative, with the implication, as to the work approved, of some pleasing archaelogical reconstruction. You can hardly make the word agreeable to English ears without this comfortable reference to the reassuring science of archaeology.

Yet if the only form of tradition, of handing down, consisted in following the ways of the immediate generation before us in a blind or timid adherence to its successes, "tradition" should positively be discouraged. We have seen many such simple currents soon lost in the sand; and novelty is better than repetition. Tradition is a matter of much wider significance. It cannot be inherited, and if you want it you must obtain it by great labour. It involves, in the first place, the historical sense, which we may call nearly indispensable to anyone who would continue to be a poet beyond his twenty-fifth year; and the historical sense involves a perception, not only of the pastness of the past, but of its presence; the historical sense compels a man to write not merely with his own generation in his bones, but with a feeling that the whole of the literature of Europe from Homer and within it the whole of the literature of his own country has a simultaneous existence and composes a simultaneous order. This historical sense, which is a sense of the timeless and of the temporal together, is what makes a writer traditional. And it is at the same time what makes a writer most acutely conscious of his place in time, of his contemporaneity. (318 words) *Part I, 2005.*

Substance: In English literature the word 'tradition' is used very sparingly. Even when it is used, it is used in a disparaging manner. When, on the other hand, it is used in an approving sense, its connotation remains confined merely within the imitation of the writing style of the past. The writer believes that this is not the proper way to be traditional. 'Tradition' involves something greater than this. Mere imitation of the past writings in the name of tradition should be discouraged. 'Tradition' has got wider ramification and significance and this requires a perception of the past in the form of historical sense which should not discard the present also. It is the perfect blending of the past and the present that makes a writer truly traditional. (127 words)

Critical Note: The passage is an attempt to interpret the term '*tradition*' and the author's approach to the subject is iconoclastic. He repudiates the common notion that following the style and manner of the past writers blindly is the path to be traditional. According to the author tradition involves a deep historical perception coupled with the understanding of present trend.

The treatment of the subject is logical and the arguments put forth are done in an objective manner. Here the personality of the writer is kept in the background and the author lets his intellect and power of mind speak for him. He arranges his arguments authoritatively, independent of his personal impressions. His arguments are factual and realistic. He remains detached from himself and remains unemotional throughout. The approach of the author is direct and despite being iconoclastic, he is never aggressive or pompous or dogmatic say, like Shaw. A refined taste is maintained throughout and this is the hall mark of ideal style of modern prose.

To sum up, the author's subject-matter is quite serious, but his style easy, and arguments convincing. His language is simple and sentences are well- constructed. What is more, his approach is argumentative as well as illustrative. This makes his tough theme quite impressive and understandable.

2. A survey of language, however superficial, makes it evident when we speak of style, we have to take into account those qualities of national character which are embodied in national speech. No man could be born of precisely the same physical, mental and precisely the same social conditions; and if these men learned different language in the cradle and used those languages in after life, they would be unable to deliver exactly the same message to the world through literature. The dominant qualities of each mother tongue would impose definite limitations on their power of expressing thoughts, however, similar or identical those thoughts might be.

We cannot conceive two men born with the same physical, mental and moral nature, at the same moments, under precisely the same conditions, and using the same language. They would be identical, and everything they uttered would be clothed with exactly the same words. The absurdity of this conception brings home to us the second aspect of style. Style is not merely a sign of those national qualities which are generic to established languages, and which constitute the so-called genius of a race. It is also the sign of personal qualities, specific to individuals which constitute the genius of a man. Whatever a man utters from his heart and head is the index of his character. The more remarkable person is, the more strongly he is differentiated from the average of human beings, the more salient will be the characteristic notes of his expression. But even the commonest people have each of them a specific style. The marks of difference become microscopical as we descend from Dante to Shakespeare to the drudges of the clerk's dress in one of the great cities. Yet these marks exist, and are no less significant of individuality than the variations between leaf and leaf upon the lime trees of an avenue. (Words 312) (*Part I, 2005*)

Substance: The writing style of a person is deeply rooted within his national character. Given the same upbringing under identical social conditions, the messages of two persons through literature cannot be the same if their languages are different. Their individual mother tongue would play the decisive role in expressing their thoughts although the same may be somewhat similar. As regards the matter of style in literature, it may be safely said that style is closely related to the characteristic genius of a race or country. But style apart from being what it is, in relation to the national character, is also the reflexion of the mind and personality of an exceptionally gifted writer. Such combination between national and individual genius makes a writer great and makes him stand apart from common people. (131 words)

Critical Note: The passage deals with the theme of literature, its style and message, which according to the author, are dependent on certain factors like his nationality, mother tongue and also his individual endowment. The conclusion drawn by the author is logical and acceptable.

The author has put forth his arguments in an objective and dispassionate manner. His derivations are based on observation of things and hence his arguments are beyond dispute. Thus his approach to the subject is scientific, factual and realistic. As regards style, the same is lucid without any jerk and it maintains a steady rhythm. The sequence of logic is natural, smooth and spontaneous and as a result of this it provides a pleasant reading to the reader. The last sentence of the passage provides an imagery in which the individuals are compared to tree leaves and such ornamentation provides a suitable finish to the passage.

3. The history of the Victorian age would never be written. We know too much about it. For ignorance is the first requisite of the historian—ignorance, which amplifies and clarifies, which selects and omits, with a placid perfection unattainable by the highest art. Concerning the age which has just passed our fathers and grandfathers have poured forth and accumulated so vast a quantity of information that the industry of a Ranke would be submerged by it, and the perspicacity of a Gibbon would quail before it. It is not by the direct method of a scrupulous narration that the explorers of the past can hope to depict that singular epoch. If he is wise, he will adopt a subtle strategy. He will attack his subject in unexpected places, he will fall upon the flank, or the rear, he will shoot a sudden, revealing search light in obscure recesses, hitherto undefined. He will row out over that green ocean of material and lower down into it, here and there, a little bucket, which will bring up to light of day some characteristic specimen from those far depths to be examined with careful curiosity. (192 words) *(C. U. part I, 1989)*

Substance: The author asserts that ignorance renders the task of a historian easy while true knowledge makes it difficult. He contends that writing the history of the Victorian age would prove an extremely difficult task because of the vast wealth of information available. He suggests that a historian of the Victorian age must adopt a novel and unconventional method. Instead of trying to present a panoramic view of the age, he would do well to deal with isolated but interesting facets or phases of the age. (85 words)

Critical Note: The interpretation of the requisite of a historian i.e. his ignorance is rather unusual and certainly open to question. It is certainly a glaring contradiction to say that ignorance constitutes the primary basis for writing history of an age. In the first half of the passage, he introduces and elaborates the main idea. Then, in the second half he suggests a way out of the problem. The passage thus somehow attains a logical structure. The language is simple and effective. The ordinary, objective prose of the first half of the passage presents a fine contrast to the subjective, imaginative prose of the second half. Towards the end of the passage, the author speaks in metaphors that make his argument all the more convincing.

4.
So shuts the marigold her leaves
At the departure of the sun;
So from the honeysuckle sheaves
The bee goes when the day is done;

So sits the turtle when she is but one,
And so all woe, as I since she is gone.

To some few birds kind Nature hath
      Made all the summer as one day;
Which once enjoyed, cold winter's wrath
      As night they sleeping pass away.
Those happy creatures are that know not yet
The pain to be deprived or to forget.

I oft have heard men say there be
      Some that with confidence profess
The helpful Art of Memory;
      But could they teach forgetfulness
I'd learn, and try what further art could do
To make me love her and forget her too.

(*C.U. Part I, 1990*)

Substance: The pain of being separated from one's beloved seems to be a universal phenomenon to one who suffers this agony. Some birds that sleep through the long winter do not suffer from the memory of the summer days that are no more. There are people who praise memory for the benefits it confers on mankind. But the poet is eager to learn the art of forgetfulness which might enable him to forget the agony of being separated from his beloved.

Critical Note: This is a conventional love poem which lacks the vital touch of genuine passion. The first stanza portrays the state of the lover's mind through three typically conventional images. The second stanza builds up what may be described as a contrast. The third stanza finally brings out the main idea, also through a contrast. But, if the poem lacks the touch of true imagination, it certainly excels in the quality of craftsmanship. The words and phrases have been carefully chosen, and then, neatly packed into lines and stanzas. The images are not particularly attractive or original, but they serve their purpose quite effectively. The verses are in the iambic metre though there are quite a number of variations. Each of the three stanzas contain six lines, of which the first four have four feet each while the rest two contain five feet each. The rhyme scheme for each stanza is as follows: *a b a b c c*.

5. The man of life upright,
      Whose guiltless hart is free

From all dishonest deeds,
Or thought of vanity,

The man whose silent days,
In harmless joys are spent,
Whom hopes cannot delude,
Nor sorrow discontent ;
That man needs neither towers
Nor armour for defence,
Nor secret vaults to fly
From thunders violence.

He only can behold
With unaffrighted eyes
The horrors of the deep
And terrors of the Skies.

Thus, scorning all the cares
That fate, or fortune brings,
He makes the heaven his book,
His wisdom heavenly things,

Good thoughts his only friends,
His wealth a well-spent age,
The earth his sober Inn
And quiet Pilgrimage.

(*C.U. Part I, 1986*)

Substance: A pious man who is honest, innocent and humble, spends his days in harmless pleasures. Hopes cannot elate him nor can sorrows depress him. Such a man is not afraid of the frowns of nature or of man. He regards with scorn the cares and evils that are the lot of men on earth. He thinks constantly of God and always entertains pure thoughts. He regards heaven as his proper home and the earth as a place of temporary sojourn.

Critical Note: This appears to be one of the professedly didactic poems which were written in great numbers in the sixteenth and seventeenth centuries. The poet speaks of so many virtues of a truly honest and upright man. His theme, naturally provides him with little scope for what we call "poetic imagination". And yet, we must admit that the poem does not at all read like a mere catalogue of the qualities of a virtuous man. In spite of its professedly didactic nature, the poem is invested with a kind of allegorical beauty. A few well-chosen phrases like 'horrors of the deep', and 'terrors of the skies' add to the grace of an otherwise unadorned style, while the metaphors in the last two lines bring the poem to the conclusion. The verse is in iambic trimeter. The rhyme scheme is simple, the second line rhymes with the fourth, the sixth with the eight, and so on.

6. How strange is the lot of us mortals! Each of us is here for a brief sojourn; for what purpose he knows not, though he sometimes thinks he senses it. But without deeper reflection one knows from daily life that one exists for other people—first of all for those upon whose smiles and well-being our own happiness is wholly dependent, and then for the many, unknown to us, to whose destinies we are bound by the ties of sympathy. A hundred times every day I remind myself that my inner and outer life are based on the labors of other men, living and dead, and that I must exert myself in order to give in the same measure as I have received and am still receiving. I am strongly drawn to a frugal life and am often oppressively aware that I am engrossing an undue amount of labor of my fellowmen.

   I do not at all believe in human freedom in the philosophical sense. Everybody acts not only under external compulsion but also in accordance with inner necessity. Schopenhauer's saying : " A man can do what he wants, but not want what he does," has been a very real inspiration to me since my youth; it has been a continual inspiration to me since my youth; it has been a continual consolation in the face of life's hardships, my own and others', and an unfailing wellspring of tolerance. The realization mercifully mitigates the easily paralyzing sense of responsibility and prevents us from taking ourselves and other people all too seriously. It is conducive to a view of life which, in particular, honour its due. (277 words) *(Part I - 2004)*

Substance: During his short life span, it should be the realization of man that his happiness is dependent on the happiness of others and also the fact that his destiny is bound by the ties of sympathy with others. The writer feels that both his inner and outer lives are the fruits of others' toil. At times, the writer feels that he is capitalizing on others.

The writer does not believe in human freedom in the philosophical sense of the term. To him, human action has got two aspects viz. inner necessity and external compulsion. It is a constant war between hardship and tolerance. Such realization makes life much bearable and meaningful in the long run. (115 words).

Critical Note: At times we require looking within ourselves to make ourselves aware of certain intrinsic values of human life. Such values may *prima facie* appear commonplace, but have got deeper implications. In the daily humdrum of life we tend to forget these values, but some time a voice from within makes us aware of the same. The passage in question is of that kind. Man's existence is dependant on the services from others and it is his duty to reciprocate the same. It is unjust to take undue advantage of others. So, the author feels, 'I must exert myself in order to give in the same measure as I have received and am still receiving.'

The opening sentence of the passage clearly indicates that the author is emotionally charged. His realization about life is uttered in the most inspired language. The presence of the author's personality is felt throughout and the writing may appropriately be termed as a subjective one. The passage is marked throughout by the personal touches, reflecting the writer's taste and temperament. His approach is impressionistic. As said earlier, the author is emotionally moved as if ready to communicate with the readers.

Emotional writing normally tends to be feminine and the language becomes less forceful. But the true merit of the passage is that the language is totally masculine by virtue of the author's conviction about the message he is going to convey. As such, language is forceful, though traditional. The sentence construction is superb. The clarity of thought and expression remains unquestioned.

7. It is not easy to make a living in India as a man of letters. People don't buy books enough, there aren't not adventurous or reliable publishers enough, book reviewing is not quick or helpful enough, and current critical standards aren't informed or exciting enough. One can turn out an occasional poem or short story or even a novel while earning one's bread and butter in a safe or steady occupation like law, medicine, teaching, business, Government Service, journalism,—that is, if one hasn't the present-day Indian equivalent of the Virginia Woolfian desiderata (for women writers) of 'a room one's own and 500 pounds year.' But to make serious writing—'creative writing', if you will—one's career is too risky anywhere, and more so in India for one who chooses to write in English. As in the United Kingdom, here in India too the writer has at least to try to supplement his income (or neutralize his losses) through journalistic hack-work or preparation of text books or translating for the Sahitya Academi. Grow the cabbages that pay at once so that some roses too may be grown to meet the soul's need for beauty. (195 words) *(Part I, 2004)*

Substance: In India taking up creative writing as a profession is a challenging proposition in the sense that an author is exposed to various hurdles like low demand for books, lack of suitable publishers, belated review of books, absence of proper critical insight and so on. One must be in some other regular earning process while resorting to creative writing. Earning a livelihood only by serious writing is uncertain in India and one has to take resort to the ways of quick earning by writing articles, text books, translating other matters to reach a break even situation. However, amidst such hack jobs, come out the real treasures of creative writing at times. (112 words)

Critical Note: The author has highlighted some very practical problems for the Indian writers, particularly those who are engaged in serious writing and also in English. He has attributed several reasons for this like 'there aren't not adventurous or reliable publishers enough, book reviewing is not quick or helpful enough, and current critical standards aren't informed or exciting enough.' So, the author feels, earning a livelihood through writing only is a difficult and challenging proposition. So the quick earning process is a must for them and these include 'journalistic hack-work or preparation of text books or translating for the Sahitya Academi.' But the concluding sentence makes an optimistic note that even in such a dismal situation, occasional creative and good writing is possible.

The approach of the writer is very clear and matter of fact. His arguments are largely true in the Indian perspective. The same situation applies to Britain also, the writer asserts. His approach is direct, straight-forward and objective. The theme being what it is, there is little scope for display of emotions. The language is clear and simple.

8. Literary style is a matter of sentiment, emotion involuntary habits of feeling and observing, constitutional sympathy with the world of men, tendencies of curiosity and liking, than of the pure intellect. The style of scientific works, affording little scope for the exercise of these psychological elements, throws less light upon their authors' temperament than does the style of poems, novels, essays, books of travel, descriptive criticism. In the former case all that need be aimed at is lucid exposition of fact and vigorous reasoning. In the latter, the fact to be stated, the truth to be arrived at, being of a more complex nature, involves a process akin to that of the figurative arts. The stylist has here to produce the desired effect by suggestion of indefinite subtlety, and to present impressions made upon his sensibility. (136 words) *(Part I, 2004)*

Substance: Literary style is different from the style adopted in scientific works. The former is a complex process involving, apart from pure intellect, psychological insight, human relationships, curiosity and observation.

Literary style demands 'suggestion of indefinite subtlety' and the sensibility of the writer. But style in works of science is matter of fact based on reasons having lucidity. (57 words)

Critical Note: The author has drawn a distinction between literary style and that adopted in writings on science. To him, the former is a complex process which is intellectual as well as psychological. In scientific writing, the writer has no scope to go beyond the realm of fact and logic and hence his style is relatively simple. The arguments put forth by the writer are true and leaves no scope for dispute. His approach is objective and impersonal. His personality is veiled in the background. His approach is factual and realistic. His style is clear and does not suffer from any obscurity or ambiguity. The sentences are compact and offer a pleasant and smooth reading.

9. When music sounds, gone is the earth I know,
And all her lovely things even lovelier grow;
Her flowers in vision flame, her forest trees
Lift burdened branches, stilled with ecstasies.

When music sounds, out of the water rise
Naiads whose beauty dims my waking eyes,
Rapt in strange dreams burns each enchanted face,
With solemn echoing stirs their dwelling-place.

When music sounds, all that I was I am
Ere to this haunt of brooding dust I came;
And from Time's woods break into distant song
The swift-winged hours, as I hasten along.

(*C.U. 1984*)

Substance: The poet speaks of the effect of music on him. He points out music transcends all his limitations and fills him with ecstatic sensations. Different natural elements appear to him lovelier and he even visualizes beautiful and mystic scenes under its effect. What is more, the sound of music seems to take him back to pre-natal state, as time rolls on, swiftly and harmoniously, leading him to his end.

Critical Note: The poem is on the effect of music. It shows the deep and mysterious effect of music on the poet, who is evidently a lover of this. Indeed, the poem bears out strongly the poet's profound attachment to music. Here he is intensely personal. Moreover, it well illustrates his love for nature and his power of visualization of strange and lovely scenes.

A romantic note is evident throughout the poem. It has got an aesthetic inspiration and imaginative propensity.

The diction of the poem is simple enough. The effect of music is clearly shown by means of some and concrete images. The poet's vision of *flowers* and *forest trees* as also of *Naiads*, rising *out of the water*, may be mentioned here. *Burdened branches, enchanted face, brooding dust, Time's woods* and *swift winged hours* are some happy expressions used by the poet with adequately suggestive images.

The poem is thoroughly melodious. This has three stanzas of four lines each. The lines are found to rhyme in couplets. The expression *when music sounds*, repeated at the beginning of each stanza is a fine case of epanaphora.

10. Happy the man, whose wish and care
A few paternal acres bound,
Content to breathe his native air,
In his own ground.

Whose herds with milk, whose fields with bread,
Whose flocks supply him with attire,
Whose trees in summer yield him shade,
In winter fire.

Blest! who can unconcern'dly find
Hours, days, and years slide soft away,
In health of body, peace of mind,
Quiet by day,

Sound sleep by night; study and ease
Together mix'd; sweet recreation,
And innocence, which most does please,
With meditation.

Thus let me live, unseen, unknown;
Thus unlamented let me die;
Steal from the world, and not a stone
Tell where I lie.

(*C.U. PART I , 1985*)

Substance: A truly happy man is one whose field and firm provide for his simple needs. Such a man is content with his lot and lives a life of serene happiness. He is free from all worries and his peace of mind is never broken. He spends his days and years in study, repose and sweet meditation. The poet wishes to live such a life and then quietly take leave of this world.

Critical Note: The theme of the poem is true happiness. One may or may not agree with the poet's concept of true happiness, but the picture he draws here of the happy man's life certainly has its charms. And these charms naturally prove particularly attractive to people besieged with thousand worries of modern city life. In these few lines the poet has conjured up a fine picture of a serene country life, free from the hurry and bustle of modern city life. We may scoff at the poet's idea of happiness as impractical and even absurd, but we cannot stifle a wistful sigh as we read through those few lines. And herein, we think, lies the success of the poem as a work of art. Images are simple but effective. The lines flow in a slow and quiet rhythm that automatically suggests the tranquil pace of the serene and secluded life portrayed. The verse is iambic tetrameter with sprinkling trochees here and there. There are five shorter lines of two feet each. The rhyme scheme is *abab; cdcd* and so on.

11. Today the study of both the classic and the Bible has dwindled to small proportions. What has taken their place? To some extent the vacuum has been filled by a more and correct knowledge of history and a wider range of literature. But I fear that the greater part of it has been filled up with rubbish.

    Similarly, and only in a lesser degree than in case of literature, the enjoyment and understanding of architecture and painting and of all the domestic art, are enhanced by the knowledge of history. The man who knows no history can travel through Italy thinking it very pretty and picturesque and queer, but understanding very little of what he sees. Foreign travel is enjoyable and instructive largely in proportion to the amount of historical knowledge which we take with us across the channel. But I am glad to observe that the power of enjoying old buildings by means of historical knowledge and imagination is very widely spread today. That is something to build on, educationally and culturally. Vast numbers of people speeding along, get out of their motor cars or buses or leave their bicycles, and walk half a mile uphill to inspect the ruin of some old Roman buildings on wild moor. There is no beauty in the ruins which are little more than foundations, but the historical imagination of the visitors is touched. Some know, more away desire to know, something of the history of the Romans in Britain.

    (248 words) (*C.U.Part I, 1988*)

Substance: There is an important point of similarity between literature and architecture, a good knowledge of history is essential for the enjoyment of both of them. Without such knowledge, the real beauty of the finest architecture will go unnoticed and unappreciated. But the author is glad to notice that a good number of visitors are today equipped with a knowledge of history. Great number of people visits the ruins of Roman buildings. While many of them possess the requisite knowledge of the history of the Romans in Britain, others feel the necessity of acquiring such knowledge once they visit these ruins. (109 words)

Critical Note: The first paragraph does not seem to have any essential connection with the rest of the passage. It merely serves to introduce the topic dealt with. The main idea has been presented clearly enough. The author balances his arguments well, so that his conclusion seems quite logical and convincing. The writer appears to be more at home when he describes a thing or narrates an incident than when he argues an abstract point. Thus, his language which, in the first part of the passage, is ordinary to the point of being trivial, suddenly becomes lively and forceful as soon as he starts describing the visits of vast number of people to the ruins of old Roman buildings.

12. There is plenty of mystery in poetry without making it mystical. And we may, perhaps, advance a step further and suggest that a poet is he in whom the vast majority of his 'thoughts'...occur with vivid emotional fields. It is probably true that in the mental activity of even the ordinary run of men thoughts are always accompanied by such emotional fields, but that they ignore them, because they have no means of distinguishing them from one another. The poet, on the contrary from the beginning, possesses such means. He has the Word. The word in the poet's mind partly arises out of the emotional field, partly is deliberately fitted to convey it. This mating of the word to the entire mental experience of thought and emotional field experienced as one is the specific poetic act. If an ordinary man were visited by Prospero's thought, which came, we may remember, to a troubled brain and a beating mind, he would strive to remember it. He would not be able to remember it.... In order that the beauty should be saved from the inequity of oblivion it is necessary not that the thought should be expressed, but that the entire mental experience—thought and emotional field—should be fixed in words. (203 words) (*Part I, 2003*)

Substance: The birth of poetry, although mysterious, does not necessarily attract mysticism. To a true poet thoughts come into his mind accompanied by emotion. Similar process takes place within an ordinary man also but he is not aware of such process because he cannot separate his emotions from thoughts. The poet, on the other hand, has got the acumen in this regard. So poetry may be defined to be a combination of emotion and deliberate thought, and poetic act is giving expression to words combining these two things. (86 words)

Critical Note: The theme of the passage is the origin of poetry in human mind. Poetry, according to the author, is a combination of thought and emotion expressed in words. The idea is very near to Wordsworth's theory of poetry of 'emotion recollected in tranquility.' However, our present author goes a step ahead that all human beings have got the elements of poetry within them i.e. they have got both thought and emotion, but what they lack is the word-power to give vent to their emotion. The logic of the author is largely true.

Apart from logical sequence, the passage is marked by clarity of thought and economy of expression. Only the concluding portion of the passage that deals with the example of Prospero creates some confusion in the minds of the readers. Otherwise the style of the author is simple and down to earth. The opening sentence of the passage using the words 'mystery' and 'mystical' immediately catches the attention of the reader. Although the approach of the author is objective, he has been able to establish some sort of nearness with the reader by virtue of the simplicity of his style and acceptability of his reasons.

13. It is easy to oversimplify in defining the character of the Restoration period because the comedies of the age stamp in our minds the picture of a frivolous society ready to trivialize the human relationships, to treat love and marriage flippantly, and to show scant regard for the virtues of hard work, sobriety and un-selfishness. Indeed the public that supported the London theatre was a very different public from the seemingly mixed cross-section of the populace who attended the Globe Theatre in Shakespeare's days. The Restoration theatre provided amusement for a leisured and dissolute society. Puritans naturally shunned it. The respectable Londoners who earned their living by honest trade or craft could scarcely be expected to throng to see themselves being made but is of upper class mockery. The court of Charles II certainly contained more than its fair share of cynical libertines who made a mockery of virtue and assumed all its advocates to be hypocrites. This was the public which relished the antics of Homer, who cleverly reduced women in Wycherley's *The Country Wife* (1675). But the latter play was not representative of the spirit of the kingdom as a whole. Milton's *Paradise Lost* and Bunyan's *Pilgrim's Progress* were published soon after. The civil struggle may have been settled politically in favour of the monarchy and the Church of England, and against the

Puritans, but the moral struggle continued in literary productivity and in commentary upon it. (239 words) (*Part I, 2003*)

Substance: The Restoration period suffers from an over-simplified notion that it is devoid of any moral value and that it is full of trivialities. This is mainly due to the fact that the dramas of that period project a picture of life and society showing little regard to the serious moral values of life. Naturally the Puritans and people with earnest moral values avoided the Restoration theatre. But such a notion is only partial as the Restoration theatre is not the only reflexion of the era. We have simultaneously notable serious literary creations from Milton, Bunyan and others that uphold true moral values. (102 words)

Critical Note: In this passage the author attempts to dispel some of the misconceptions about the Restoration Age from the minds of the readers. The author is of the opinion that the Restoration theatre is not the only reflection of the true literary signals of the age. Serious attempts in literature involving greater moral values could be found in the writings of Milton, Bunyan and others. The view point of the author is a matter of fact based on history and therefore not to be disputed. However, it may be said to the credit of the author that he has provided a new angle to the readers towards the true assessment of the age.

The author's style is clear and his approach, objective and direct. His choice of words is suitable to the subject he deals with. With a few strokes of words like *frivolous flippantly*, *scant regard for the virtues* the author brings out the popular notion of the age.

14. O talk not to me of a name great in story;
The days of our youth are the days of our glory;
And the myrtle and ivy of sweet two-and-twenty
Are worth all your laurels, though ever so plenty.

What are garlands and crowns to the brow that is wrinkled?
'Tis but as a dead flower with May-dew besprinkled:
Then away with all such from the head that is hoary—
What care I for the wreaths that can only give glory?

Oh Fame! — if I e'er took delight in thy praises,
'Twas less for the sake of thy high-sounding phrases,
Than to see the bright eyes of the dear one discover
She thought that I was not unworthy to love her.

There chiefly I sought thee, there only I found thee;
Her glance was the best of the rays that surround thee;

When it sparkled o'er aught that was bright in my story,
I knew it was love, and I felt it was glory.

(*C.U. Part I, 1978*)

Substance: The fame and glory of youth appear hollow and unsubstantial to the poet, now that he is old and infirm. In his youth he ran after those worthless things, not because he set much store by them, but only because his beloved wanted to see him famous. Love impelled him to win laurels in his youth. To sober eyes of old age, these appear quite frivolous and meaningless. The poet seeks glory or fame not for its own sake; he seeks it so that it may make his beloved feel he is worthy of being her lover.

Critical Note: This is a typically conventional love poem, devoid of all the throbbing passions of true love. The first eight lines constitute of falsely impassioned repudiation of glory when divorced from youth. The rest of the poem lays bare the reason behind the lover's quest for glory. In spite of the artificial note that runs through all the sixteen lines of the verse, the poem may be regarded as a finished product of art.

The third line of the poem has a genuine ring of poetic imagination, and the contrast between *the myrtle and ivy* on the one hand and *laurels* on the other, proves truly effective in bringing about the desired effect.

15. So may the outward shows be least themselves:
The world is still deceived with ornament.
In law, what plea so tainted and corrupt,
But, being seasoned with a gracious voice,
Obscures the show of evil? In religion,
What damned error, but some sober brow
Will bless it and approve it with a text,
Hiding the grossness with fair ornament?
There is no vice so simple but assumes
Some mark of virtue on his outward parts:
How many cowards, whose hearts are all as false
As stairs of sand, wear yet upon their chins
The beards of Hercules and frowning Mars;
Who, inward search'd, have livers white as milk.

(*C.U. 1997*)

Substance: Everywhere external glamour dazzles and deceives mankind. Eloquence in legal matters as also holy sermons in religion is found to sanction and justify criminality and impiety respectively. Utter cowardice is often concealed by the sheer pose of gallantry. In fact, vice becomes truly dangerous under the feigning of virtue.

Critical Note: The present verse passage conveys a profound thought. This serves to expose the hypocrisy of the world that is not seldom ruled by outward shows. The idea is struck in the very second line:

The world is still deceived with ornament.

The poet appears rather cynical about the way of the world that prizes corruption and wickedness and turns away virtue and nobleness. He brings out categorically how evil and mischief are found to dominate the present-day worlds in different worlds.

Of course, a moral note underlies the poet's cynical tone. He is definitely didactic, though not very directly.

The passage is rich in technique and contains several figurative expressions. The personification in *the world* (*The world is still deceived*), and *vice* ('assumes some marks of virtue'), the synecdoche in the *sober brow* and the simile in 'hearts are all as false as stairs of sand') and 'livers as white as milk' may be mentioned in particular.

The poetic diction here is quite plain and melodious. There are fourteen lines in the poem which is, however, not a sonnet. There is no rhyme as the lines are written in blank verse.

16. Yes, I remember Adlestrop—
The name because one afternoon
Of heat the express-train drew up there
Unwontendly. It was late June.
The steam hissed. Someone cleared his throat.
No one left and no one came
On the bare platform. What I saw
Was Adlestrop —only the name
And willows, willow-herb, and grass,
And meadow sweet, and haycocks dry,
No whit less still and lonely fair
Than the high cloudlets in the sky.
And for that minute a blackbird sang
Close by, and round him, mistier,
Farther and farther, all the birds
Of Oxfordshire and Gloucestershire.

(*C.U. Part I, 1987*)

Substance: The poet remembers Adlestrop, a small station where his train has suddenly halted for a while. His memory of Adlestrop is crowded with a number of fragmentary images. The images of willows, meadow sweets, haycocks and cloudlets merge in his memory with a blackbird's song the refrain of which was taken up, as it were, by all the birds of the area.

Critical Note: This is not a great poem nor does it attempt to be one. This is a simple but sincere recapitulation in verse of the scene at a small railway station. The poem is like a wayside flower that has no pretension to flamboyant colours, but, which, nevertheless, offers its sweet fragrance to a chance visitor. The language of the poetry here happily identifies itself with the language of speech. The simple words and phrases are endowed with an evocative power that is seldom achieved through ingeniously contrived metaphors.

The verse is composed chiefly of iambic tetrameters, though there are frequent variations. The third and the fifth lines contain five feet each.

17. We have curious ideas about ourselves. We think of ourselves as a body with a spirit in it, or a body with a soul in it, or a body with a mind in it. The years drink up the wine, and at last throw the bottle away, the body, of course, being the bottle.

It is a funny sort of superstition. Why should I look at my hand, as it so cleverly writes these words, and decide that it is mere nothing compared to the mind that directs it? Is there really any huge difference between my hand and my brain? Or my mind? My hand is alive, it flickers with a life of its own. It meets all the strange universe in touch, and learns a vast number of things. My hand as it writes these words , slips gaily along , jumps like a grasshopper to dot an i, feels the table rather cold, gets a little bored if I write too long, has its own rudiments of thoughts , and is just as much me as is my brain , my mind or my soul. Why should I imagine that there is a me which is more me than my hand is? Since my hand is absolutely alive, me alive.

Whereas, of course, as far as I am concerned, my pen isn't alive at all. My pen isn't me alive. My alive ends at my finger-tips.

Whatever is me alive, is me. Every tiny bits of my hands is alive, every little freckle and hair and fold of skin. And whatever is me alive is me. Only my finger-nails, those ten little weapons between me and an inanimate universe, they cross the mysterious Rubicon between me alive and things like my pen which are not alive, in my own sense. (303 words) (*Part I, 2002*)

Substance: Common people suffer from a superstition that human body contains such elements like spirit or soul or mind which regulate the functions of the various parts of the body. This, according to the writer, is a wrong concept. Various parts of human body are as much alive as mind or soul. There is no reason to believe that the hand that writes words so efficiently is nothing compared to our mind.The hand has got its separate existence and it is no less a living object than mind or soul is.The writing instrument, however, is not alive as it is not a part of human body. So every part of human body, however, little it may be, is an integral part of one's self so long as it is alive. (131 words)

Critical Note: The passage deals with an unconventional subject in an unusual way. The author takes resort to his own logic to propound his thesis. He challenges the prevailing notion that the spirit or mind or soul within human body is the real existence of man. He opines that each and every part of human body is alive as a part of human existence having separate entity. His arguments which obviously defy scientific logic do evoke a curiosity in the minds of the readers. The readers may not agree with his view point, but to appreciate the writing as such, we have to maintain the 'willing suspension of disbelief'.

Assuming, though not accepting the arguments of the writer, it has to be admitted that he has arranged his arguments in a very 'logical' manner. He denies that each part of human body is subordinate to our soul. He takes the example of his hand and puts forth his arguments from his own stand point.

The above passage makes a beautiful piece of subjective writing ; we feel the presence of the writer reflecting his personality. The sentence structure, though unconventional at times, is fitting to the subject that is unconventional too. The style is simple and the writer's approach is authoritative and straight-forward. The use of simile, 'jumps like a grasshopper' is apt and picturesque.

18. It can be said then that the common distinctive characteristic that unites many of the best modern writers is the plainness of style: they aim at saying what they intend to say and no more, and deliberately avoid artifice and ornament. Some of them who in their various ways and for their different purposes achieve greatest simplicity are Somerset Maugham, G.B. Shaw Aldous Huxley, George Orwell and H.E.Bates. They avoid the out-of-the-way world, the elaborate sentences, and all suspicion of 'poetry'. Obviously, these could be an ideal of dullness. A plain style should not be undistinguished as common speech: it will be closet to common speech in approximating to speech rhythms or the ease of good talk, as in the prose of Shaw and Orwell, and closet to plain expression in choice of exactly right words or constructions that will convey the writer's thought most clearly. Simplicity is no less difficult to attain than a complex structure: the writer needs an

exceptionally accurate eye, and ear for natural rhythms, and the critical judgement to avoid hackneyed or commonplace expressions. Whilst aiming at his ideal of clarity and naturalness, he will remember that the original writer puts fresh life into language and keeps up its standards. He will not use clichés because they are closed to common speech, unless he puts them into the mouth of a character who would naturally use them: If he uses them himself, it is more a defect then a virtue. (248 words) (*Part I, 2002*)

Substance: Plainness of style is the common distinctive feature among the best modern writers. Their approach to the subject is direct without 'artifice or ornament'. But such simplicity of style does not make their writings a bad reading. Their style is somewhat different from the day-to-day hackneyed common speech. Their language and style are something alien to the commoners. But to attain simplicity is a difficult task. For this the writer requires power of keen observation, a sense of 'natural rhythms' and above all a power of sound critical judgement. He will put in fresh life in his language and will avoid clichés in the normal course. (108 words)

Critical Note: The main idea in the passage is about the simplicity and plainness of prose writing. This has been presented with admirable clarity, but some of the details remain a bit obscure. The author adopts a balanced approach to the subject under discussion. He shows both the similarity and the difference between plain style and common speech. He cites examples and makes comparisons in order to drive home the point. His style is clear, direct and traditional and it does not lack rhythm or cadence. His approach is objective in the sense that he keeps his personality in the background and projects his theme with authority and clarity. He remains unemotional in handling his subject. Then while advocating plain style in prose, the writer himself had adopted the same and avoids jerky expressions. If clarity is a yardstick of good prose, the passage is an example of the same.

19. Say not the struggle naught availeth,
The labour and the wounds are vain,
The enemy faints not, nor faileth,
And as things have been they remain.

If hopes were dupes, fears may be liars;
It may be, in yon smoke concealed,
Your comrades chase e'en now the fliers,
And, but for you, possess the field.

For while the tired waves, vainly breaking,
Seem here, no painful inch to gain,
Far back, through creeks and inlets making,
Comes silent, flooding in, the main.

And not by eastern windows only,
When daylight comes, comes in the light,
In front, the sun climbs slow, how slowly,
But westward, look, the land is bright.

Arthur Hugh Clough (*C.U. Part I, 2001*)

Substance: In this poem the poet rebukes the despondency of people who give up the battle of life in sheer exhaustion of spirit. No sincere effort is ever lost in this world. We should never say that inspite of all our efforts we have achieved nothing and things have remained the same, and no efforts of ours can alter them. But on deep thinking we find that failures are the only earnest of success. The poet makes it clear by two images. The waves of the sea dashing against the shore to enter inland seem apparently unsuccessful. But farther off, their efforts yield result and the sea is rushing into the land through narrow creeks. Again, the sun climbs slowly in the east but it reddens not only the eastern sky, the west also becomes bright with the sunshine. Thus the results of our efforts may be slow and invisible, but it is inevitable.

Critical Note: The poem is an example of restrictive poetry for its moralistic note. His purpose behind the composition of such poem is to fill the sagging hearts of his countrymen with inspiration and hope by asking them to continue their struggle which alone can ensure their success.

The poem is written in a serious tone. It is remarkable for its high and noble aim. The solemnity of the poet's voice can be felt almost throughout. A note of confidence is perceptible which makes the poet support his viewpoint through a number of images. In form the poem is a lyric expressing the poet's own viewpoint. It is didactic in nature, and solemn in its mode of expression.

The poem is rich in imagery. As many as three pictorial images have been used to buttress the theme of the poem—hope and success follow when struggle is continued.

The poem consists of four stanzas, each having four lines which rhyme alternately in couplets. The lines are iambic pentameter with variations to save it from dullness.

20. Remember me when I am gone away,
Gone far away into the silent land;

When you can no more hold me by the hand,
Not I half turning to go, yet turning to stay.
Remember me when no more day by day
You tell me of our future that you planned:
Only remember me; you understand
It will be too late to counsel or pray.
Yet if you should forget me for a while
And afterwards remember, do not grieve:
For if the darkness and corruption leave
A vestige of thoughts I once had,
Better by far you should forget and smile
Than that you should remember and be sad.

(*C.U. 1974, 1982*)

Substance: The beloved entreats her lover to remember her when she is dead and gone for ever , and when the sweet scenes of love can no longer be enacted between them. He need not be sorry if he forgets her for a while, she assures him. And, if her memory pains him sometimes, it would be better for him to forget her.

Critical Note: This fine sonnet vividly portrays the yearnings of the beloved as she dwells on the painful thought of being parted from her lover by the cruel hand of death. The octave conjures up a beautiful picture of their life. The sestet relates what the beloved desires her lover to do when she would be dead and gone. The fine details in the octave as well as the subtle suggestions in the sestet clearly indicate that it is a kind of love in which affection decidedly predominates over passion—a love that is ready to make any sacrifice for the object of love. The line, 'Not I half turning to go, yet turning to stay' effectively portrays the lovers' unwillingness to part from one another even though for a brief while. The whole poem is vibrant with notes of true affection. Not a single artificially conceived phrase or metaphor mars the sweet and absolutely genuine tone of the poem. A breath of sweet sadness seems to envelop the entire poem, and the shadow of a tragic parting of the lovers invests the poem, as it were, with the last glow of a setting sun.

21. Learn to be good readers—which are perhaps a more difficult thing than you can imagine. Learn to be discriminative in your reading; to read faithfully and with your best attention, all kinds of things which you have a real interest in, a real not an imaginary, and which you find to be really fit for what you are engaged in. Of course, at the present time, in a great deal of the reading incumbent on you, you must be

guided to the books recommended by your professors for assistance towards the effect their selections. And then, when you leave the University, and go into studies of your own, you will find it very important that you have chosen a field, some province specially suited to you, in which you can study and work. The most unhappy of all men is the man who cannot tell what he is going to do, who has got no work cut out for him in the world, and does not go into it. For work is the grand cure of all maladies and miseries that ever beset mankind—honest work, which you intend getting done. (Carlyle) (192 words) *(Part I, 2001)*

Substance: To be a good reader, one must be choosy, faithful and attentive to one's subject for which one has got real interest. Guidance from the professors in selection of books is a must. The real effect of such exercise will be felt when he completes his academic life and starts working in independent field for a specific goal. Without a specific goal, life is a bundle of miseries and maladies. (71)

Critical Note: The theme of the passage is twofold, (i) selection of right books and (ii) the choice of career in future. The treatment of the theme is quite logical, as the author starts from the academic and then switches over to career path of the students.

A perusal of the passage makes it clear that the author is addressing the students of a university. It is therefore natural that the message conveyed is didactic in nature. The true merit of the passage is that the message conveyed is clear and specific without any ambiguity. The arguments put forth are logical and forceful. The author has maintained an objective approach throughout without betraying emotion and therefore, and it can be classified as an objective piece of writing. The prose style is in keeping with the subject. It is simple apparently but the seriousness of tone is maintained throughout the passage. No doubt, the author is pragmatic in his approach and he offers his argument keeping in view the needs of the students. The prose style is traditional and the choice of words are in keeping with the subject. Clarity of expression is one of the merits of the passage.

22. I take it, then, that nine out of ten of us desire more freedom, and that is why we listen to wireless talks about it. As long as we go on as we are—content with a vote and a dole...the only advice we can give one another is that Shakespeare's Iago: 'Put money in thy purse.' But we get very little money into our purse on the pay-day, and all the rest of the week other people are taking money out of it, Iago's advice is

not very practical. We must change our politics before we can get what we want; and meanwhile we must stop gossiping about freedom, because the people of England in the lump don't know what freedom is, never having had any. Always call freedom by its old name of leisure and keep clamoring for more leisure and more money to enjoy it in return for an honest share of work. And let us stop singing Rule, Britannia! until we make it true. Until we do, let us never vote for a parliamentary candidate who talks about our freedom and our love of liberty, for whatever political name he may give himself, he is sure to be at bottom an Anarchist who wants to live on our labour without being taken up by the police for it as he deserves. (227 words)

(*Part I, 1994*)

Substance: Most people desire freedom but they do not know what true freedom is or how to seek for it. Freedom consists not in a vote and a dole, but in leisure and the means to enjoy it. People of England should stop all idle talks about freedom. They should also stop voting for all parliamentary candidates who talk about freedom only to deceive the people. (65 words)

Critical Note: The idea of true freedom as enunciated in the passage is a very valid one, not only for England, but also for other countries, particularly in the third world countries. Common people are not very clear about what true freedom is; a dole or some charity is commonly mistaken as freedom. The author points out, and very rightly, that true freedom is something different. It is the economic freedom that really matters for the people. And true freedom is dependant on financial stability which only can bring leisure and enjoyment.

The author's presentation of the main idea is clear, precise and forceful. His approach is logical and presentation certainly convincing. The reference to Shakespeare's Iago vividly brings out the miserable state in which the people of England found themselves at that time. The concluding sentence contains a witty sarcasm directed against dishonest politicians. The language is simple but forceful, and is finely wedded to the subject-matter.

23. One cannot argue about the return to theology in literature. If one believes, it will make sense, if one does not, one will talk, like Sir Herbert Read, about 'the attempt to revive medieval theocracy'.....But there can be no genuine discussion between belief and unbelief. What one may note, however, is that in the work of the writers who have gone back to older dogmas, there seems a weakening of their hold on the idiom of contemporary life, corresponding to the increase of their

power to express their beliefs. Mr. Eliot and Mr. Auden might well retort that if they seem less concerned with contemporary life, this is because they have enlarged their understanding of a life outside time altogether. Nevertheless, these efforts do not resolve the problem of putting poetry back at the centre of the unconditioned imagination, and the reason is that although the weakening in daily life of the symbolism of the church is no argument against religious belief, it has deprived religious poetry of its common language. Compared with their early, secular poems, the later Eliot and Auden seem curiously specialized in an age of specialization. (190 words)

(*C.U. Part I, 1994*)

Substance: The return of theology to literature is a matter of personal belief or disbelief. Such return, however, is not welcomed by the writer. The upholders of such return have got their own arguments.The author, however, observes that the writers in whose works such a return is visible, appear to lose their hold on the contemporary literary idiom.That such great writers like Eliot and Auden suffer from such shortcoming becomes amply clear from a comparison of their later religious writings with their early secular ones. (72 words)

Critical Note: The theme of the passage relates to desirability or otherwise of the inclusion of theocracy in literature.The writer has expressed his opinion in unequivocal terms. In support of his view, he has cited the examples of Eliot and Auden drawing reference to their earlier and later writings.The view expressed is subjective in the sense that it is based on his personal perception of the writer. Hence his view is impressionistic. Although subjective, the writer's approach to the subject is unemotional and he maintains a sense of detachment.As regards style, the same is clear and simple and hence it may be termed as masculine. Economy of expression seems to be one of the leading features of the author's style. He uses contrasts, comparisons and arguments to reach his conclusion, and his conclusion indeed carriesconviction.

24. There are words made, not for, but with music, and the art is dead, and it is a chance if anything like it will again revisit literature.The body of our joy has sensibly shrunken from the old Greek and the old human unity of words, music and dance, we have dropped to mere verse; and already we are asking whether it need scan; and yet again, whether poetry need be verse at all.About the answer, I have no doubts: it need not; perhaps one day it will not. But the soul of man will have lost, in that day, something of its lilt. Of the fortunes of poetic speech, of the

actual words which poets employ, the account is more difficult. Words wear out faster than numbers, than tunes quicker cease to be vital, and pass into convention. Hence periodic revolution in diction; when some great and original poet takes us back to simpler elements, to a more human speech, and perhaps with the naiveté of this class tells us that the speech of poetry and of prose is one and the same thing. Between the language of prose and the language of poetry there is no difference at all - save a difference of poetry; and that is why so long as there is poetry, there will be poetic diction. (204 words) (*Part I, 1993*)

Substance: The essential music of words which is an integral part of poetry is fast missing today. Poetry is now reduced to mere verse and it may dispense with metre altogether. This has happened because words lose their musical charm and vitality through constant and repeated use. The periodic revolutions in diction set things right. Such a revolution brought about by some great, original poet, reveals the apparent similarity and essential difference between the language of prose and the language of poetry.

Critical Note: The evolution of poetry from ancient times to its present state is the theme of the passage. The approach of the author is controversial and debatable. Many of his readers may not, rather will not, agree with the author that poetry has slipped down to mere verse in the present day, and he makes no attempt to substantiate his argument. His approach is rather generalized. He simply takes for granted that the essence of poetry has steadily evaporated since the time of the ancient Greeks. The author is more emotional than logical. Some readers may initially find it difficult to ascertain whether the author recognizes any difference between the language of poetry and the language of prose. But a reading of the last sentence with deeper attention makes the reader realize that the author believes that there is a fundamental difference between the two.

As stated earlier, the approach of the author is emotional and therefore, it is subjective rather than objective. Objective writing is realistic and is supported with valid and sound reasons which are conspicuously absent in the passage. The language, thought not pompous, may appear to be jerky at times. The beginning sentence 'There are words made, not for, but with music, and the art is dead...' is an example in point. All said and done, it is a novel theme that keeps the interest of the reader aroused throughout.

25. I have no wish, however, to disparage a classical education. I have not myself enjoyed its benefits, and my knowledge of Greek and Latin

authors is derived almost wholly from translations. But I am firmly persuaded that the Greeks fully deserve all the admiration that is bestowed upon them, and that it is a very great and serious loss to be unacquainted with their writings. One defect, however, does seem inherent in a purely classical education—namely, a too exclusive emphasis on the past. By the study of what is absolutely ended and can never be renewed, a habit of criticism towards the present and the future is endangered. The qualities in which the present excels are qualities which, therefore, the student of Greek civilization may easily become blind. In what is new and growing, there is apt to be something crude, insolent, even a little vulgar, which is shocking to the man of sensitive tastes; quivering from the rough contact, he retires to the trim garden of the polished past, forgetting that they were reclaimed from the wilderness by men as rough and earth-solid as those from whom he shrinks in his own day.The habit of being unable to recognize merit until it is dead is too apt to a purely bookish life, and a culture based wholly on the past will seldom be able to pierce through everyday surroundings to the essential splendour of contemporary things or to the hope of greater splendour in the future.(251words) (*C.U. part I, 1993*)

Substance: The author is fully aware of the great merits of the classical learning.Yet he cannot but disapprove of its too exclusive preoccupation with the past.A student of Greek and Latin is apt to become blind to the excellences of what is new and growing. He sees a touch of vulgarity in all contemporary developments and promptly seeks refuge in what he considers the untainted glory of the classical past. He remains unaware of the essential splendour of the present and cherishes no hope for the greater splendour that the future holds for humanity. (95 words)

Critical Note: The writer makes a two-way assessment of classical writing i.e. its merits and also its inherent shortcomings that may befall a student of Greek and Latin who may not be in a position to appreciate the present and may not cherish any hope for the future.Whether we agree with the viewpoint of the author is a matter for consideration. But within the framework of the theme, the author makes a balanced approach to the question he deals with. His exposition to the main idea is logical in his own way and the conclusion drawn is convincing.

The language is lucid and simple and this makes the author's arguments forceful and convincing. He makes his presence felt in his writing as is apparent at the beginning of the passage and therefore, it falls under the category of subjective writing. The passage is marked by some metaphorical figures of speech like 'the trim garden of the polished past...'

26. Prose is the achievement of people who have learnt to discuss without blows or invective, who know that truth is hard to find and worth finding, who do not begin by accusing an opponent of wickedness, but elicit reasons and patience by displaying them. You cannot say in poetry what best prose says, or accomplish what the best prose accomplishes. Civilization may not surpass a primitive society in heights of rapture or heroism, but it is better for everyday life; kinder, more rational, more sustained in effort. The French understood this long ago, because they prize civilization and enjoy it. Pascal, writing his Provincial Letters in 1656 upon a subject obscured by medieval subtleties and distorted by party passions, is already just, polite and lucid. He does not even affect the magnificent disdain of Gibbon, but is a civilized man talking to other civilized men, and, therefore, all the more deadly in debate. But it is fallacies that he would kill, not those who maintain them. He knows not that the art of controversy is not to begin with invective, but to state your case in such a way that those who like invective will supply in themselves against your adversity. (201 words) *(C.U. part I, 1992)*

Substance: Prose is the product of civilization. It is the natural medium of expression of those who seek truth and reach reason and patience among men. Poetry cannot adequately accomplish these objects which prose can do. Kindness, reason and sustained efforts on which the life of the civilized community is based are expressed in the masterpieces of prose writers. The French were the first to realize the truth of this; hence French prose-writing is a pioneer work. Pascal, though he wrote on controversial subjects, did not openly attack his adversary but presented his case with reason and argument. It is in this appeal to reason that his chief strength lay. (109 words)

Critical Note: The point the author tries to prove in the passage is about the superiority of prose over poetry. In his opinion, for reaching and establishing truth and reason, prose is the ideal medium. Prose, according to him, is best suited to express in polite, logical and urbane manner. He finds the French writers as the best exponents for this.

The author presents his idea in a somewhat roundabout way and the reader may find it a bit difficult to grasp the main idea contained in the passage. However, he presents his idea in a clear logical manner and uses comparisons and contrasts to justify it. He clearly states that prose and reason are the achievements of civilization. This, by implication, suggests that poetry and emotion are the peculiar properties of primitivism. This point also is a matter of debate and controversy. But the writer certainly argues his point in a logical and convincing manner. His prose is lucid and simple. He himself appears to a good master of the art of civilized debate.

27. I love all beauteous things,
I seek and adore them;
God hath no better praise,
And man in his hasty days
Is honoured for them.
I too will something make
And joy in the making!
Altho' tomorrow it seem'
Like the empty words of a dream
Remembered, on waking.

(*C.U. Part I, 1994*)

Substance: The poet is a lover of beauty because it is the crowning glory of God's creation. It helps man overcome his sufferings. As a worshipper of beauty, the poet too, is eager to create something beautiful even though his creation may sink into oblivion.

Critical Note: This little poem praises beauty as the crowning glory of creation. It has the tone and structure of a prayer which perfectly suits its content. It expresses a fundamental idea of our existence with Biblical simplicity. The comparison between the thing will make and the 'empty words of dream' has been drawn with fine poetic skill.

The dominating metre is iambic though there are frequent variations. The second, fifth, seventh and tenth line contain two feet each. The first and the sixth are unrhymed. The rhyme scheme may be stated as follows: *a b c c b d e f f c.*

28. Death is a fisherman; the world we see
His fish-pond is, and we the fishes be,
He, sometimes, angler-like, doth with us play,
And slyly takes us one by one away;
Diseases are the murdering hooks which he
Doth catch us with, the bait mortality,
Which we poor fish devour, till snook
At last, too late, we feel the bitter hook.
At other times he brings his net, and then
At once sweeps up whole cities full of men,

Drawing up thousands a draught and saves
Only some few to make the others' graves,
His net some raging pestilence. Now he
Is not so kind as other fishers be;
For if they take one of the smaller fry,
They throw him in again, he shall not die;
But death is sure to kill all he can get,
And all is fish with him that comes to net.

(*C.U. Part I, 1992*)

Substance: Death is personified as and compared to a fisherman. Diseases and mortality are the hook and bait which Death uses to kill human beings who are compared to fishes. Pestilence is the net which Death uses to wipe out population of the whole cities. But Death is crueler than an angler and he would not spare even a small fry he catches with his hook.

Critical Note: It is a simple poem that conveys the simple message that death is inevitable to everyone and that no one can escape its clutches. Here Death is the fisherman and human beings are the fishes. The poem is a continuous and extended metaphor. It should not be termed as an allegory because there is no story element in it as such. As a matter of fact, the poet makes no attempt to allegorise the idea he expressed in the poem. But the metaphorical approach remains constant throughout the poem. The likeliness between Death and an angler is demonstrated through well-conceived comparisons. The metaphorical contrast between Death and an angler towards the end of the poem constitutes a welcome variation. The simple language and the absolutely unaffected style effectively counter-balance the veiled didactic tone of the poem. The verse is with iambic pentameter with certain variations. Each line rhymes with the next.

29. Oh for a poet—for a beacon bright
To rift this changless glimmer of dead gray;
To spirit back the Muses, long astray,
And flush Parnassus with a newer light;
To put these little sonnet-men to flight
Who fashion, in a shrewd mechanic way,
Songs without souls, that flicker for a day,
To vanish in irrevocable night.
What does it mean, this barren age of ours?
Here are the men, the women, and the flowers,
The seasons, and the sunset, as before.
What does it mean? Shall there not one arise

To wrench one banner from the western skies,
And mark it with his name forevermore?

(*C.U. Part I, 1992*)

Substance: The poet laments the present deplorable state of poetry. He is thoroughly tired of the sonnet-mongers whose compositions are devoid of the essential spirit of poetry. The poet eagerly awaits the arrival of a truly great poet whose mighty pen would set things right and bring poetry back to life again.

Critical Note: This is a fine sonnet of the Petrarchan type. It expresses the ardent longing by the poet for someone who would bring back true poetry that is lacking in the hands of the contemporary sonnet-mongers. The sonnet is the true reflection of the poet's genuine desire to re-establish the lost glory of poetry. It genuinely expresses the poet's sincerity and depth of feeling. The idea denoted in the octave has been properly elaborated and reiterated in the sestet. The poem abounds in metaphors that are aptly conceived and efficiently executed. Throughout the poem, passion and craftsmanship have been wedded to each other in due proportions. The metre and the rhyme schemes conform to the standard conventions of the Petrarchan variety of sonnet.

30. The love that is given to ships is profoundly different from the love men feel for every other works of their hands - the love they bear to their houses, for instance - because it is untainted by the pride of possession. The pride of skill, the pride of responsibility, the pride of endurance there may be, but otherwise it is a disinterested sentiment. No seaman ever cherished a ship, even if she belonged to him, merely because of the profit he put in his pocket. No one I think, ever did it, for a ship-owner, even of the best, has always been outside the pale of that sentiment, embracing a feeling of intimate, equal fellowship between the ship and the man, backing each other against the implacable, if sometimes dissembled, hostility of their world of waters. The sea—this truth must be confessed—has no generosity. No display of manly qualities—courage, hardihood, endurance, faithfulness—has ever been known to touch its irresponsible consciousness of power. The ocean has a conscienceless temper of savage autocrat spoiled by much adulation. He cannot brook the slightest appearance of defiance, and has remained the irreconcilable enemy of ships and men ever since ships and men had the unheard of audacity to go afloat together in the face of his frown. From that day he has gone on swallowing up the fleets and men without his resentment being glutted by a number

of victims—by so many wrecked ships and wrecked lives. Today, as ever, he is ready to beguile and betray, to smash and to drown the incorrigible option of men who backed by the fidelity of ships are trying to wrest from him the fortune of their houses, the dominion of their world, or only a dole of food for their hunger. If not always in the hot mood to smash, he is always ready for a drowning. The most amazing wonder of the deep is its unfathomable cruelty. (328 words)

(C.U. , 1998)

Substance: There exists an intensely human relationship between men and ships. It is not based on material considerations for, it is a kind of pure and selfless psychological attachment. This attachment results from a profound sense of comradeship between the man and the ship which is engendered by their continuous battle against the cruel and hostile sea. Ever since men and ships have ventured to defy the powers of the deep, the sea has been retaliating by drowning men and wrecking ships. And, it is these shared misfortunes that have cemented the intensely human relationship between men and ships. (98 words)

Critical Note: This is a highly imaginative piece of writing that has an unmistakable flavour of allegory about it. The writer deals with two separate but inter-related ideas in the paragraph—love of men for ships and the savage cruelties of the sea. But the two sides have been so skillfully welded to each other that we scarcely notice where exactly in the paragraph the writer leaves the one and takes up the other. The writer has a rich vocabulary and he uses his words and phrases with the wisdom of a true artist. Without using a single metaphor, the writer succeeds in transforming the latter part of the paragraph into a kind of sustained metaphor. The comparison of the sea with an autocrat vividly conjures up the image of a rough, violent sea, forever ready to wreck ships and destroy life. The passage, indeed, is very akin to poetry and has got its own rhythm and cadence that are sure to catch the ear of a sensitive reader.

—o—

CHAPTER VI

A Note on Shakespeare's Sonnets

We do not know when Shakespeare composed his sonnets, though it is possible that he wrote them over a period of several years, beginning, perhaps, in 1592 or 1593. Some of them were being circulated in manuscript form among his friends as early as 1598, and in 1599 two of them-138 and 144-were published in *The Passionate Pilgrim*, a collection of verses by several authors. The sonnets as we know them were certainly completed no later than 1609, the year they were published by Thomas Thorpe under the title Shakespeare's Sonnets. Most scholars believe that Thorpe acquired the manuscript on which he based his edition from someone other than the author. Few believe that Shakespeare supervised the publication of this manuscript, for the text is riddled with errors. Nevertheless, Thorpe's 1609 edition is the basis for all modern texts of the sonnets.

With only a few exceptions-Sonnets 99, 126, and 145-Shakespeare's verses follow the established English form of the sonnet. Each is a fourteen-line poem in iambic pentameter, comprising four sections: three quatrains, or groups of four lines, followed by a couplet of two lines. Traditionally, a different-thought related-idea is expressed in each quatrain, and the argument or theme of the poem is summarized or generalized in the concluding couplet. It should be noted that many of Shakespeare's couplets do not have this conventional effect. Shakespeare did, however, employ the traditional English sonnet rhyme-scheme: *abab, cdcd, efef, gg.*

Shakespeare's 154 sonnets, taken together, are frequently described as a sequence, and this is generally divided into two sections. Sonnets 1-126 focus on a young man and the speaker's friendship with him, and Sonnets 127-52 focus on the speaker's relationship with a woman. However, in only a few of the poems in the first group is it clear that the person being addressed is a male. And most of the poems in the sequence as a whole are not direct addresses to another person. The two concluding sonnets, 153 and 154, are free translations or adaptations of classical verses about Cupid; some critics believe they serve a specific purpose—though they disagree about what this may be—but many others view them as perfunctory.

The English sonnet sequence reached the height of its popularity in the 1590s, when the posthumous publication of Sir Philip Sidney's *Astrophel* and *Stella* (1591) was widely celebrated and led other English poets to create their own sonnet collections. All of these, including Shakespeare's, are indebted to some degree to the literary conventions established by the *Canzoniere*, a sonnet sequence composed by the fourteenth-century Italian poet Petrarch. By the time Shakespeare wrote his sonnets, there was also an anti-Petrarchan convention, which satirized or exploited traditional motifs and styles. Commentators on Shakespeare's sonnets frequently compare them to those of his predecessors and contemporaries, including Sidney, Sir Thomas Wyatt, Henry Howard, Earl of Surrey, Samuel Daniel, and Edmund Spenser.

The principal topics of twentieth-century critical commentary on the sonnets, however, are their themes and poetic style. Analyses of formal elements in the poems include examinations of the rhetorical devices, syntax, and diction Shakespeare employed here. The multiple and indefinite associations of his words and phrases have proved especially intriguing-and problematic-for scholars as well as general readers. The complexity and ambiguity of Shakespeare's figurative language is also a central critical issue, as is the remarkable diversity of tone and mood in the sequence. Shakespeare's departures from or modifications of the poetic styles employed by other sonneteers have also drawn a measure of critical attention.

Many of Shakespeare's themes are conventional sonnet topics, such as love and beauty, and the related motifs of time and mutability. But Shakespeare treats these themes in his own, distinctive fashion-most notably by addressing the poems of love and praise not to a fair maiden but instead to a young man; and by including a second subject of passion: a woman of questionable attractiveness and virtue. Critics have frequently called attention to Shakespeare's complex and paradoxical representation of love in the sonnets. They have also discussed at length the poet-speaker's claim that he will immortalize the young man's beauty in his verses, thereby defying the destructiveness of time. The themes of friendship and betrayal of friendship are also important critical issues, as is the nature of the relationship between the speaker and the youth. The ambiguous eroticism of the sonnets has elicited varying responses, with some commentators asserting that the relationship between the two men is asexual and others contending that it is sexual.

Because these lyrics are passionate, intense, and emotionally vivid, over the centuries many readers and commentators have been convinced that they must have an autobiographical basis. There is, however, no evidence that this is so. Nevertheless, there has been endless speculation about what these sonnets may tell us about their creator, and researchers have attempted to identify the persons who were the original or historical models for the persons the speaker refers to and addresses. The fact remains, however, that we do not know to what degree Shakespeare's personal experiences are reflected in his sonnets; nor do we know with any measure of certainty whether the persons depicted in these poems are based on specific individuals or are solely the product of Shakespeare's observation, imagination, and understanding of the human heart.

Contradictions and uncertainties are implicit in Shakespeare's sonnets. Both individually and as a collection, these poems resist generalities and summations. Their complex language and multiple perspectives have given rise to a number of different interpretations, all of which may at times seem valid-even when they contradict each other. Few critics today read the sonnets as personal allegory. Indeed, most commentators assert that speculation about what these verses may imply about Shakespeare's life, morals, and sexuality is a useless exercise. The speaker is as closely identified with each reader as he is with the writer who created him. His confused and ambiguous expressions of thought and emotion heighten our own ambivalent feelings about matters that concern us all: love, friendship, jealousy, hope, and despair.

1. **Sonnet 1**

From fairest creatures we desire increase,
That thereby beauty's rose might never die,
But as the riper should by time decease,
His tender heir might bear his memory:
But thou, contracted to thine own bright eyes,
Feed'st thy light'st flame with self-substantial fuel,
Making a famine where abundance lies,
Thyself thy foe, to thy sweet self too cruel.
Thou that art now the world's fresh ornament
And only herald to the gaudy spring,
Within thine own bud buriest thy content
And, tender churl, makest waste in niggarding.
Pity the world, or else this glutton be,
To eat the world's due, by the grave and thee.

Substance: Shakespeare begins his sonnets by introducing four of his most important themes-immortality, time, procreation, and selfishness-which are interrelated in this first sonnet both thematically and through the use of images associated with business or commerce.

Critical Note: The sonnet's first four lines relate all of these important themes. Individually, each of these four lines addresses a separate issue. Line 1 concerns procreation, especially in the phrase "we desire increase"; line 2 hints at immortality in the phrase "might never die"; line 3 presents the theme of time's unceasing progress; and line 4 combines all three concerns: A "tender heir" represents immortality for parents, who will grow old and die. According to the sonnet's poet, procreating ensures that our names will be carried on by our children. If we do not have children, however, our names will die when we do.

But, the scenario the poet creates in these four lines apparently has been rejected by the young man, whom the poet addresses as "thou," in lines 5-12. Interested only in his own selfish desires, the youth is the embodiment of narcissism, a destructively excessive love of oneself. The poet makes clear that the youth's self-love is unhealthy, not only for himself but for the entire world. Because the young man does not share himself with the world by having a child to carry on his beauty, he creates "a famine where abundance lies" and cruelly hurts himself. The "bud" in line 11 recalls the "rose" from line 2: The rose as an image of perfection underscores the immaturity of the young man, who is only a bud, still imperfect because he has not fully-bloomed.

The final couplet—the last two lines reinforces the injustice of the youth's not sharing his beauty with the world. The "famine" that he creates for himself is furthered in the phrase "To eat the world's due," as though the youth has the responsibility and the world has the right to expect the young man to father a child. Throughout the sonnets, Shakespeare draws his imagery from everyday life in the world around him. In Sonnet 1, he writes of love in terms of commercial usury, the practice of charging exorbitant interest on money lent. For example, in the first line, which reads, "From fairest creatures we desire increase," "increase" means not only nature's gain through procreation but also commercial profit, an idea linked to another trade term, "contracted," in line 5. In line 12, by using the now-antiquated term "niggarding," which means hoarding, the poet implies that the youth, instead of marrying a woman and having children, is selfishly wasting his love all for himself.

2. **Sonnet 18**

Shall I compare thee to a summer's day?
Thou art more lovely and more temperate:
Rough winds do shake the darling buds of May,
And summer's lease hath all too short a date:
Sometime too hot the eye of heaven shines,
And often is his gold complexion dimm'd;
And every fair from fair sometime declines,
By chance or nature's changing course untrimm'd;
But thy eternal summer shall not fade
Nor lose possession of that fair thou owest;
Nor shall Death brag thou wander'st in his shade,
When in eternal lines to time thou growest:
    So long as men can breathe or eyes can see,
    So long lives this, and this gives life to thee.

Substance: The speaker opens the poem with a question addressed to the beloved: "Shall I compare thee to a summer's day?" The next eleven lines are devoted to such a comparison. In line 2, the speaker stipulates what mainly differentiates the young man from the summer's day: he is "more lovely and more temperate." Summer's days tend toward extremes: they are shaken by "rough winds"; in them, the sun ("the eye of heaven") often shines "too hot," or too dim. And summer is fleeting: its date is too short, and it leads to the withering of autumn, as "every fair from fair sometime declines." The final quatrain of the sonnet tells how the beloved differs from the summer in that respect: his beauty will last forever ("Thy eternal summer shall not fade...") and never die. In the couplet, the speaker explains how the beloved's beauty will accomplish this feat, and not perish because it is preserved in the poem, which will last forever; it will live "as long as men can breathe or eyes can see."

Critical Note: This sonnet is certainly the most famous in the sequence of Shakespeare's sonnets; it may be the most famous lyric poem in English. Among Shakespeare's works, only lines such as "To be or not to be" and "Romeo, Romeo, wherefore art thou Romeo?" are better-known. This is not to say that it is at all the best or most interesting or most beautiful of the sonnets; but the simplicity and loveliness of its praise of the beloved has guaranteed its place.

On the surface, the poem is simply a statement of praise about the beauty of the beloved; summer tends to unpleasant extremes of windiness and heat, but the beloved is always mild and temperate. Summer is incidentally personified as the "eye of heaven" with its "gold complexion"; the imagery throughout is simple and unaffected, with the "darling buds of May" giving way to the "eternal summer", which the speaker promises the beloved.The language, too, is comparatively unadorned for the sonnets; it is not heavy with alliteration or assonance, and nearly every line is its own self-contained clause—almost every line ends with some punctuation, which effects a pause.

Sonnet 18 is the first poem in the sonnets not to explicitly encourage the young man to have children.The "procreation" sequence of the first 17 sonnets ended with the speaker's realization that the young man might not need children to preserve his beauty; he could also live, the speaker writes at the end of Sonnet 17, "in my rhyme." Sonnet 18, then, is the first "rhyme"—the speaker's first attempt to preserve the young man's beauty for all time.An important theme of the sonnet (as it is an important theme throughout much of the sequence) is the power of the speaker's poem to defy time and last forever, carrying the beauty of the beloved down to future generations. The beloved's "eternal summer" shall not fade precisely because it is embodied in the sonnet: "So long as men can breathe or eyes can see," the speaker writes in the couplet, "So long lives this, and this gives life to thee."

3. **Sonnet 60**

Like as the waves make towards the pebbled shore,
So do our minutes hasten to their end;
Each changing place with that which goes before,
In sequent toil all forwards do contend.
Nativity, once in the main of light,
Crawls to maturity, wherewith being crown'd,
Crooked elipses 'gainst his glory fight,
And Time that gave doth now his gift confound.
Time doth transfix the flourish set on youth
And delves the parallels in beauty's brow,
Feeds on the rarities of nature's truth,
And nothing stands but for his scythe to mow:
    And yet to times in hope my verse shall stand,
    Praising thy worth, despite his cruel hand.

Substance: This sonnet attempts to explain the nature of time as it passes, and as it acts on human life. In the first quatrain, the speaker says that the minutes replace one another like waves on the "pebbled shore," each taking the place of that which came before it in a regular sequence. In the second quatrain, he tells the story of a human life in time by comparing it to the sun: at birth ("Nativity"), it rises over the ocean ("the main of light"), then crawls upward toward noon (the "crown" of "maturity"), then is suddenly undone by "crooked eclipses", which fight against and confound the sun's glory. In the third quatrain, time is depicted as a ravaging monster, which halts youthful flourish, digs wrinkles in the brow of beauty, gobbles up nature's beauties, and mows down with his scythe everything that stands. In the couplet, the speaker opposes his verse to the ravages of time: he says that his verse will stand in times to come, and will continue to praise the "worth" of the beloved despite the "cruel hand" of time.

Critical Note : This poem is organized very neatly into the quatrain/ quatrain/quatrain/couplet structure that defines the Shakespearean sonnet. Each quatrain presents a relatively self-contained metaphorical description of time's passage in human life, while the couplet offers a twist on the poem's earlier themes. In the first quatrain, the metaphor is that of the tide; just as waves cycle forward and replace one another on the beach, so do minutes struggle forward in "sequent toil." In the second quatrain, the focus shifts from the passage of time to the passage of human life, using the metaphor of the sun during the span of a day: first it crawls forward out of the sea (an image linking this quatrain to the previous one), then is crowned with maturity in the sky, then, suddenly, it is darkened by the "crooked eclipses" of age, as time retracts his original gift. In the third quatrain, the metaphor becomes one of time as a personified force, a ravaging monster, who digs trenches in beauty, devours nature, and mows down all that stands, with his scythe.

Clearly, these images develop from one another: the first describes the way time passes, the second describes the way a human life passes, and the third describes the way time is responsible for the ravages in human life. Each quatrain is a single four-line sentence, developing a single argument through metaphor: time passes relentlessly, human life is cripplingly short before it quickly succumbs to age and decay, time is the ravager responsible for the downfall of men's lives. This is one of the great themes of the sonnets. In the couplet, the speaker then stunningly declares that he has found a way to confound time: his verse, despite time's "cruel hand," will live on, and continue to praise the worth of the beloved. This is the often-invoked corrolary to the great theme of time's passage: the speaker, disappointed that the young man will not defy time by having children, writes poem after poem about the mighty power of the "bloody tyrant" time, then declares that his poems will remain immortal, and will enable the young man's beauty to live forever. Sonnets 18, 19, 55, 63, and 65 all follow this formula, and echoes of it appear in countless of many other sonnets.

4. **Sonnet 64**

When I have seen by Time's fell hand defaced
The rich proud cost of outworn buried age,
When sometime lofty towers I see down razed,
And brass eternal slave to mortal rage;
When I have seen the hungry ocean gain
Advantage on the kingdom of the shore,
And the firm soil win of the wat'ry main,
Increasing store with loss, and loss with store;
When I have seen such interchange of state,
Or state itself confounded to decay,
Ruin hath taught me thus to ruminate:
That Time will come and take my love away.
This thought is as a death which cannot choose
But weep to have that which it fears to lose.

Substance: In Sonnet 64, the poet is portrayed as a historian, philosopher, and antiquarian who dreams of time's relentless destruction of ancient glories. Monuments that reflect the noblest ideas of human kind—castles, churches, and cities—will one day be "confounded to decay."

Critical Note: Sonnet 64 is remarkably similar to Sonnet 60, yet each sonnet concludes in a very different tone. Many of the same images are found in both sonnets: the ocean's tireless pounding of the shore; the give-and-take battle between water and the land; and the use of the word "confound" to characterize time's ceaseless progress. However, whereas Sonnet 60's concluding couplet evokes feelings of high-spirited joy and confidence, Sonnet 64 ends in despair: The poet is now certain that death will "take my love away," but he no longer seems satisfied that his verse will ensure the youth's immortality. The sonnet's last two lines convey a grievous, depressing tone: "This thought is as a death, which cannot choose/ But weep to have that which it fears to lose." The poet finally acknowledges the youth's—and his own—mortality.

5. **Sonnet 73**

That time of year thou mayst in me behold
When yellow leaves, or none, or few, do hang
Upon those boughs which shake against the cold,
Bare ruin'd choirs, where late the sweet birds sang.

In me thou seest the twilight of such day
As after sunset fadeth in the west,
Which by and by black night doth take away,
Death's second self, that seals up all in rest.
In me thou see'st the glowing of such fire
That on the ashes of his youth doth lie,
As the death-bed whereon it must expire
Consumed with that which it was nourish'd by.
This thou perceivest, which makes thy love more strong,
To love that well which thou must leave ere long.

Substance: In this poem, the speaker invokes a series of metaphors to characterize the nature of what he perceives to be his old age. In the first quatrain, he tells the beloved that his age is like a "time of year," late autumn, when the leaves have almost completely fallen from the trees, and the weather has grown cold, and the birds have left their branches. In the second quatrain, he then says that his age is like late twilight, "As after sunset fadeth in the west," and the remaining light is slowly extinguished in the darkness, which the speaker likens to "Death's second self." In the third quatrain, the speaker compares himself to the glowing remnants of a fire, which lies "on the ashes of his youth"—that is, on the ashes of the logs that once enabled it to burn—and which will soon be consumed "by that which it was nourished by"—that is, it will be extinguished as it sinks into the ashes, which its own burning created. In the couplet, the speaker tells the young man that he must perceive these things, and that his love must be strengthened by the knowledge that he will soon be parted from the speaker when the speaker, like the fire, is extinguished by time.

Critical Note: Sonnet 73 takes up one of the most pressing issues of the first 126 sonnets, the speaker's anxieties regarding what he perceives to be his advanced age, and develops the theme through a sequence of metaphors each implying something different. The first quatrain, which employs the metaphor of the winter day, emphasizes the harshness and emptiness of old age, with its boughs shaking against the cold and its "bare ruined choirs" bereft of bird song. In the second quatrain, the metaphor shifts to that of twilight, and emphasizes not the chill of old age, but rather the gradual fading of the light of youth, as "black night" takes away the light "by and by". But in each of these quatrains, with each of these metaphors, the speaker fails to confront the full scope of his problem: both the metaphor of winter and the metaphor of twilight imply cycles, and impose cyclical motions upon the objects of their metaphors, whereas old age is final. Winter follows spring, but spring will follow winter just as surely;

and after the twilight fades, dawn will come again. In human life, however, the fading of warmth and light is not cyclical; youth will not come again for the speaker. In the third quatrain, he must resign himself to this fact. The image of the fire consumed by the ashes of its youth is significant both for its brilliant disposition of the past—the ashes of which eventually snuff out the fire, "consumed by that which it was nourished by"—and for the fact that when the fire is extinguished, it can never be lit again.

In this sense, Sonnet 73 is more complex than it is often considered supposed by critics and scholars. It is often argued that Sonnet 73 and sonnets like it are simply exercises in metaphor--that they propose a number of different metaphors for the same thing, and the metaphors essentially mean the same thing. But to make this argument is to miss the psychological narrative contained within the choice of metaphors themselves. Sonnet 73 is not simply a procession of interchangeable metaphors; it is the story of the speaker slowly coming to grips with the real finality of his age and his impermanence in time.

The couplet of this sonnet renews the speaker's plea for the young man's love, urging him to "love well" that which he must soon leave. It is important to note that the couplet could not have been spoken after the first two quatrains alone. No one loves twilight because it will soon be night; instead they look forward to morning. But after the third quatrain, in which the speaker makes clear the nature of his "leav[ing] ere long," the couplet is possible, and can be treated as a poignant and reasonable exhortation to the beloved.

6. **Sonnet 94**

They that have power to hurt and will do none,
That do not do the thing they most do show,
Who, moving others, are themselves as stone,
Unmoved, cold, and to temptation slow,
They rightly do inherit heaven's graces
And husband nature's riches from expense;
They are the lords and owners of their faces,
Others but stewards of their excellence.
The summer's flower is to the summer sweet,
Though to itself it only live and die,
But if that flower with base infection meet,
The basest weed outbraves his dignity:
For sweetest things turn sourest by their deeds;
Lilies that fester smell far worse than weeds.

Substance: The first eight lines of this rather difficult sonnet are devoted to the description of a certain kind of impressive, restrained person: "They that have pow'r to hurt" and do not use that power. These people seem not to do the thing they are most apparently able to do--they "do not do the thing they most do show"—and while they may move others, they remain themselves "as stone," cold and slow to feel temptation. People such as this, the speaker says, inherit "heaven's graces" and protect the riches of nature from expenditure. They are "the lords and owners of their faces," completely in control of themselves, and others can only hope to steward a part of their "excellence."

The next four lines undergo a remarkable shift, as the speaker turns from his description of those that "have pow'r to hurt and will do none" to look at a flower in the summer. He says that the summer may treasure its flower (it is "to the summer sweet") even if the flower itself does not feel terribly cognizant of its own importance ("to itself it only live and die"). But if the flower becomes sick—if it meets with a "base infection"—then it becomes more repulsive and less dignified than the "basest weed." In the couplet, the speaker observes that it is behaviour that determines the worth of a person or a thing: sweet things which behave badly turn sour, just as a flower that festers smells worse than a weed.

Critical Note: Sonnet 94 is one of the most difficult sonnets in the sequence, at least in terms of the reader's ability to know what exactly the speaker is talking about. He jumps from an almost opaque description of these mysterious people who "have pow'r to hurt and will do none" to an almost inexplicable description of a flower in the summer. The two parts of the poem seem almost unconnected. In order to understand them, both on their own and in relation to one another, it is necessary to understand something about the tradition out of which the first 126 sonnets were written.

In Elizabethan England, it was very difficult for poets to make money simply by writing and selling their poetry. Many writers sought out aristocratic patrons, who supported them in return for the prestige of having a poet at their beck and call. Very often, poets courted their patrons, and ensured their places in their patrons' good graces, by writing fawning verses in praise of the patron's beauty, valor, power, and so on. The first 126 of Shakespeare's sonnets, while not exactly fawning praise aimed at an infinitely higher-up aristocrat (the speaker often seems quite intimate with the young man), do come from this tradition of patronage and praise. The speaker's lengthy invocations to the beloved's beauty, sweetness, and worth, and the occasional intimations of power differences between him and his beloved (as in Sonnet 87, where the speaker says that the young man is "too dear for my possessing"), hint at this tradition. Certain other poems—such as the sequence from 82 to 86, in which the speaker reacts to the presence of a rival poet competing for his patron's favours—express it outright. Sonnet 94 is a reaction to the conditions of the speaker's patronage.

An aristocrat was in no way obligated to treat the poet he supported as an equal; in fact, his superiority was in some ways the entire point of the exchange. The speaker, genuinely in love with the young man, is forced to relate to him not as an equal, but as an inferior. To him, the young man can often seem cold, distant, and grave, and the speaker, who loves him, is forced to try to explain this behaviour in a way that will enable him to continue loving the young man. The solution is to praise his very distance and reserve: he is not only "unmoved, cold, and to temptation slow," he is "the lord and owner" of his face, and the inheritor of "heaven's graces." But praise of this chilly detachment seems inadequate (after all, the speaker's tone seems to imply that he has been hurt by the young man's behaviour, so how can he say that the young man "will do none"?), so he makes his argument even more oblique by turning to the metaphor of the flower.

The summer's flower, like the cold aristocrats of the first two quatrains, is beautiful only in and for itself; it has no interest in the fact that the summer loves it, because "to itself it only live and die." Like the summer, the speaker hopes he can love the young man simply for his beauty without expecting anything in return. But he is forced to acknowledge that the young man is not so neutral and inactive: he has committed hurtful deeds, which act like a "base infection" in the flower to render it lower than a weed. The couplet brilliantly brings the two parts of the poem into full relation: the first line refers specifically to the first part of the poem ("Sweetest things turn sourest by their deeds"—as opposed to the perfect creatures who "do not do" hurtful deeds), and the second half refers to the metaphor of the flower ("Lilies that fester"—a sour deed—"smell far worse than weeds").

The major themes of this poem are continued in the far simpler Sonnet 95, in which the metaphoric relation between the hurtful, aristocratic young man and the festering flower is developed: "How sweet and lovely dost thou make the shame/Which, like a canker in the fragrant rose,/ Doth spot the beauty of thy budding name!"

7. **Sonnet 97**

How like a winter hath my absence been
From thee, the pleasure of the fleeting year!
What freezings have I felt, what dark days seen!
What old December's bareness every where!
And yet this time removed was summer's time,
The teeming autumn, big with rich increase,
Bearing the wanton burden of the prime,
Like widow'd wombs after their lords' decease:
Yet this abundant issue seem'd to me
But hope of orphans and unfather'd fruit;
For summer and his pleasures wait on thee,
And, thou away, the very birds are mute;
    Or, if they sing, 'tis with so dull a cheer
    That leaves look pale, dreading the winter's near.

Substance: The speaker has been forced to endure a separation from the beloved, and in this poem he compares that absence to the desolation of winter. In the first quatrain, the speaker simply exclaims the comparison, painting a picture of the winter: "How like a winter hath my absence been/From thee, the pleasure of the fleeting year!/What freezings have I felt, what dark days seen!/What old December's bareness everywhere!" In the second quatrain, however, he says that, in reality, the season was that of late summer or early autumn, when all of nature was bearing the fruits of summer's blooming. In the third quatrain, he dismisses the "wanton burden of the prime"—that is, the bounty of the summer—as unreal, as the "hope of orphans." It could not have been fathered by summer, because "summer and his pleasures" wait on the beloved, and when he is gone, even the birds are silent. In the couplet, the speaker says that the birds may sing when the beloved is gone, but it is with "so dull a cheer" that the leaves, listening, become fearful that winter is upon them.

Critical Note: The seasons, so often invoked as a metaphor for the passage of time in the sonnets, are here metaphorized, and function as a kind of delusional indication of how deeply the speaker misses the company of the beloved. As the second quatrain reveals, the speaker spends some time apart from the beloved in "summer's time," in late summer, when the natural world is heavy with the fruits of the summer. But without the young man's presence, the world of abundance and plenty instead resembles "old December's bareness," not the pleasures of summer attendant upon the young man's presence.

The linguistic richness of this poem is the cause of its prominence and popularity among the sonnets. With an economy of imagery, the speaker manages to evoke the "freezings" and "dark days" of winter, the warmth and luxury of the "teeming autumn, big with rich increase," and, in the third quatrain, the uneasy coexistence of the two in the lonely speaker's mind. The poem makes use of its strong alliteration (*fl*eeting and *fr*eezings, *da*rk days and *De*cember, *ti*me and *te*eming, *wi*dowed *wo*mbs, "*or*phans" and "un*fa*thered *fr*uit") to give it linguistic weight and pacing, and its lines seem stuffed full with of evocative words.

Probably because of this sensory and imagistic luxury, Sonnet 73 has become the ancestor of a great many other important poems, most notably Keats's ode *To Autumn*. Its sense and its images are also present in Keats's sonnet *When I have fears that I may cease to be*, Wallace Stevens's *The Snow Man* and *No Possum, No Sop, No Taters*, many of Robert Frost's autumn lyrics, and other important poems.

8. **Sonnet 116**

Let me not to the marriage of true minds
Admit impediments. Love is not love
Which alters when it alteration finds,
Or bends with the remover to remove:
O no! it is an ever-fixed mark
That looks on tempests and is never shaken;
It is the star to every wandering bark,
Whose worth's unknown, although his height be taken
Love's not Time's fool, though rosy lips and cheeks
Within his bending sickle's compass come:
Love alters not with his brief hours and weeks,
But bears it out even to the edge of doom.
If this be error and upon me proved,
I never writ, nor no man ever loved.

Substance: This sonnet attempts to define love, by telling both what it is and is not. In the first quatrain, the speaker says that love—"the marriage of true minds"—is perfect and unchanging; it does not "admit impediments," and it does not change when it find changes in the loved one. In the second quatrain, the speaker tells what love is through a metaphor: a guiding star to lost ships ("wand'ring barks") that is not susceptible to storms (it "looks on tempests and is never shaken"). In the third quatrain, the speaker again describes what love is not: it is not susceptible to time. Though beauty fades in time as rosy lips and cheeks come within "his bending sickle's compass," love does not change with hours and weeks: instead, it "bears it out ev'n to the edge of doom." In the couplet, the speaker attests to his certainty that love is as he says: if his statements can be proved to be error, he declares, he must never have written a word, and no man can ever have been in love.

Critical Note: Along with Sonnets 18 ("Shall I compare thee to a summer's day?") and 130 ("My mistress' eyes are nothing like the sun"), Sonnet 116 is one of the most famous poems in the entire sequence. The definition of love that it provides is among the most often quoted and anthologized in the poetic canon. Essentially, this sonnet presents the extreme ideal of romantic love: it never changes, it never fades, it outlasts death and admits no flaw. What is more, it insists that this ideal is the only love that can be called "true"—if love is mortal, changing, or impermanent, the speaker writes, then no man ever loved. The basic division of this poem's argument into the various parts of the sonnet form is extremely simple: the first quatrain says what love is not (changeable), the second quatrain says what it is (a fixed guiding star unshaken by tempests), the third quatrain says more specifically what it is not ("time's fool"—that is, subject to change in the passage of time), and the couplet announces the speaker's certainty. What gives this poem its rhetorical and emotional power is not its complexity; rather, it is the force of its linguistic and emotional conviction.

The language of Sonnet 116 is not remarkable for its imagery or metaphoric range. In fact, its imagery, particularly in the third quatrain (time wielding a sickle that ravages beauty's rosy lips and cheeks), is rather standard within the sonnets, and its major metaphor (love as a guiding star) is hardly startling in its originality. But the language is extraordinary in that it frames its discussion of the passion of love within a very restrained, very intensely disciplined rhetorical structure. With a masterful control of rhythm and variation of tone—the heavy balance of "Love's not time's fool" to open the third quatrain; the declamatory "O no" to begin the second—the speaker makes an almost legalistic argument for the eternal passion of love, and the result is that the passion seems stronger and more urgent for the restraint in the speaker's tone.

9. **Sonnet 129**

The expense of spirit in a waste of shame
Is lust in action; and till action, lust
Is perjured, murderous, bloody, full of blame,
Savage, extreme, rude, cruel, not to trust,

Enjoy'd no sooner but despised straight,
Past reason hunted, and no sooner had
Past reason hated, as a swallow'd bait
On purpose laid to make the taker mad;
Mad in pursuit and in possession so;
Had, having, and in quest to have, extreme;
A bliss in proof, and proved, a very woe;
Before, a joy proposed; behind, a dream.
All this the world well knows; yet none knows well
To shun the heaven that leads men to this hell.

Substance: This complex poem grapples with the idea of sexual desire as it exists in longing, fulfilment, and memory. (That is to say, it deals with lust as a longing for future pleasure; with lust as it is consummated in the present; and with lust as it is remembered after the pleasurable experience, when it becomes a source of shame.) At the beginning of the poem, the speaker says that "lust in action"—that is, as it exists at the consummation of the sexual act—is an "expense of spirit in a waste of shame." He then devotes the rest of the first quatrain to characterizing lust as it exists "till action"—that is, before the consummation: it is "perjured, murd'rous, bloody, full of blame / Savage, extreme, rude, cruel, not to trust."

In the second quatrain, the speaker jumps between longing, fulfilment, and memory. No sooner is lust "enjoyed" than it is "despised." When lust is longing, the fulfilment of that longing is hunted "past reason"; but as soon as it is achieved, it becomes shameful, and is hated "past reason." In the third quatrain, then, the speaker says that lust is mad in all three of its forms: in pursuit and possession, it is mad, and in memory, consummation, and longing ("had, having, and in quest to have") it is "extreme." While it is experienced it might be "a bliss in proof," but as soon as it is finished ("proved") it becomes "a very woe." In longing, it is "a joy proposed," but in memory, the pleasure it afforded is merely "a dream." In the couplet, the speaker says that the whole world knows these things well; but nevertheless, none knows how to shun lust in order to avoid shame: "To shun the heaven that leads men to this hell."

Critical Note: The situation of the speaker of this poem is that of a person who has experienced each stage of lust, and who is therefore able to articulate the shame he now feels with reference to his past desire and its consummation. Though the lust of this poem is not explicitly sexual, it is described in highly carnal language—bloody, full of blame, savage, rude, swallowed bait. The most important device of this poem is its rapid oscillation between tenses and times; it jumps between the stages of lust almost uncontrollably, and in so doing creates a composite picture of its subject from all sides—each tinged by the shameful "hell" the speaker now occupies.

Another important device, and a rare one in the sonnets, is the poem's impersonal tone. The speaker never says outright that he is writing about his own experience; instead, he presents the poem as an impersonal description, a catalogue of the kinds of experience offered by lust. But the ferocity of his description belies his real, expressive purpose, which is to rue his own recent surrender to lustful desire. (The impersonal tone is exceedingly rare in the sonnets, and is invoked only when the speaker seeks most defensively to deflect his words away from himself—as in Sonnet 94, where his tone of impersonal description covers a deep-seated vulnerability.)

10. **Sonnet 130**

My mistress' eyes are nothing like the sun;
Coral is far more red than her lips' red;
If snow be white, why then her breasts are dun;
If hairs be wires, black wires grow on her head.
I have seen roses damask'd, red and white,
But no such roses see I in her cheeks;
And in some perfumes is there more delight
Than in the breath that from my mistress reeks.
I love to hear her speak, yet well I know
That music hath a far more pleasing sound;
I grant I never saw a goddess go;
My mistress, when she walks, treads on the ground:
And yet, by heaven, I think my love as rare
As any she belied with false compare.

Substance: This sonnet compares the speaker's lover to a number of other beauties—and never in the lover's favour. Her eyes are "nothing like the sun," her lips are less red than coral; compared to white snow, her breasts are dun-coloured, and her hairs are like black wires on her head. In the second quatrain, the speaker says he has seen roses separated by colour ("damasked") into red and white, but he sees no such roses in his mistress cheeks; and he says the breath that "reeks" from his mistress is less delightful than perfume. In the third quatrain, he admits that, though he loves her voice, music "hath a far more pleasing sound," and that, though he has never seen a goddess, his mistress—unlike goddesses—walks on the ground. In the couplet, however, the speaker declares that, "by heav'n," he thinks his love as rare and valuable "As any she belied with false compare"—that is, any love in which false comparisons were invoked to describe the loved one's beauty.

Critical Note: This sonnet, one of Shakespeare's most famous, plays an elaborate joke on the conventions of love poetry common to Shakespeare's day, and it is so well-conceived that the joke remains funny today. Most sonnet sequences in Elizabethan England were modeled after that of Petrarch. Petrarch's famous sonnet sequence was written as a series of love poems to an idealized and idolized mistress named Laura. In the sonnets, Petrarch praises her beauty, her worth, and her perfection using an extraordinary variety of metaphors based largely on natural beauties. In Shakespeare's day, these metaphors had already become cliche (as, indeed, they still are today), but they were still the accepted technique for writing love poetry. The result was that poems tended to make highly idealizing comparisons between nature and the poets' lover that were, if taken literally, completely ridiculous. My mistress' eyes are like the sun; her lips are red as coral; her cheeks are like roses, her breasts are white as snow, her voice is like music, she is a goddess. In many ways, Shakespeare's sonnets subvert and reverse the conventions of the Petrarchan love sequence: the idealizing love poems, for instance, are written not to a perfect woman but to an admittedly imperfect man, and the love poems to the dark lady are anything but idealizing ("My love is as a fever, longing still / For that which longer nurseth the disease" is hardly a Petrarchan conceit.) Sonnet 130 mocks the typical Petrarchan metaphors by presenting a speaker who seems to take them at face value, and somewhat bemusedly, decides to tell the truth. Your mistress' eyes are like the sun? That's strange—my mistress' eyes aren't at all like the sun. Your mistress' breath smells like perfume? My mistress' breath reeks compared to perfume. In the couplet, then, the speaker shows his full intent, which is to insist that love does not need these conceits in order to be real; and women do not need to look like flowers or the sun in order to be beautiful.

The rhetorical structure of Sonnet 130 is important to its effect. In the first quatrain, the speaker spends one line on each comparison between his mistress and something else (the sun, coral, snow, and wires)—the one positive thing in the whole poem—some part of his mistress is like. In the second and third quatrains, he expands the descriptions to occupy two lines each, so that roses/cheeks, perfume/breath, music/voice, and goddess/ mistress each receive a pair of unrhymed lines. This creates the effect of an expanding and developing argument, and neatly prevents the poem--which does, after all, rely on a single kind of joke for its first twelve lines--from becoming stagnant.

11. **Sonnet 146**

Poor soul, the centre of my sinful earth,
[My sinful earth] these rebel powers that thee array;
Why dost thou pine within and suffer dearth,
Painting thy outward walls so costly gay?
Why so large cost, having so short a lease,
Dost thou upon thy fading mansion spend?
Shall worms, inheritors of this excess,
Eat up thy charge? is this thy body's end?
Then soul, live thou upon thy servant's loss,
And let that pine to aggravate thy store;
Buy terms divine in selling hours of dross;
Within be fed, without be rich no more:
So shalt thou feed on Death, that feeds on men,
And Death once dead, there's no more dying then.

Substance: The speaker addresses this poem to his soul, asking it in the first stanza why it, the centre of his "sinful earth" (that is, his body), endures misery within his body while he is so concerned with maintaining its "paint[ed]" outward appearance—that is, why his soul allows his exterior vanity to wound its interior life. He asks his soul why, since it will not spend long in the body ("having so short a lease" in the "fading mansion"), it spends "so large cost" to decorate it, and he asks whether worms shall be allowed to eat the soul's "charge" after the body is dead. In the third quatrain, the speaker exhorts his soul to concentrate on its own inward well-being at the expense of the body's outward walls ("Let that [i.e., the body] pine to aggravate [i.e., increase] thy store"). He says that the body's hours of "dross" will buy the soul "terms divine"; and admonishes the soul to be fed within, and not to be rich without. In the couplet, the speaker tells the soul that by following his advice, it will feed on death, which feeds on men and their bodies; and once it has fed on death, it will enjoy eternal life: "And Death once dead, there's no more dying then."

Critical Note: Sonnet 146, an austerely moralizing self-exhortation to privilege the inner enrichment of the soul over the outer decoration of the body, is also the site of the most virulent textual controversy of any of Shakespeare's poem in the sequence. The way the poem is printed in its first edition, its first two lines read: Poor soule, the centre of my sinful earth, My sinful earth these rebel powers that thee array... The repetition of the phrase "my sinful earth" at the start of the second line has long been chalked up to a printer's mistake; it almost certainly could not have been Shakespeare's intention to break his meter so egregiously for the sake of such a heavy-handed repetition. (In the 1590s, any text that was to be printed had to be set into the printing press letter by letter, a painstaking and often mind-numbing process that resulted in many mistakes of this nature.) As a result, critics have debated for what seems the better part of four centuries over what the "missing" text might have been. "Trapp'd by these rebel powers"? "Ring'd" by them? "Fenced"? "Foil'd"? "Pressed with"? Possible alternatives are literally endless; most recent editors of the sonnets have avoided conjecture for that very reason.

Apart from the textual controversy, Sonnet 146 presents the relatively simple idea that the body exists at the expense of the soul, so that decorating or adorning the body, or even worrying about its beauty, can only be accomplished at the soul's expense. The speaker of this sonnet feels trapped by his preoccupation with his outward appearance, and urges himself—by addressing his neglected soul, which he concedes has the decision-making power over the body—to neglect the body as a way to enrich the soul and help it toward heaven ("Buy terms divine in selling hours of dross"). In this sense, Sonnet 146 is one of comparatively few sonnets to strike a piously religious tone: in its overt concern with heaven, asceticism, and the progress of the soul, it is quite at odds with many of the other sonnets, which yearn for and celebrate sensory beauty and aesthetic pleasure.

12. **Sonnet 150**

O, from what power hast thou this powerful might
With insufficiency, my heart to sway?
To make me give the lie to my true sight,
And swear that brightness doth not grace the day?
Whence hast thou this becoming of things ill,
That in the very refuse of thy deeds
There is such strength and warrantize of skill
That, in my mind, thy worst all best exceeds?
Who taught thee how to make me love thee more
The more I hear and see just cause of hate?
O, though I love what others do abhor,
With others thou shouldst not abhor my state:
If thy unworthiness raised love in me,
More worthy I to be beloved of thee.

Substance: The poet wonders where from had his beloved got the power to rule him with her very defects. She even had the capability to direct his sight so that he could not see thinks clearly. His sight could not distinguish between black and white. From where he wonders, she had got the ability to make bad things appear good, so that in the worst of her deeds there was such conviction that her worst appeared to be better than other's best. The more he hears others talk of her lack of beauty, and find the cause of hating her, the more he loved her. Though he loved in her what others hated; she should not hate him in such a predicament, because of his inability to see correctly. She should consider him more worthy of her love. In fact, it was for her unworthiness that he loved her.

Critical Note: Using a more rational tone than in the previous sonnet, the poet tries to understand why he cannot completely break from the woman. He shifts his approach asking what incredible power the woman uses to enslave him; earlier he had asked himself what his own character flaws were that bound him to her. Again written as a series of questions to the woman, the poet asks the woman. "O, from what pow'r hast thou this pow'rful might/with insufficiency my heart to sway?" Contrary to all sense, the poet appeals for pity from his mistress. Her sexual powers have unbalanced his judgement and inflamed his imagination. Promiscuity, the least flattering thing about the woman, is what he loves.

13. Sonnet 10

For shame deny that thou bear'st love to any,
Who for thy self art so unprovident.
Grant, if thou wilt, thou art beloved of many,
But that thou none lov'st is most evident:
For thou art so possessed with murderous hate,
That 'gainst thy self thou stick'st not to conspire,
Seeking that beauteous roof to ruinate
Which to repair should be thy chief desire.
O! change thy thought, that I may change my mind:
Shall hate be fairer lodged than gentle love?
Be, as thy presence is, gracious and kind,
Or to thyself at least kind-hearted prove:
    Make thee another self for love of me,
    That beauty still may live in thine or thee.

Substance: The poet declares a personal interest in the youth, and addresses by saying if he (the youth) has any sense of shame, he should admit that he does not have any love in his heart for anyone, since he so unwilling to care about himself. The poet admits, if he likes, that many people love him, but it's also obvious that he loves no one. For he is so possessed with murderous hatred that he has no problem plotting against himself, seeking to destroy the house that he should want to repair. The youth should change his way of thinking, so the poet can change his mind about him. Hate should not have a more beautiful home than love. The poet implores the youth to be gracious and kind, like his appearance—or at least be kind-hearted to himself, to have a child out of love for the poet, so his beauty will live on in his children, if not in him.

Critical Note: Sonnet 10 repeats and extends the argument of Sonnet 9, with the added suggestion that the youth really loves no one. Clearly, the poet does not seriously believe the young man to be incapable of affection, for then there would be no point in the poet's trying to maintain a relationship with him. However, underneath the mock-serious tone is the poet's suggestion that the youth's self-love wastes himself. Narcissism means infatuation with one's own appearance, but the youth's absorption with his own image is really an attachment to nobody. He therefore loses the power of returning the creative force of love in a relationship. The poet considers the youth's unwillingness to marry a form of homicide against his potential progeny, which he suggested in Sonnet 9: "The world will wail thee like a makeless wife;/The world will be thy widow, and still weep..." And in Sonnet 10, the poet writes, "For thou art so possessed with murderous hate/That 'gainst thyself thou stick'st not to conspire." Here, Sonnet 10 creates the image of marriage as a house with a roof falling in decay that the youth should seek to repair, but the poet uses the house imagery less to indicate marriage than to suggest the youth's beauty would reside in his offspring: "Make thee another self for love of me,/ That beauty still may live in thine or thee."

14. Sonnet 16

But wherefore do not you a mightier way
Make war upon this bloody tyrant, Time?
And fortify yourself in your decay
With means more blessed than my barren rhyme?
Now stand you on the top of happy hours,
And many maiden gardens yet unset
With virtuous wish would bear your living flowers,
Much liker than your painted counterfeit:
So should the lines of life that life repair,
Which this, Time's pencil, or my pupil pen,
Neither in inward worth nor outward fair,
Can make you live yourself in eyes of men.
    To give away yourself keeps yourself still,
    And you must live, drawn by your own sweet skill.

Substance: Why don't you fight time with weapons more powerful than my poetry? Right now you are in your prime, and many women would be willing to bear you a child, who would copy you better than any work of art. The life of your child would renew your own beyond my own power (Lines 9-12 are doubtful and contested). Giving your self away (that is, in marriage and procreation) will allow you to keep yourself (in life), and only your own skill can cause this to happen.

Critical Note: Sonnet 16 continues the arguments for the youth to marry and at the same time now disparages the poet's own poetic labours, for the poet concedes that children will ensure the young man immortality more surely than will his verses because neither verse nor painting can provide a true reproduction of the "inward worth" or the "outward fair" of youth.

Although the poet has tried to immortalize the youth's beauty in his sonnets, the youth's sexual power is, as line 4 states, endowed "With means more blessed than my barren rhyme." The poet concedes that his poetry ("painted counterfeit") is "barren" because it is a mere replica of the young man's beauty and not the real thing itself, whereas a child ("the lines of life") will keep the young man's beauty alive and youthful in a form more substantial than art can create.

15. Sonnet 25

Let those who are in favour with their stars
Of public honour and proud titles boast,
Whilst I, whom fortune of such triumph bars
Unlook'd for joy in that I honour most.
Great princes' favourites their fair leaves spread
But as the marigold at the sun's eye,
And in themselves their pride lies buried,
For at a frown they in their glory die.
The painful warrior famoused for fight,
After a thousand victories once foiled,
Is from the book of honour razed quite,
And all the rest forgot for which he toiled:
    Then happy I, that love and am beloved,
    Where I may not remove nor be removed.

Substance: Let fortunate people boast about their prizes and their titles, while the poet—who is not lucky enough to get such rewards—experiences unexpected joy in what he honours most: the love of his beloved. Those courtiers who enjoy high status because they are the favourites of great princes are like marigolds. They bloom as long as the sun shines on them, but their pride is fragile—one frown will kill them. And once a famous warrior who has painfully endured and won a thousand battles is defeated, he is stripped of all his honours, and all of the successes that he worked for are forgotten. The poet is much happier, who loves and is loved in a place he cannot leave and from which others cannot remove him.

Critical Note: In Sonnet 25, which has as its theme mortality versus immortality, the poet contrasts himself with those "who are in favour with their stars," implying that, though he is not numbered among those famous, fortunate people, their fame will not last, while his love will. Therefore, he is happy in his love. Most important, the poet is comforted in the knowledge that his love for the young man grants him permanence: "Then happy I, that love and am beloved / Where I may not remove nor be removed." Requited love between him and the youth replaces his need for fame.

16. Sonnet 55

Not marble, nor the gilded monuments
Of princes, shall outlive this powerful rime;
But you shall shine more bright in these contents
Than unswept stone, besmear'd with sluttish time.
When wasteful war shall statues overturn,
And broils root out the work of masonry,
Nor Mars his sword nor war's quick fire shall burn
The living record of your memory.
'Gainst death and all-oblivious enmity
Shall you pace forth; your praise shall still find room
Even in the eyes of all posterity
That wear this world out to the ending doom.
So, till the judgment that yourself arise,
You live in this, and dwell in lovers' eyes.

Substance: Neither marble nor the gold-plated monuments of princes will outlive this powerful poetry. You will shine more brightly in these poems than those stones that crumble to dust, blackened by time. When devastating war overturns statues, with its battles uprooting buildings, neither the god of war nor his quick-burning fires shall destroy this record of you. Despite death and ignorant enmity, you shall continue on. All those generations to come, down to the weary end of time, will devote space to praising you. So until Judgment Day, when you are raised up, you will live in this poetry, and in the eyes of lovers who read this.

Critical Note: Sonnet 55 is one of Shakespeare's most famous works and a noticeable deviation from other sonnets in which he appears insecure about his relationships and his own self-worth. Here we find an impassioned burst of confidence as the poet claims to have the power to keep his friend's memory alive evermore.

Although the poet's previous pride in writing verse is missing in this sonnet, he still manages to demonstrate a superbly confident spirit: "Not marble, nor the gilded monuments / Of princes, shall outlive this powerful rime." He clearly abandons, at least for the time being, his earlier depressing opinion of his verse as "barren rime," for next he contrasts his verses' immortality to "unswept stone, besmeared with sluttish time," meaning that the young man will be remembered longer because of the poet's having written about him than if descriptions of his beauty had been chiseled in stone.

The next four lines address the same theme of immortality, but now the poet boasts that not only natural forces but human wars and battles cannot blot out his sonnets, which are a "living record" of the youth. Monuments and statues may be desecrated during war, but not so these rhymes.

Some critics argue that Shakespeare's sudden-swell of pride in his poetry was strictly artificial—a blatant attempt to mimic the style of the classical poets. "It is difficult on any other hypothesis to reconcile the inflated egotism of such a one as 55 with the unassuming dedications to the Venus and Lucrece, 1593 and 1594, or with the expressions of humility found in the sonnets themselves, e.g. 32 and 38" (Halliwell-Phillipps, 304).

However, many believe that such an analysis ignores Shakespeare's paramount desire to immortalize his friend in verse, and not himself (as was the motive of most classical poets). "The Romans say: Because of my poem I will never die. Shakespeare says: Because of my poem you will never die.... What distinguishes Shakespeare is that he values the identity of the beloved; he recognizes that the beloved has his own personal immortality, in no way dependent on poetry" (Martin, 158). By focusing on the word "live", Shakespeare uses the language itself to emphasize his authorial intentions. Notice the word choices of *outlive* (2), *living* (8), *oblivious* (9), and *live* (14).

—o—

CHAPTER VII

Passages For Practice (Prose)

1. There can be little question that the attainment of a federation of all humanity, together with a sufficient measure of social justice, to ensure health, education, and a rough equality of opportunity to most of the children born into the world, would mean such a release and increase of human energy as to open a new phase in human history. The enormous waste caused by military preparation and the mutual annoyance of competing great powers and the still more enormous waste due to unproductiveness of great masses of people, either because they are too wealthy for stimulus or too poor for efficiency, would cease. There would be a vast increase in the supply of human necessities, a rise in the standard of life and in what is considered a necessity, a development of transport and every kind of convenience; and a multitude of people would be transferred from low-grade production to such higher work as art of all kinds, teaching, scientific work and the like. All over the world there would be a setting free of human capacity, such as here has occurred hitherto only in small places and through precious limited phases of prosperity and security. Unless we are to suppose that spontaneous outbreaks of supermen have occurred in the past, it is reasonable to conclude that the Athens of Pericles, the Florence of the Medicis, Elizabethan England, the great deeds of Asoka, the Tang and Ming periods in art, are but samples of what a whole world of sustained security would yield continuously cumulatively. Without supposing any change in human quality, but merely its release from the present system of inordinate waste, history justifies this expectation. (H. G. Wells)

Idea: The establishment of a world federation will bring about the golden age of the world, and end the present war and wastage of human energy.

2. The old statesman was now entering upon the penultimate period of his enormous career. He who had once been the rising hope of the

stern and the unbending Tories, had at length emerged, after a lifetime of transmutations, as the champion of militant democracy. He was at the apex of his power. His great rival was dead; he stood preeminent in the eye of the nation; he enjoyed the applause, the confidence, the admiration, the adoration, even of multitudes. Yet—such was the peculiar character of the man, and such the intensity of the feelings which he called forth—at this very moment, at the height of his popularity, he was distrusted and loathed; already an unparalled animosity was gathering its forces against him. For, indeed, there was something in his nature which invited-which demanded-the clashing reactions of passionate extremes. It was easy to worship Mr. Gladstone; to see him the perfect model of the upright man whose life had been devoted to the application of high principles to affairs of state-the man, too, whose sense of right and justice was invigorated and ennobled by an enthusiastic heart. It was also easy to detest him as a hypocrite, to despise him as a demagogue and to dread him as a crafty manipulator of men and things for the purpose of his own ambition. It might have been supposed that one or the other of these conflicting judgements must have been palpably absurd, that nothing short of gross prejudice and wilful blindness, on one side or other, could reconcile such contradictory conception of a single human being. (Lytton Strachey)

Idea: The character of Gladstone was a mixture of such opposite qualities that some admired him as an ideal gentleman, while others condemned him as a hypocrite.

3. Lenin was the Grand Repudiator. He repudiated everything. He repudiated God, King, Country, morals, treaties, debts, rents, interest, the laws and customs of centuries, all contracts written or implied, the whole structure—such as it is—of human society. In the end he repudiated himself. He repudiated the communist system. He confessed its failure in all important spheres. He proclaimed the New Economic Policy and recognized private. He repudiated what he had slaughtered so many trade. He repudiated what he had slaughtered so many for not believing. They were right, it seemed after all. They were lucky that he did not find it out before. But these things happen sometimes; and how great is the man who acknowledges his mistake! Back again to wash the dishes and give the child a sweetmeat. Thence once more to the rescue of mankind. This time perhaps the shot will be better aimed. It may kill those who are wrong; not those who are right. But

after all, what are men? If Imperialism has its cannon of food, should the Communist laboratory be denied the raw material for sociological experiment? (Winston Churchill)

Idea: Lenin was a perfect revolutionary, who denied everything that was so long held dear to human heart.

4. Great men of science, literature, and art—apostles of great thoughts and lords of the great heart—have belonged to no exclusive class nor rank in life. They have come alike from colleges, workshops, and farmhouses,—from the huts of poor men and the mansions of the rich. Some of God's greatest apostles have come from "the ranks." The poorest have sometimes taken the highest places; nor have difficulties apparently the most insuperable proved obstacles in their way. Those very difficulties, in many instances, would ever seem to have been their best helpers, by evoking their powers of labour and endurance, and stimulating into life faculties which might otherwise have lain dormant. The instances of obstacles thus surmounted, and of triumphs thus achieved, are indeed so numerous, as almost to justify the proverb that "With will one can do anything."

Idea: Poetry is no curse; it has produced some of the greatest men of the earth.

5. In a remote village among some wild hills in the province of Lorraine, there lived a countryman whose name was Jacques d'Arc. He had a daughter, Joan of Arc, who was at this time in her twentieth year. She had been a solitary girl from her childhood; she had often tended sheep and cattle for whole days where no human figure was seen or human voice heard; and she had often knelt, for hours together, in the gloomy, empty, little village chapel, looking up at the altar and at the dim lamp burning before it, until she fancied that she saw shadowy figures standing there, and even that she heard them speak to her. The people in that part of France were very ignorant and superstitious, and they had many ghostly tales to tell about what they had dreamed, and what they saw among the lonely hills when the clouds and the mists were resting on them. So, they easily believed that Joan saw strange sights, and they whispered among themselves that angels and spirits talked to her.

Idea: Joan spent her childhood days tending sheep and praying in lonely places. People of France believed that she had visions and she could hear the voices of the angels.

6. The death of Nelson was felt in England as something more than a

public calamity; men started at the intelligence, and turned pale, as if they had heard of the loss of a dear friend. An object of our admiration and affection, of our pride and of our hopes, was suddenly taken from us; and it seemed as if we had never, till then, known how deeply we loved and reverenced him. What the country had lost in its great naval hero—the greatest of our own, and of all former times—was scarcely taken into the account of grief. So perfectly, indeed, had he performed his part, that the maritime war, after the battle of Trafalgar, was considered at an end: the fleets of the enemy were not merely defeated but destroyed; new navies must be built, and a new race of seamen reared for them, before the possibility of their invading our shores could again be contemplated. It was not, therefore, from any selfish reflection upon the magnitude of our loss that we mourned for him: the general sorrow was of a higher character.

Idea: The death of Nelson was a great national catastrophe. An object of love admiration for the whole nation was gone. He completely annihilated the navy of the enemy in the battle of Trafalgar. But the death of Nelson was grieved more from a sense of personal loss than from a sense of the loss to the nation.

7. The Great War arose out of a state of opinion which regarded war as a legitimate and normal method of promoting national interests; and to prevent opinion slipping back into that atmosphere is perhaps the greatest task before the coming generation. It is a good thing, if only it lasts, that we should all be so impressed with the horrors of war as to speak of the war-makers and militarists as criminals, but we did not speak or think in that way before the war. Let me take as an example the case which is commonly made against the Russians, for having, it is alleged, precipitated the war by mobilizing in July, 1914. This may, in a sense, be true, but at the time, not one person in a hundred would have imputed 'guilt' to Russia if it had been true. We might have called her precipitate or impolite, but we should not have called her guilty. For, according to the ideals of the time, Russia was fully entitled to mobilize after Austria had done so, and if she had left Serbia to her fate without moving, she would have afterwards incurred much of the same approach as we should have, if at the later stage we had left Belgium to her fate. I myself felt, as I still feel, that the rally of Russia to Serbia was one of the few spirited acts of the Czardom, and though (if I had known all the facts) I might have wished to restrain her from motives of prudence, I should certainly not have held her morally to blame, when she persisted.

Idea: War is regarded as the legitimate means of advancing national interests. Unless this curious mentality is got rid of, there can be no true world peace.

8. Education ought to teach us how to be in love always and what to be in love with. The great things of history have been done by the great lovers, by the saints and men of science and artists, and the problem of civilization is to give every man a chance of being a saint, a man of science, or an artist. But the problem cannot be attempted, much less solved, unless men desire to be saints, men of science and artists. And if they are to desire that continuously and consciously they might be taught what it means to be these things. We think of the man of science or the artist, if not of the saint, as a being with peculiar gifts, not as one who exercises, more precisely and incessantly perhaps, activities which we all ought to exercise. It is commonplace now that art has ebbed away out of our ordinary life, out of all things which we use, and that it is practised no longer by workmen, but only by a few painters and sculptors. That has happened because we no longer recognize the aesthetic activity as an activity of the spirit and common to all men. We do not know that when a man makes anything he ought to make it beautiful for the sake of doing so, and that when a man buys anything he ought to demand beauty in it, for the sake of that beauty. We think of beauty, if we think of it at all, as a mere resource of pleasure, and therefore it means to us ornament added to things for which we can pay extra as we choose. But beauty is not an ornament to life, or to the things made by man. It is an essential part of both. (Arthur Clutton-Brock)

Idea: The object of education is to create in us a sense of beauty. All great things of the world have proceeded from that. But unfortunately this sense of beauty has now disappeared from life.

9. Another point on which it seems necessary to insist is that a writer or an artist works primarily for his own time. This is, of course, a commonplace, but current modes of literary study largely neglect it. The artistic product, like the intellectual product of any age, is the individual response of the artist to the circumstances of his own time. In a sense all art is journalism. The greatest artists reach beyond their age to the minds of timeless humanity; but in them the transitory mingles with the permanent and the appeal which they make varies from generation to generation. In the lesser men the transitory

predominates. By laborious historical research we may be able to recapture something of the spirit that produced their work; we may think ourselves back into an alien culture, we may even be able to induce in ourselves a feeble glow of the emotion which the first audience experienced; but the game is scarcely worth the candle. If Spenser's poetry cannot be read by most people today, it is because he has nothing to say to the twentieth century; and no amount of critical exposition will help him. A Donne may find a second audience three centuries after his death. A Blake or an El Greco may miss recognition by his contemporaries and come up into his own much later; such solitary spirits born out of due season must wait until the whirling of time brings in a temper of mind with which they are sympathetic. Even the feeble poet may once by a fortunate chance touch the lyre to immortal music. Gray gave us the Elegy, and Drayton the sonnet, "Since there is no help, come let us kiss and part". But these exceptional cases only serve to enforce the fact that most of the works of the minor artists of the past as well as some of the work of the major artists has only an antiquarian interest. (Alderton Pink)

Idea: A work of art is the artist's reaction to contemporary life. But the great artists transcend the limitations of time and space. Their works live for all ages.

10. It is impossible to imagine, even after allowing for changes of diction, a Gray's Elegy or an Ode on Intimations of Immortality, still less a Prelude or a Paradise Lost, as the product of the early twentieth century. It may be argued that we have no great poetry today because we have no great poets; that is a perfectly defensible argument. Still, I do not believe that even a great poet, were one to arise, would or could move upon the plane, or breathe the air of Milton and of Wordsworth. This is simply another way of saying that sublimity has gone out of fashion. Or I might say, again, that we have no passion, because we have no convictions. And it is very difficult to see what is to take place of that passion, which in the past, and according to the temperament of the writer, has clothed itself in the garments of reverence, awe and faith. We have nothing but doubt and uncertainty—both negative elements; and above all, we have over-developed that destructive sense of proportion—destructive to poetry, I mean—which we are pleased to call our sense of humour. It has been frequently suggested of late, indeed, that science might provide some material for poetry, but

although this idea seems plausible and fertile enough at first sight, on second thought it is apparent that it represents only a very journalistic conception. I allude to it, and to the fact that such suggestion has been made, merely to support my contention that something, something constructive, meaning, some ideal, if you like to call it, that is lacking in poetry of today and that the critics have felt the lack of it, and are casting round for something which may take the place of the quality which I characterized as reverence, awe and faith. And when I say faith, I need scarcely say that I do not necessarily mean religious faith; I mean what I call passion—the sense that some things are more important than other things; and by that I do not mean, again, the fine frenzy, but a quieter and deeper thing, which is unaffected by our sense of humour, and expresses itself without the deterrent fear of ridicule. (Victoria Sackville-West)

Idea: The twentieth century is very poor in the political achievement because it has no faith and reverence. Passion is also needed for the production of great poetry.

11. A book is essentially not a talked thing but a written thing; and written not with a view of mere communication, but of permanence. The book of talk is printed only because its author cannot speak the thousands of people at once; if he could, he would—the volume is a mere multiplication of his voice. You cannot talk to your friend in India; if you could, you would; you write instead; that is mere conveyance of voice. But a book is written, not to multiply the voice merely, not to carry it merely, but to perpetuate it. The author has something to say which he perceives to be true and useful or helpfully beautiful. So as far he knows, no one can say it. He is bound to say it, clearly and melodiously, if he may; clearly at all events. In the sum of his life he finds this to be the thing, or group of things, manifest to him,—this is the piece of true knowledge, or sight, which his share of sunshine and earth has permitted him to seize. He would fain set it down for ever; engrave it on rock, if he could; saying, 'this is the best of me; for the rest I ate and drank, and slept, loved and hated like another; my life was as the vapour , and is not; But this I saw and knew: this, if anything of mine, is worth your memory'. That is his 'writing'; it is in his small human way, and with whatever degree of true inspiration is in him, his inscription and scriptures. This is a 'Book'. (John Ruskin)

Idea: Books contain the best that an author is capable of giving. Mere printed matter does not constitute a book.

12. The student should forward to his examination not as a solemn ordeal which he is compelled to go through with the prospect of a degree, should he be successful, but as a means of showing his teacher and his fellows how he has profited by the work which he has done; those who pursue knowledge in this spirit and those, be it remarked, who examine in this spirit will look forward to examination with no apprehension; not perhaps with joy, for after all it is a bore to be examined and perhaps a still greater bore to examine, but it is a necessary step for the student in gaining self-assurance and the conviction of having profited by his exertions; and for the teacher, as a means of insuring that his instruction has not been profitless to his student. In this connection I cannot refrain from remarking that genius for competition which as over-ridden our nation of England appears to me to be misplaced. For too much is thought of the top man; very likely the second, or even the tenth or it may be the fiftieth, has a firmer grasp of his subject, and in the long run would display more talent. Let us take comfort, however, in the thought, that the day of examinations, for the sake of examinations, is approaching an end. (Sir William Ramsay)

Idea: Examinations are the tests as to how far a student has profited by lecture of teachers. A great premium is set on examinations, but the days of examinations are coming to an end.

—o—

CHAPTER VIII

Passages for Practice (Poetry)

1. It is not growing like a tree
In bulk doth make Man better be;
Or standing long an oak, three hundred year,
To fall a log at last, dry, bald, and sere:
A lily of a day
Is fairer far in May,
Although it fall and die that night—
It was the plant and flower of light.
In small proportions we just beauties see;
And in short measures life may perfect be.

(Ben Jonson)

Idea: Beauty consists not in bulk but in proportion.

2. Under the greenwood tree
Who loves to lie with me,
And turn [his] merry note
Unto the sweet bird's throat,
Come hither, come hither, come hither:
Here shall he see
No enemy
But winter and rough weather.

Who doth ambition shun,
And loves to live i' the sun,
Seeking the food he eats,
And pleas'd with what he gets,
Come hither, come hither, come hither:
Here shall he see
No enemy
But winter and rough weather.

(William Shakespeare)

Idea: Life in the bosom of nature is joyful. It is free from the evils of society to heir it.

3 How happy is he born and taught
That serveth not another's will;
Whose armour is his honest thought,
And simple truth his utmost skill!
Whose passions not his masters are;
Whose soul is still prepared for death,
Untied unto the world by care
Of public fame or private breath;
Who envies none that chance doth raise,
Nor vice; who never understood
How deepest wounds are given by praise;
Nor rules of state, but rules of good;
Who hath his life from rumours freed;
Whose conscience is his strong retreat;
Whose state can neither flatterers feed,
Nor ruin make oppressors great;
Who God doth late and early pray
More of His grace than gifts to lend;
And entertains the harmless day
With a religious book or friend;
—This man is freed from servile bands
Of hope to rise or fear to fall:
Lord of himself, though not of lands,
And having nothing, yet hath all.

(Sir Henry Watton)

Idea: The various elements of human happiness are freedom from all passions, honesty of thought, faith in God, preparedness for death, etc.)

4. Who is the strong? Not he who puts to test
His sinews with the strong and proves the best;
But he who dwells where weaklings congregate,
And never lets his splendid strength abate.
Who is the wise? Not he who from the start
With wisdom's followers has taken part;
But he who looks in Folly's tempting eyes
And turns away, perceiving her disguise.
Who is serene? Not he who flees his kind
Some mountain fastness, or some cave to find;

But he who, in the city's noisiest scene,
Keeps calm within—he only is serene.

Idea: The poet here expresses wherein lie real strength, wisdom and sincerity.

5. He that has grown to wisdom hurries not,
But thinks and weighs what Reason bids him do
And after thinking he retains his thought
Until as he conceived the fact ensue.
Let no man to o'erweening pride be wrought,
But count his state as Fortune's gift and due.
He is a fool who deems that none has sought
The truth, save he alone, or knows it true.
Many strange birds are on the air abroad,
Nor all are of one flight or of one force,
But each after his kind dissimilar:
To each was portioned of the breath of God,
Who gave them divers instincts from one source.
Then judge not thou thy fellows what they are.

Idea: A truly wise man always follows the dictates of reason. Truth is not the monopoly of anybody; but every man approaches truth according to his capability.

6. The Glories of our blood and state
Are shadows, not substantial things;
There is no armour against fate;
Death lays his icy hand on kings:
Sceptre and Crown
Must tumble down,
And in the dust be equal made
With the poor crooked scythe and spade.
Some men with swords may reap the field,
And plant fresh laurels where they kill:
But their strong nerves at last must yield;
They tame but one another still:
Early or late
They stoop to fate,
And must give up their murmuring breath
When they, pale captives, creep to death.

Idea: Death levels all distinctions between man and man. All are laid low by death.

7.
FAME is a food that dead men eat,—
I have no stomach for such meat.
In little light and narrow room,
They eat it in the silent tomb,
With no kind voice of comrade near
To bid the banquet be of cheer.
But Friendship is a nobler thing,—
Of Friendship it is good to sing.
For truly, when a man shall end,
He lives in memory of his friend,
Who doth his better part recall,
And of his faults make funeral.

(Austin Dobson)

Idea: Friendship is preferable to fame, for friends remember the good forgetting the evil, of the dead man.

8.
Life! I know not what thou art,
But know that thou and I must part;
And when, or how, or where we met
I own to me's a secret yet.
Life! We've been long together
Through pleasant and through cloudy weather,
'Tis hard to part when friends are dear,—
Perhaps 'twill cost a sigh, a tear;
—Then steal away, give little warning,
Choose thine own time;
Say not Good Night, -- but in some brighter clime
Bid me Good Morning.

(A.L. Barbauld)

Idea: Life is a mystery. Death is painful.

9.
He came today, our whilom [former] foe—
An enemy ten years ago—
At least our country's enemy,
Even as I was forced to be
An enemy of his: he came;
And by the hearth we watched the flame
Flourish [embellish] the logs with gold, as we

Together talked of poetry,
Or sat, each silent in his seat,
Rapt in the healing quiet, sweet
Companionship of kindred minds.
And human fellowship that binds
The broken spirit and makes whole
The horror-lacerated soul.
We, who'd been forced by fate to dwell
Four years in opposite camp of hell,
Were liberated now, and free
Of the sweet heaven of poetry,
After long years of exile come
To our true native country, home.

Idea: Human nature may be embittered by war, but with the return of peace man swings back to civilized life and enjoys good things in life even with his erstwhile enemies.

10. Why, why repine, my pensive friend,
At pleasures slipp'd away?
Some the stern Fates will never lend,
And all refuse to stay.
I see the rainbow in the sky,
The dew upon the grass;
I see them, and I ask not why
They glimmer or they pass.
With folded arms I linger not
To call them back; 'twere vain:
In this, or in some other spot,
I know they'll shine again.

Idea: Man should not lament over the pleasures that have passed away. All beautiful things pass away only to reappear.

11. Out of the night that covers me,
Black as the pit from pole to pole,
I thank whatever gods may be,
For my unconquerable soul.
In the fell clutch of circumstance
I have not winced , nor cried aloud.
Under the bludgeonings of chance
My head is bloody, but unbowed

Beyond the place of wrath and tears
Looms but the Horror of the shade
And yet the menace of the years
Finds, and shall find, me unafraid.
It matters not how strait the gate,
How charged with punishment the scroll.
    I am the master of my fate:
    I am the captain of my soul.

Idea: The poet retains a fearless soul in the gloom and horror of this world. He is never cowed down with fear.

12. Earth has not anything to show more fair;
Dull would he be of soul who could pass by
A sight so touching in its majesty:
A city now doth like a garment wear
The beauty of the morning: silent, bare,
Ships, towers, domes, threats and temples lie
Open unto the fields, and to the sky—
All bright and glittering in the smokeless air.

Never did the sun more beautifully steep
In his first splendour valley, rock, or hill;
Ne'er saw I, never felt, a calm so deep!
The river glideth at his own sweet will:
Dear God! The vey houses seem asleep;
And all that mighty heart is lying still!

Idea: London in the early morning presents a beautiful sight. The silence of the city is deeply impressive.

—o—

Glossary of Technical Terms and Literary Expressions

Abstract: of style and diction without actual or particular examples (as opposed to *concrete*)

Alliteration: sometimes called *head rhyme* or *initial rhyme.* It is the close repetition of the same sound, not necessarily of the same letter.

Alliterative verse: alliteration is the practice of using two or more words beginning with the same letter near together. Alliterative verse is the Old English verse-form based on this practice, first appearing in Anglo-Saxon times and continuing into the fourteenth century (Langland) and later. It is unrhymed, the lines are loosely dactylic four-stressed lines, containing as a rule two words beginning with the same letter in the first half, and one or two in the second.

Antithesis: form of expression, in verse or prose, in which contrasting words emphasize a contrast in ideas (e.g. 'to live a sinner or to die a saint'.)

Apostrophe: direct address to person or idea, usually absent or dead, in course of poem, or speech.

Appositional phrase: group of words, usually equivalent to a noun, placed beside a noun and having the same grammatical function (e.g. 'Mr. Atkins, a *man of sterling character*, was elected to the vacant office')

Archaic: use of word, phrase, or style, no longer in ordinary use; old-fashioned or antiquated in flavour.

Assonance: near rhyme; similarity of sound without actual rhyme (e.g. 'Full fathom *five Thy* father *lies*.)

Asyndeton: absence of syntactical sequence in the construction of a sentence, especially in which conjunctions are omitted. The passage from *Hamlet* is an example:

> O, what a noble mind is here o'erthrown
> *the courtier's, soldier's, scholar's, eye, tongue, sword.*

Blank Verse: an indefinite number of unrhymed iambic pentameters (see *iambic*, and *pentameter*).

Caesura: pause or break in rhythmic flow of a line of verse (e.g. after the second to *be* in 'To be or not to be/that is the question')

Circumlocution: round about and evasive speech; the use of many words where few would be clearer. It is also known as *periphrasis.*

Clause: group of words consisting of a subject and a predicate. *Simple sentence* consists of one main clause, a *double* or *multiple sentence* contains two or more main clauses. A *complex sentence* consists of one main clause and one or more dependent or subordinate clauses.

Concrete: of style, expression or diction, containing particular examples, as opposed to *abstract.* (see above)

Couplet: consists of two consecutive lines of verse rhyming together, usually in the same meter. A *closed couplet* is one that is logically and grammatically complete.

Dactyl: a foot or measure in verse, consisting of one strong syllable followed by two weak ones (e.g. *fortunate, horribly*)

Diction: vocabulary, choice of words, especially in poetry. Diction may be simple, homely, learned, pedantic, archaic, colloquial, etc.

Didactic: with a propagandist intention, of poetry, fiction, etc. The didactic intention may be moral, social, religious, political, etc. A *fable* is a short story having a moral purpose, and is therefore didactic.

Elision: dropping out or suppressing of a vowel or syllable in pronunciation; so that the line may conform to the metrical scheme as shown in the line:

What was th' impediment that broke this off?

Ellipsis: the shortening of a sentence or phrase by omission of certain words which can easily be understood from the rest of the sentence or by the reader's common sense (e.g. 'If found, return to Post Office' for 'If this document is found, please return it to the Post Office.')

Epic Simile: It is an elaborate and long-tailed simile which is not confined to just comparing two different things on one point of similarity; but in the process goes beyond the specific task of a simile, and presents a detailed picture of the scene or situation called up for the purpose of comparison, and sometimes takes our mind away from the thing which was originally the main concern of the composition.

Epithet: an adjective expressing the quality or attribute considered characteristic of a person or thing.

Erotesis: in the form of a question to which no answer is expected. It is a sort of *rhetorical question*.

Euphuism: a literary style developed in the Elizabethan period by John Lyly, of which the marks are balance of phrase, expressive alliteration and a systematic use of similes drawn especially from natural history.

Heroic couplet: iambic pentameters rhyming in pairs—*aa bb cc* etc. Some critics regard all verse written in this form as heroic couplets (e.g. Chaucer's *Prologue*, Keats's *Endymion* and Rupert Brook's *The Great Lover*.) It is, however, preferable to restrict the use of the term to that type of couplet perfected by Pope in the early eighteenth century which, modeled on Pope's immediate predecessor Dryden, is distinguished by extreme balance and antithesis, so that each couplet is in itself almost an epigram.

Hypallage: transference of an epithet from its appropriate noun to another to which it does not properly belong. It is also called *transferred epithet*. It is a common poetic device, eg. 'a restless night', 'the condemned cell'.

Hyperbaton: where words are transposed from their normal order, there seems to be a grammatical disorderliness in the sentence, as in *Othello*:

> Yet I'll not shed her blood,
> Nor scar that whiter skin of hers than snow.

Hyperbole: a figure of speech in which exaggeration is used deliberately for the sake of emphasis (e.g. Marlowe's 'Is this the face that launched a thousand ships?')

Iambic: consisting of a series of iambuses, or relating to the iambus, a measure or foot in verse consisting of one weak syllable followed by one strong one (e.g. repent, at home, connive).

Imagery: the images used by a writer of poetry or prose, an image being a picture or other sense-impression conveyed in words. Thus an image in poetry is a word or expression which appeals directly to the eye, the ear, or the senses of taste, touch, and smell. Keats's imagery was strongly sensuous, appealing more often than that of most poets to the sense of taste. Tennyson's imagery appeals often to the ear or the eye, Herrick's imagery often appeals to the sense of touch. Wordsworth's imagery is less rich and vivid than that of some poets, for instance Coleridge, and his appeal is thus less directly to the senses than to intellect.

Innuendo: way of suggesting instead of stating openly what is meant, e.g. 'Honesty is the best policy but advertising also helps.'

Irony: irony in speech or writing is present wherever the real meaning is to some extent concealed under language of opposite meaning. In its simplest form it is often called sarcasm—'You are in a good temper to-day, aren't you?' (meaning exactly the opposite).In its subtler form it is part of the usual method of highly civilized writers such as Swift, Jane Austen and Thomas Hardy.

Loose Sentence: a sentence in which the main clanse comes first, followed by subordinate clauses. The sentence is grammatically complete at one or more points before its end.

Lyric: a short song-like poem, often of a musical character, usually in verses or stanzas, expressing directly the poet's imagination or feelings. The term is very loosely used in English poetic criticism, and is most useful when the writer wishes to distinguish poems of this kind from those in some other forms—e.g. epic, narrative or dramatic.

Metaphor: the application in prose or poetry, of a word or expression to some other word to which it does not apply literally. There is always an implied, or compressed, comparison.

Metaphysicals: the name given to certain English poets of the late sixteenth and seventeenth centuries, notably Donne, Cowley, and in a lesser degree Herbert, Vaughan and Crashaw. The name, first used by Dryden and later adopted by Johnson, referred to their use of far-fetched imagery from intellectual ideas beyond physical appearances.

Metonymy: substitution of the name of an attribute of a thing for the name itself, as *crown* for *king*, *city* for *inhabitants.*

Octave: the first eight lines of a sonnet of the Petrarchan type, the remaining six lines being the *sestet.*

Onomatopoeia: matching sound to the sense. Certain words are in themselves of onomatopoeic origin, being attempt to reproduce the sound intended by the word (e.g. *splash*, *fizz*, *cuckoo*). The word also applies to deliberate poetic effect, such as Tennyson's 'The *murmur* of innumerable bees'.

Paradox: a statement or a pair of statements whose meaning is made clear by reconciliation of apparently irreconcilable ideas (e.g. the proverbial saying ' A short cut is often the longest way round). The profoundest truths are often concealed in paradoxes, a form favoured by, for instance, Jesus who often used to hide his meaning from the ignorant and thoughtless and appeal to those who were prepared to think about truth and try to solve his riddles by reflection and discussion.

Pathetic fallacy: this may be applied to those cases of Nature personification where Nature or some objects of Nature sympathizes with human sorrow or calamity by weeping, sighing, murmuring, or expressing concern. e.g.

Earth felt the wound; and Nature from her seat,
Sighing through all her works, gave signs of woe.

Pentameter: a line in verse consisting of five feet or measures, usually iambic in rhythm.

Periodic Sentence: a complete sentence consisting of several clauses which are so arranged that the sense is not finished till the close. Thomas Fuller, in *Church History of Britain*, calls it 'long and pithy, the author driving on a whole flock of several clauses before he came to the close of a sentence'.

Periphrasis: a roundabout way of saying something. It is sometimes used by a writer as a mild display of vanity or affectation, as when a cook is referred to as 'practitioner of culinary art'.

Personification: in prose and especially poetry, referring to an abstract ideas or quality as if it were a person.

Polysyndeton: consists in the use of a number of conjunctions close together; usually the repetition of the same conjunction, as in Shelley's *Adonais*:

He has out-soared the shadow of our night;
Envy and calumny *and* hate *and* pain,
And what unrest which men miscall delight.

Pun or **Paronomasia:** play upon words for humorous or serious purposes, e.g. 'When the husband died, the wife cried for a *second*.'

Quatrain: a stanza consisting of four lines, which may have various rhyme schemes. It is the commonest stanza form in English verse:

As from the power of sacred lays
The spheres began to move,
And sung he great Creator's praise
To all the blest above.

Refrain: is a burden which comprises a phrase or a line recurring usually after each stanza, sometimes within the stanza. An instance of this, we have in John Masefield's 'Sea-Fever':

I must go down to the seas again...
recurring at the beginning of each stanza.

Satire: literary or artistic expression whose general aim is to amuse, and sometimes to correct or reform, by means of ridicule.

Sestet or **Sextet:** a poem or stanza of six lines; the term frequently refers to the second part of the Petrarchan sonnet.

Simile: a figure of speech in which a comparison is introduced for the sake of added vividness or clarity. e.g. Coleridge, *The Ancient Mariner*:

Day after day, day after day,
We stuck, nor breath nor motion;
As idle as a painted ship
Upon a painted ocean.

Sonnet: a poem consisting of fourteen iambic pentameters rhyming in one of several ways. The two main forms are Petrarchan, as used mainly after the Elizabethan age by Milton, Wordsworth, Keats and others; and the Shakespearean. The latter consists of three quatrains (four-line verse) followed by a rhymed couplet. The Petrarchan form consists of an octave followed by a sestet. It avoids the necessity for the final rhymed couplet, which too often reads like an after-thought tagged on at end.

Synecdoche: a part of an object or idea stands for the whole; or the whole stands for a part. For example:

'Give us this day our daily *bread*'
'All *hands* to the pumps;'

India for *India XI.*

Trochaic: a metrical foot of two syllables with the stress on the first foot, as in 'daily'.

Zeitgeist: spirit of the age; applied to the feeling and the reactions of the writers of the time.

—o—

Select Bibliography

Literary Criticism: Malcolm Hicks & Bill Hutchings

The Critical Sense: James Reeves

Literary Appreciation: Peter Westland

A Glossary of Literary Terms: M. H. Abrams

English Prose Style: Herbert Read.

English Prose Style: Bonamy Dobree

The Poet's Defence: J. Bronowski

Reading & Criticism: Raymond Williams

Modern Poetry: Studies in Practical Criticism: C. B. Cox & A.E. Dyson

Literary Appreciation: H. L. B. Moody.

—o—